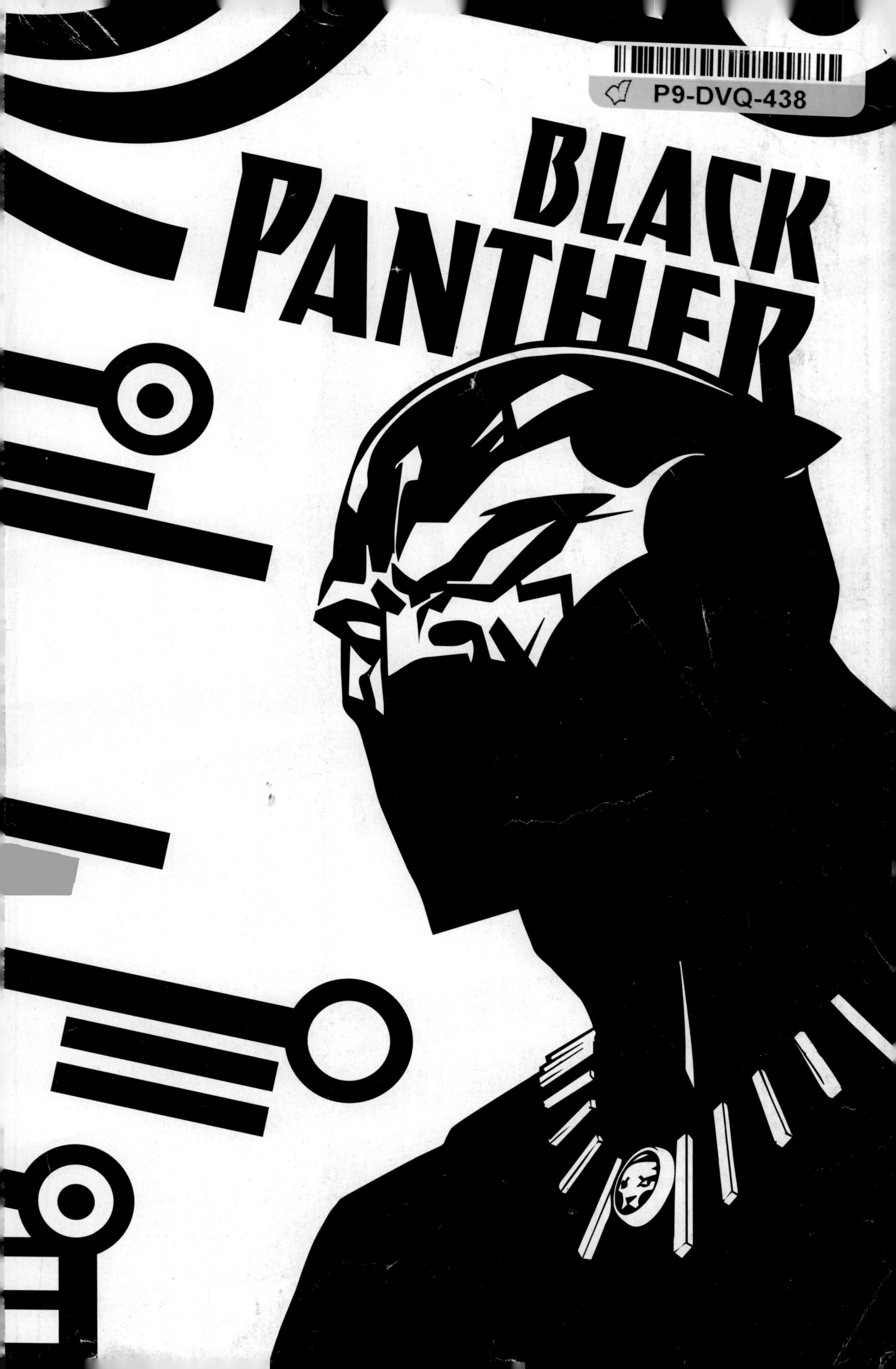
BLACK
PANTHER

BLACK P

WRITER
TA-NEHISI COATES

ARTIST
BRIAN STELFREEZE

COLOR ARTIST
LAURA MARTIN

LETTERER
VC'S JOE SABINO

COLLECTION EDITOR **JENNIFER GRÜNWALD**
ASSOCIATE EDITOR **SARAH BRUNSTAD**
EDITOR, SPECIAL PROJECTS **MARK D. BEAZLEY**
VP, PRODUCTION & SPECIAL PROJECTS **JEFF YOUNGQUIST**
SVP PRINT, SALES & MARKETING **DAVID GABRIEL**
BOOK DESIGNER **JAY BOWEN**

EDITOR IN CHIEF **AXEL ALONSO**
CHIEF CREATIVE OFFICER **JOE QUESADA**
PUBLISHER **DAN BUCKLEY**
EXECUTIVE PRODUCER **ALAN FINE**

BLACK PANTHER: A NATION UNDER OUR FEET BOOK 1. Contains material originally published in magazine form as BLACK PANTHER #1-4 and FANTASTIC FOUR #52. First printing 2016. ISBN# 978-1-302-90053-3. Published by MARVEL WORLDWIDE, INC., a subsidiary of MARVEL ENTERTAINMENT, LLC. OFFICE OF PUBLICATION: 135 West 50th Street, New York, NY 10020. **Printed in the U.S.A.** ALAN FINE, President, Marvel Entertainment; DAN BUCKLEY, President, TV, Publishing & Brand Management; JOE QUESADA, Chief Creative Officer; TOM BREVOORT, SVP of Publishing; DAVID BOGART, SVP of Business Affairs & Operations, Publishing & Partnership; C.B. CEBULSKI, VP of Brand Management & Development, Asia; DAVID GABRIEL, SVP of Sales & Marketing, Publishing; JEFF YOUNGQUIST, VP of Production & Special Projects; DAN CARR, Executive Director of Publishing Technology; ALEX MORALES, Director of Publishing Operations; SUSAN CRESPI, Production Manager; STAN LEE, Chairman Emeritus. For information regarding advertising in Marvel Comics or on Marvel.com, please contact Vit DeBellis, Integrated Sales Manager, at vdebellis@marvel.com. For Marvel subscription inquiries, please call 888-511-5480. **Manufactured between 7/8/2016 and 8/15/2016 by R.R. DONNELLEY, INC., SALEM, VA, USA.**

10 9 8 7 6 5 4 3 2 1

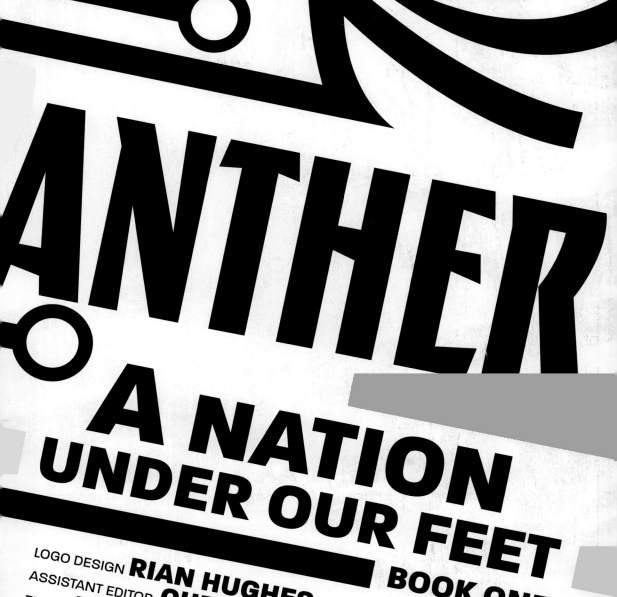

ANTHER

A NATION UNDER OUR FEET

BOOK ONE

LOGO DESIGN **RIAN HUGHES**
ASSISTANT EDITOR **CHRIS ROBINSON**
EDITOR **WIL MOSS**
EXECUTIVE EDITOR **TOM BREVOORT**

BLACK PANTHER CREATED BY
STAN LEE & **JACK KIRBY**

BLACK PANTHER

is the ancestral ceremonial title of **T'CHALLA**, the king of Wakanda. T'Challa splits his time between protecting his kingdom, with the aid of his elite female royal guard, the **DORA MILAJE**, and helping protect the entire world, as a member of super-hero teams such as the Avengers and the Ultimates.

The African nation **WAKANDA** is the most technologically advanced society on the globe. It sits upon a large deposit of an extremely rare natural resource called Vibranium. Wakanda long boasted of having never been conquered. But recent events — a biblical flood that killed thousands, a coup orchestrated by Doctor Doom, an invasion by the villain Thanos -- have humbled the kingdom.

T'Challa recently spent some time away from the throne. His sister **SHURI** had been ruling as both queen and Black Panther in his absence, but she died defending Wakanda against Thanos' army.

Now T'Challa is king once more, but the people of Wakanda are restless...

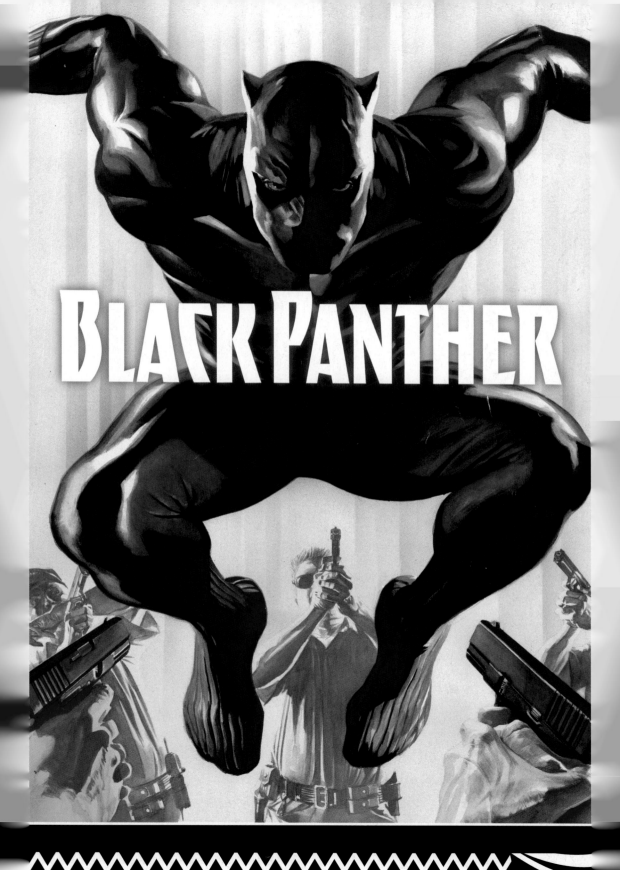

BLACK PANTHER

#1 VARIANT BY **ALEX ROSS**

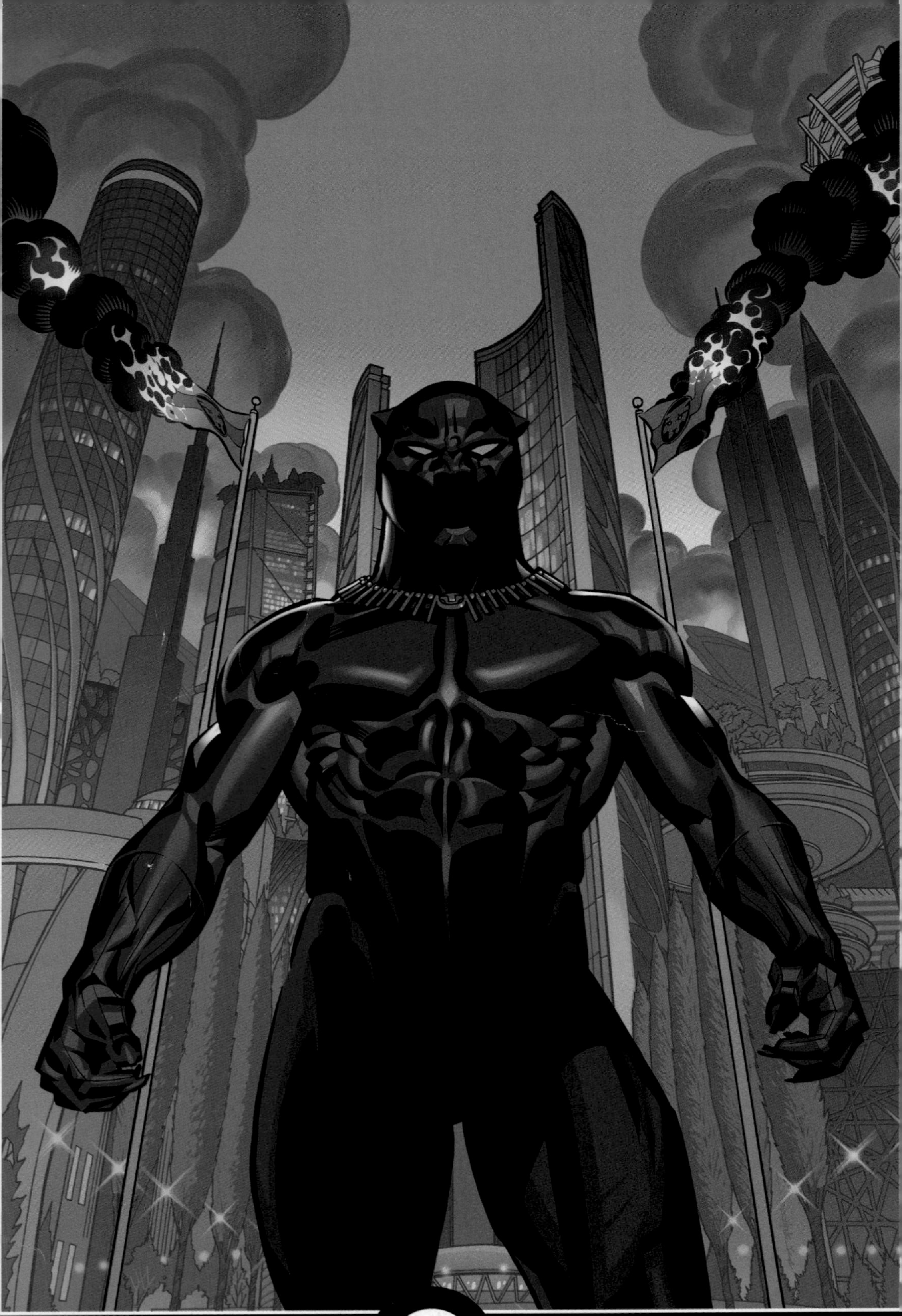

1

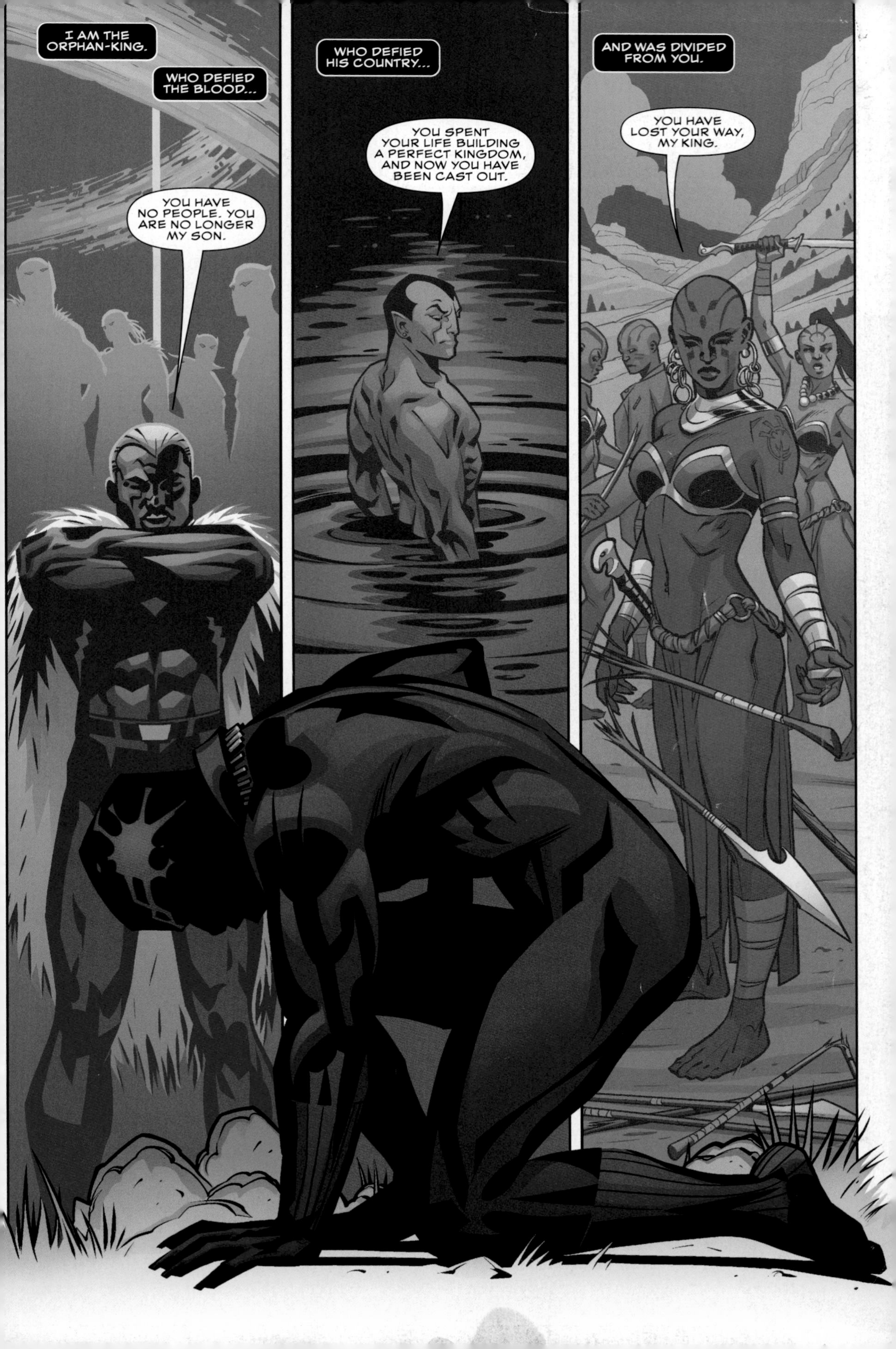
I AM THE ORPHAN-KING.
WHO DEFIED THE BLOOD...
YOU HAVE NO PEOPLE. YOU ARE NO LONGER MY SON.
WHO DEFIED HIS COUNTRY...
YOU SPENT YOUR LIFE BUILDING A PERFECT KINGDOM, AND NOW YOU HAVE BEEN CAST OUT.
AND WAS DIVIDED FROM YOU.
YOU HAVE LOST YOUR WAY, MY KING.

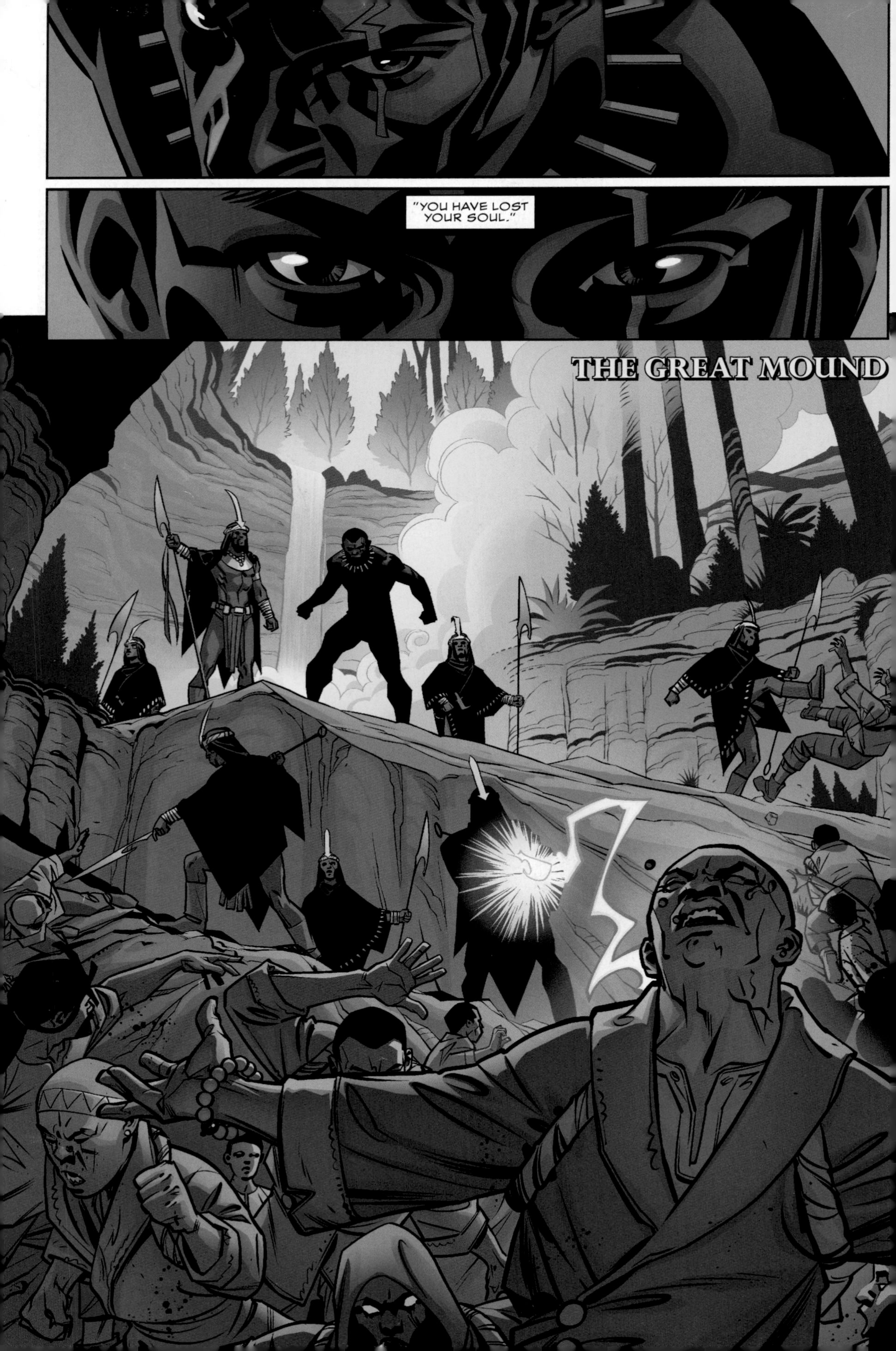
"YOU HAVE LOST YOUR SOUL."
THE GREAT MOUND

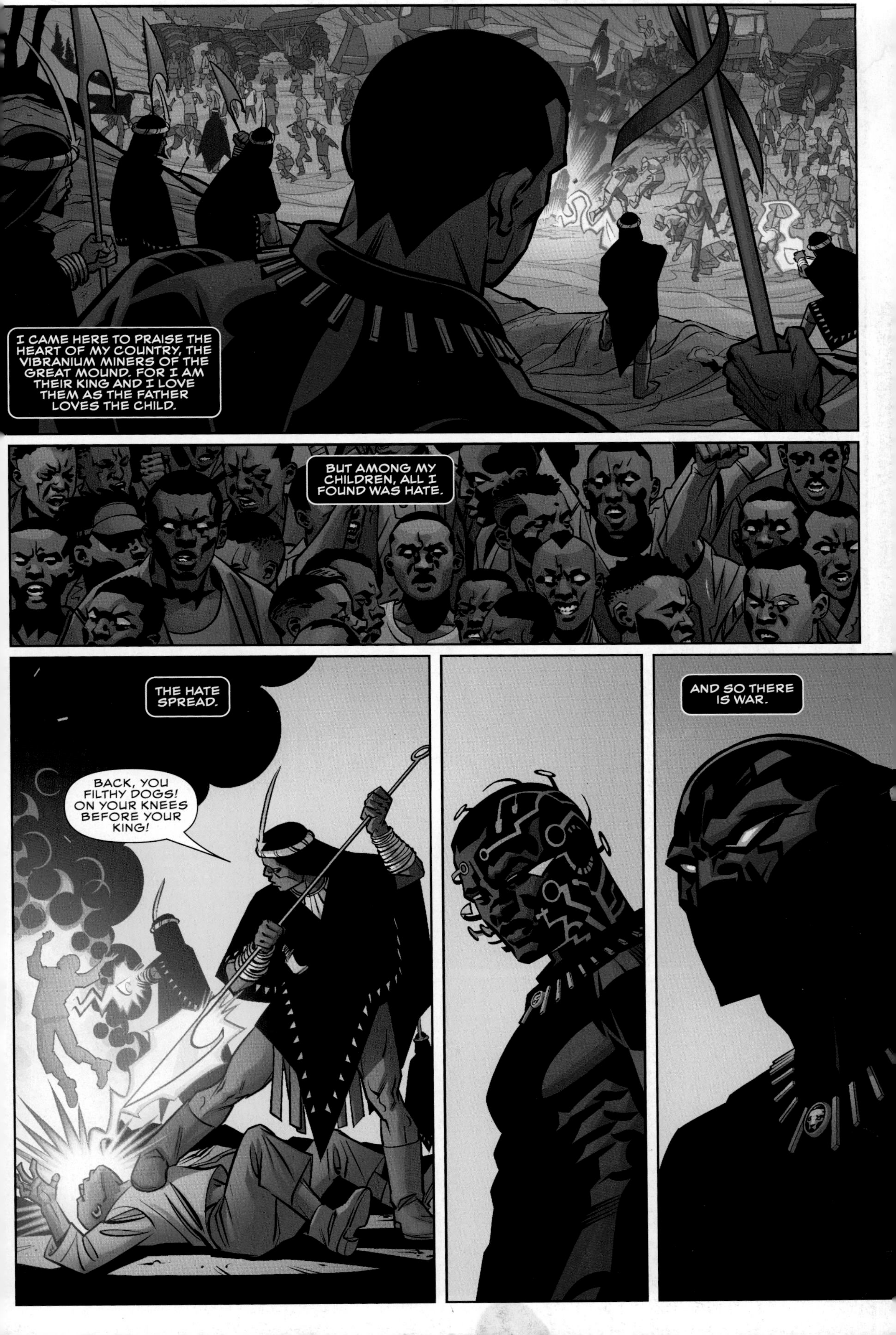
I CAME HERE TO PRAISE THE HEART OF MY COUNTRY, THE VIBRANIUM MINERS OF THE GREAT MOUND. FOR I AM THEIR KING AND I LOVE THEM AS THE FATHER LOVES THE CHILD.
BUT AMONG MY CHILDREN, ALL I FOUND WAS HATE.
THE HATE SPREAD.
BACK, YOU FILTHY DOGS! ON YOUR KNEES BEFORE YOUR KING!
AND SO THERE IS WAR.

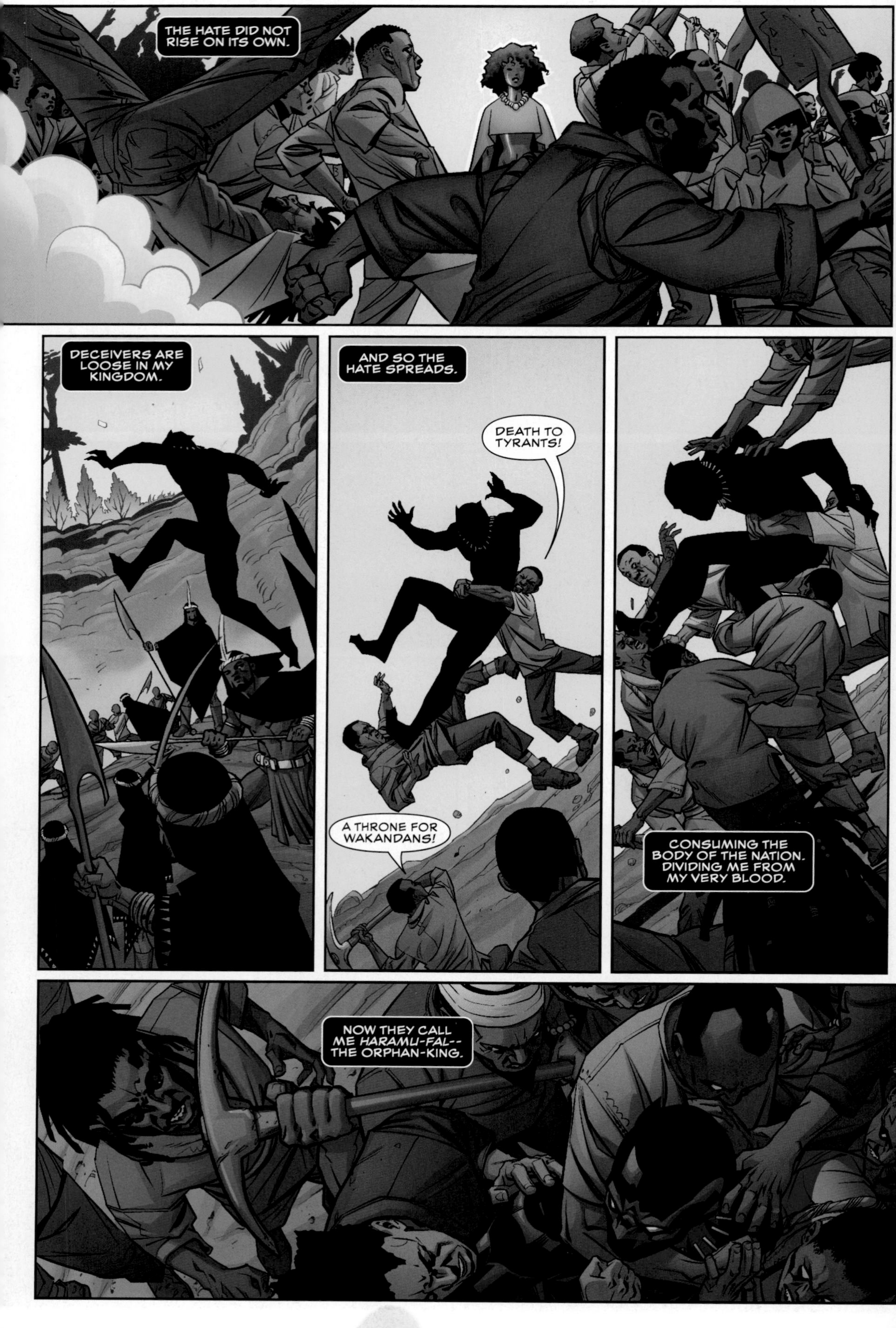
THE HATE DID NOT RISE ON ITS OWN.
DECEIVERS ARE LOOSE IN MY KINGDOM.
AND SO THE HATE SPREADS.
DEATH TO TYRANTS!
A THRONE FOR WAKANDANS!
CONSUMING THE BODY OF THE NATION. DIVIDING ME FROM MY VERY BLOOD.
NOW THEY CALL ME *HARAMU-FAL*-- THE ORPHAN-KING.

BUT I HAVE NOT FORGOTTEN MY NAME.

DAMISA-SARKI-- THE PANTHER.

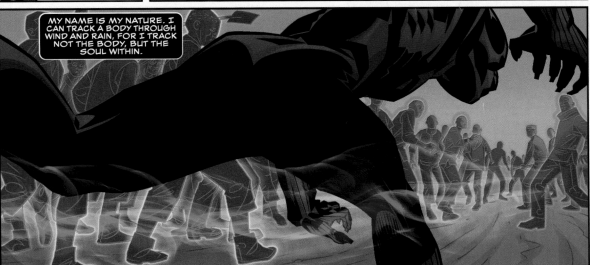

MY NAME IS MY NATURE. I CAN TRACK A BODY THROUGH WIND AND RAIN, FOR I TRACK NOT THE BODY, BUT THE SOUL WITHIN.

BUT THE DECEIVER'S SCENT HAS GONE STALE.

MY KING, WE MUST GO!

HER POWER FADES.

CALL THE SOLDIERS BACK, MY KING! WE MUST NOT MASSACRE OUR OWN PEOPLE!

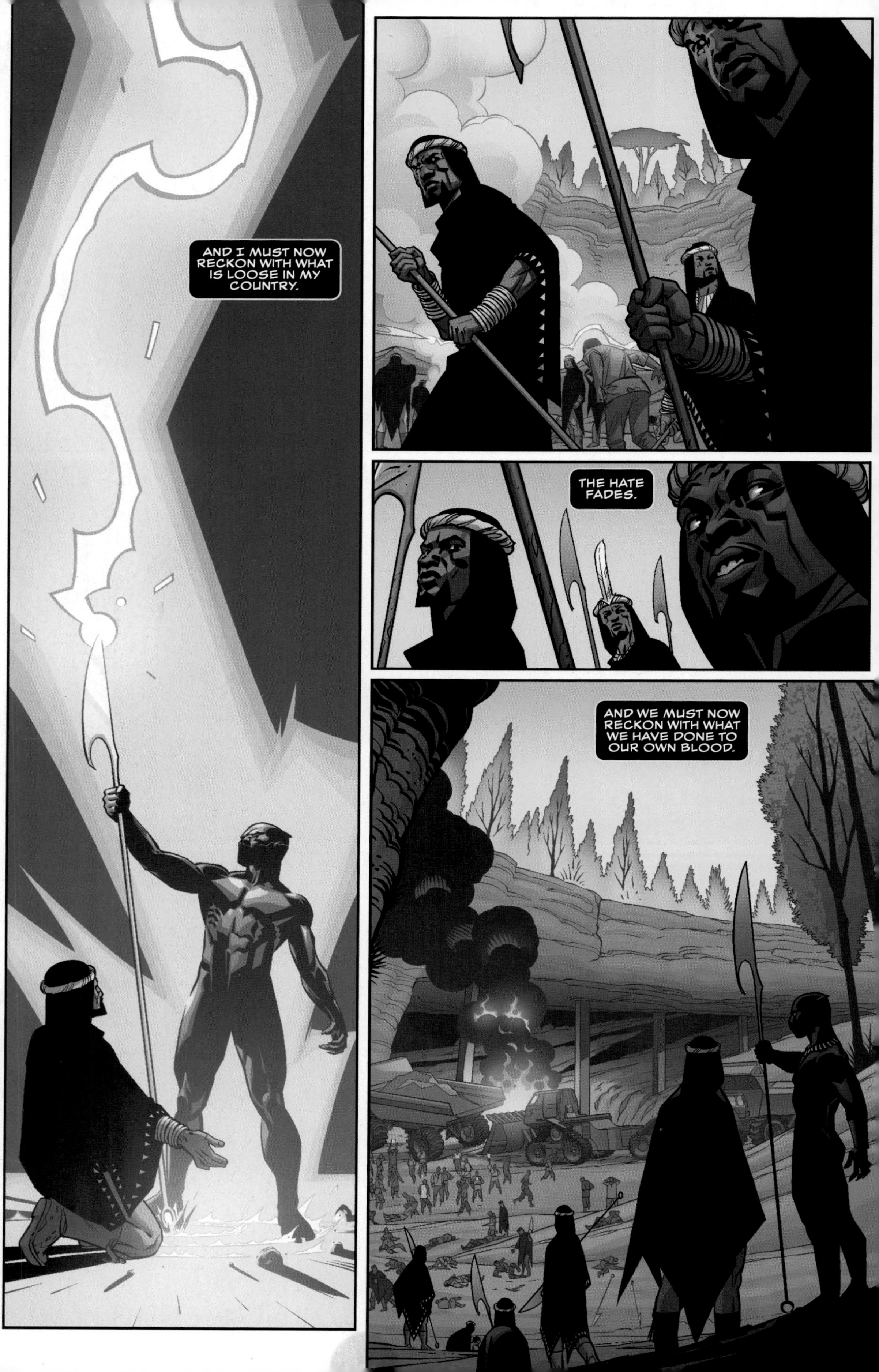
AND I MUST NOW RECKON WITH WHAT IS LOOSE IN MY COUNTRY.
THE HATE FADES.
AND WE MUST NOW RECKON WITH WHAT WE HAVE DONE TO OUR OWN BLOOD.

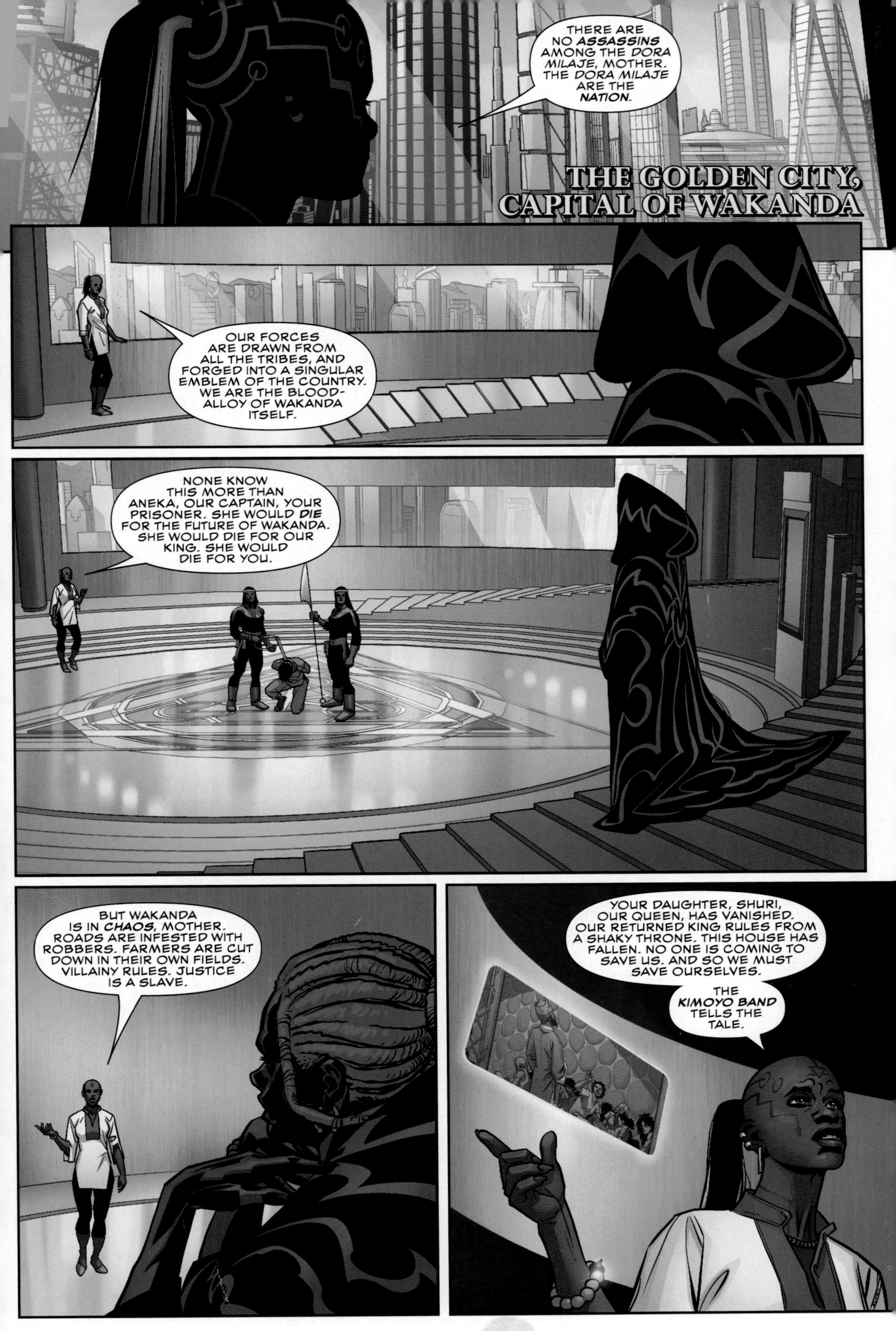
THERE ARE NO ASSASSINS AMONG THE DORA MILAJE, MOTHER. THE DORA MILAJE ARE THE NATION.
THE GOLDEN CITY, CAPITAL OF WAKANDA
OUR FORCES ARE DRAWN FROM ALL THE TRIBES, AND FORGED INTO A SINGULAR EMBLEM OF THE COUNTRY. WE ARE THE BLOOD-ALLOY OF WAKANDA ITSELF.
NONE KNOW THIS MORE THAN ANEKA, OUR CAPTAIN, YOUR PRISONER. SHE WOULD DIE FOR THE FUTURE OF WAKANDA. SHE WOULD DIE FOR OUR KING. SHE WOULD DIE FOR YOU.
BUT WAKANDA IS IN CHAOS, MOTHER. ROADS ARE INFESTED WITH ROBBERS. FARMERS ARE CUT DOWN IN THEIR OWN FIELDS. VILLAINY RULES. JUSTICE IS A SLAVE.
YOUR DAUGHTER, SHURI, OUR QUEEN, HAS VANISHED. OUR RETURNED KING RULES FROM A SHAKY THRONE. THIS HOUSE HAS FALLEN. NO ONE IS COMING TO SAVE US. AND SO WE MUST SAVE OURSELVES.
THE KIMOYO BAND TELLS THE TALE.

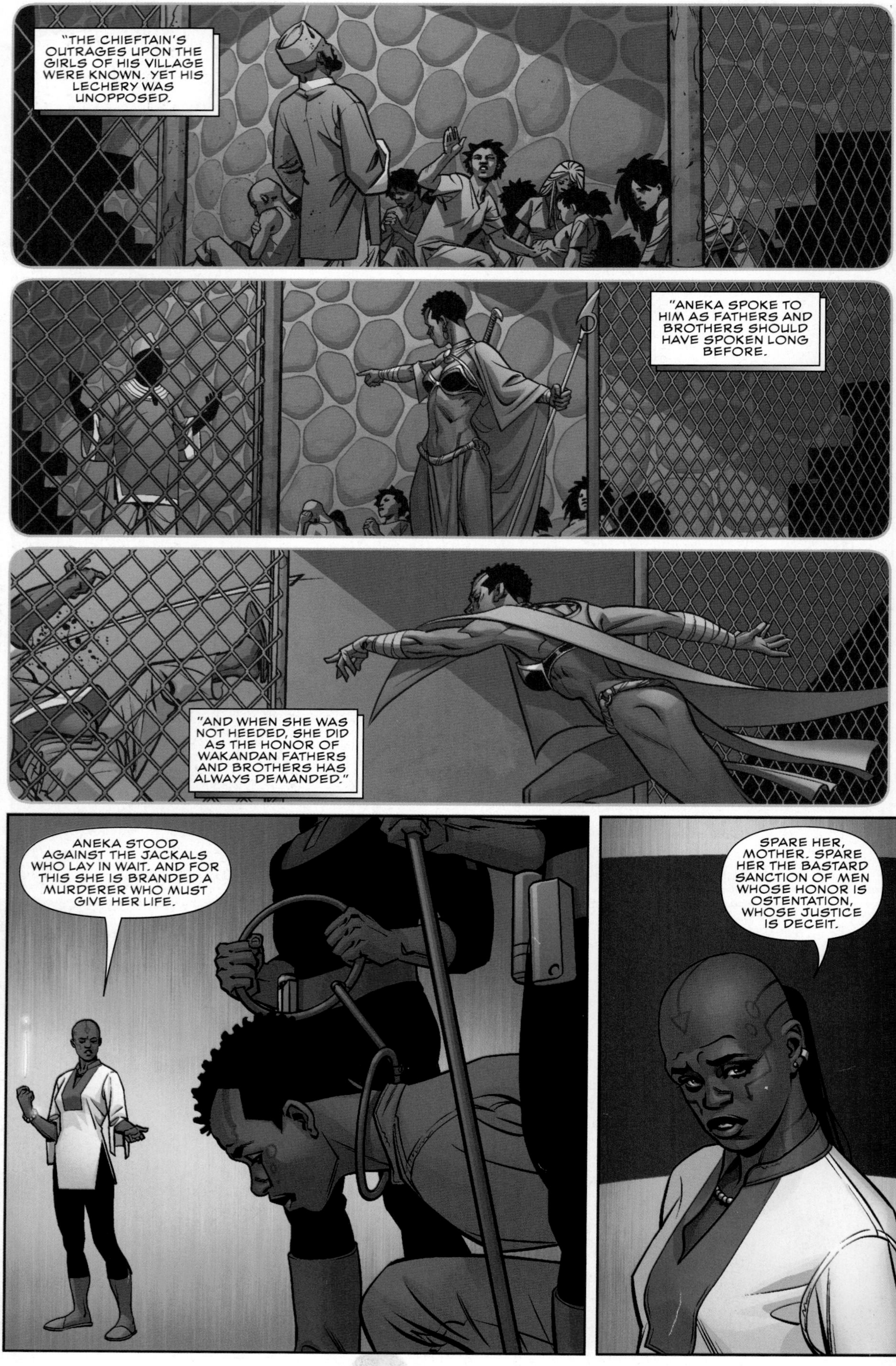
"THE CHIEFTAIN'S OUTRAGES UPON THE GIRLS OF HIS VILLAGE WERE KNOWN. YET HIS LECHERY WAS UNOPPOSED.
"ANEKA SPOKE TO HIM AS FATHERS AND BROTHERS SHOULD HAVE SPOKEN LONG BEFORE.
"AND WHEN SHE WAS NOT HEEDED, SHE DID AS THE HONOR OF WAKANDAN FATHERS AND BROTHERS HAS ALWAYS DEMANDED."
ANEKA STOOD AGAINST THE JACKALS WHO LAY IN WAIT. AND FOR THIS SHE IS BRANDED A MURDERER WHO MUST GIVE HER LIFE.
SPARE HER, MOTHER. SPARE HER THE BASTARD SANCTION OF MEN WHOSE HONOR IS OSTENTATION, WHOSE JUSTICE IS DECEIT.

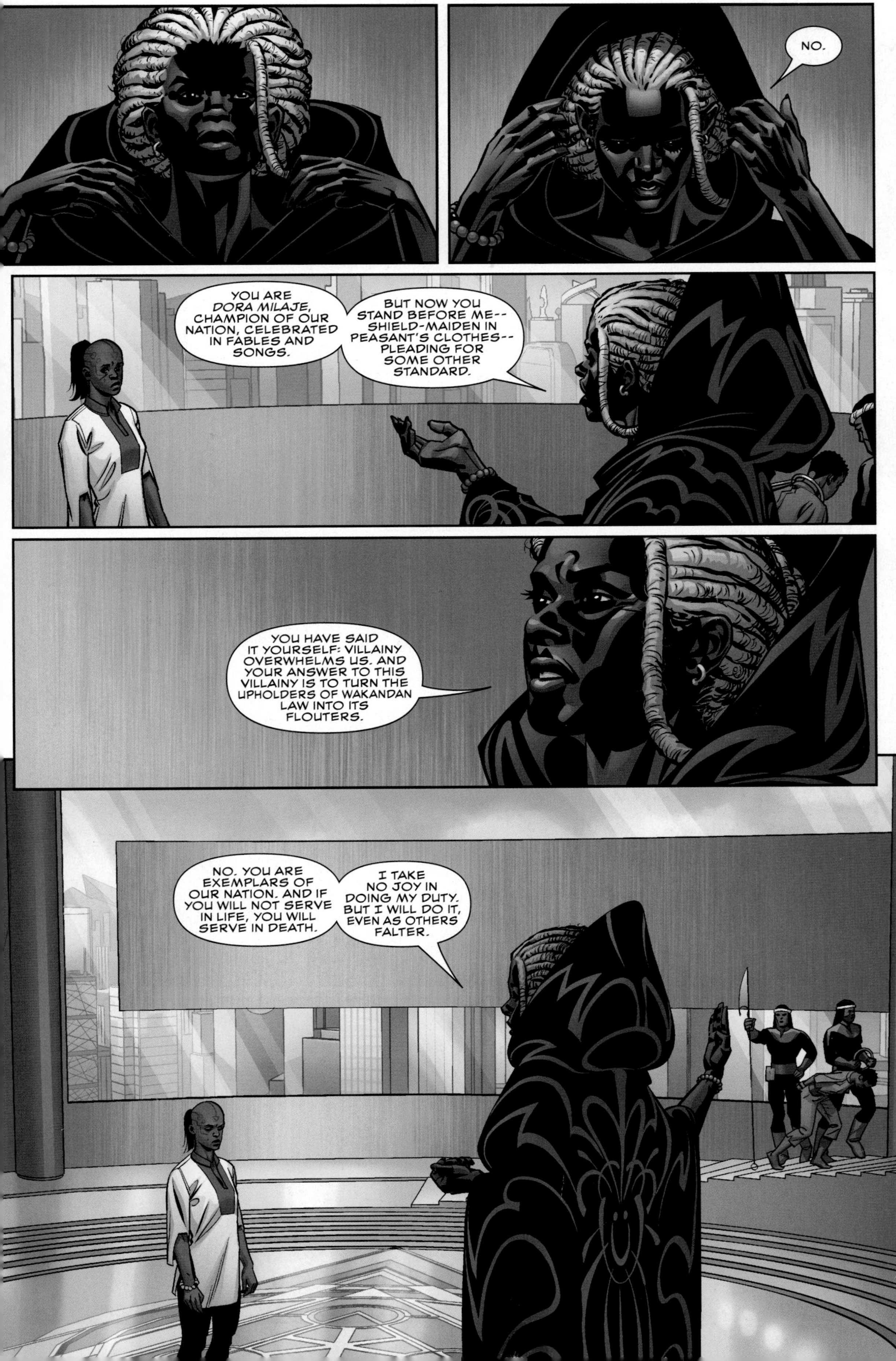
NO.
YOU ARE DORA MILAJE, CHAMPION OF OUR NATION, CELEBRATED IN FABLES AND SONGS.
BUT NOW YOU STAND BEFORE ME-- SHIELD-MAIDEN IN PEASANT'S CLOTHES-- PLEADING FOR SOME OTHER STANDARD.
YOU HAVE SAID IT YOURSELF: VILLAINY OVERWHELMS US. AND YOUR ANSWER TO THIS VILLAINY IS TO TURN THE UPHOLDERS OF WAKANDAN LAW INTO ITS FLOUTERS.
NO. YOU ARE EXEMPLARS OF OUR NATION. AND IF YOU WILL NOT SERVE IN LIFE, YOU WILL SERVE IN DEATH.
I TAKE NO JOY IN DOING MY DUTY. BUT I WILL DO IT, EVEN AS OTHERS FALTER.

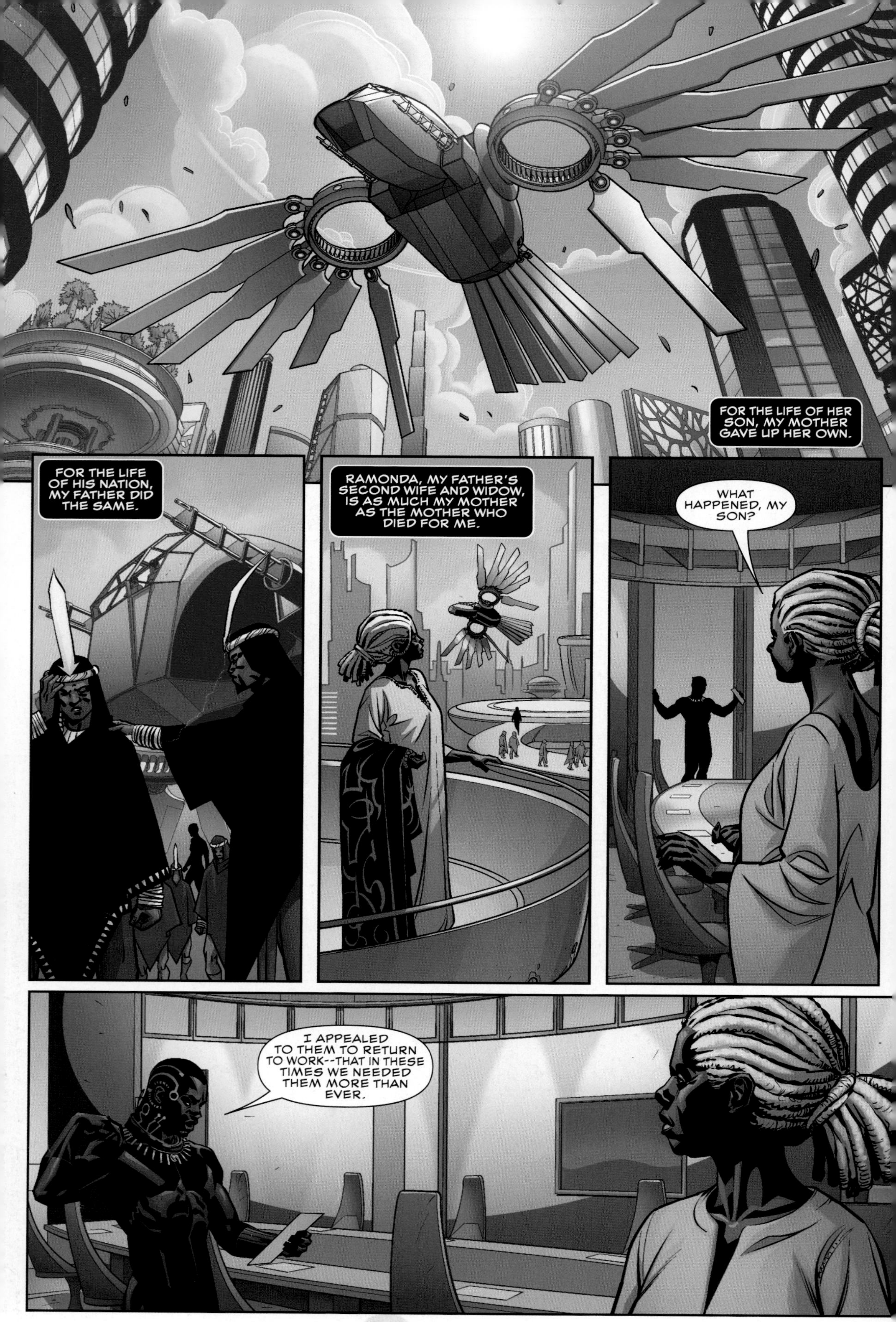
FOR THE LIFE OF HER SON, MY MOTHER GAVE UP HER OWN.
FOR THE LIFE OF HIS NATION, MY FATHER DID THE SAME.
RAMONDA, MY FATHER'S SECOND WIFE AND WIDOW, IS AS MUCH MY MOTHER AS THE MOTHER WHO DIED FOR ME.
WHAT HAPPENED, MY SON?
I APPEALED TO THEM TO RETURN TO WORK--THAT IN THESE TIMES WE NEEDED THEM MORE THAN EVER.

AND DID THEY HEAR YOU?

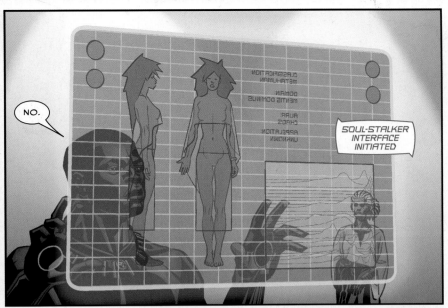

NO.

SOUL-STALKER INTERFACE INITIATED

THEY WERE LISTENING TO SOMEONE ELSE.

I SAW HER, MOTHER. THE ONE WHO DREW OUT THIS HATE. SHE TURNED US AGAINST OUR OWN PEOPLE. FOR FEAR OF MORE LIVES LOST, I LET HER GO.

BUT I WILL FIND HER. AND I WILL KILL HER FOR THIS.

MORE DEATH, T'CHALLA?

TODAY I UPHELD AN EXECUTION FOR ONE OF OUR OWN ADORED ONES. IT WAS MY DUTY, AND I WOULD DO IT AGAIN. BUT I AM NOT BLIND TO WHAT THIS MEANS.

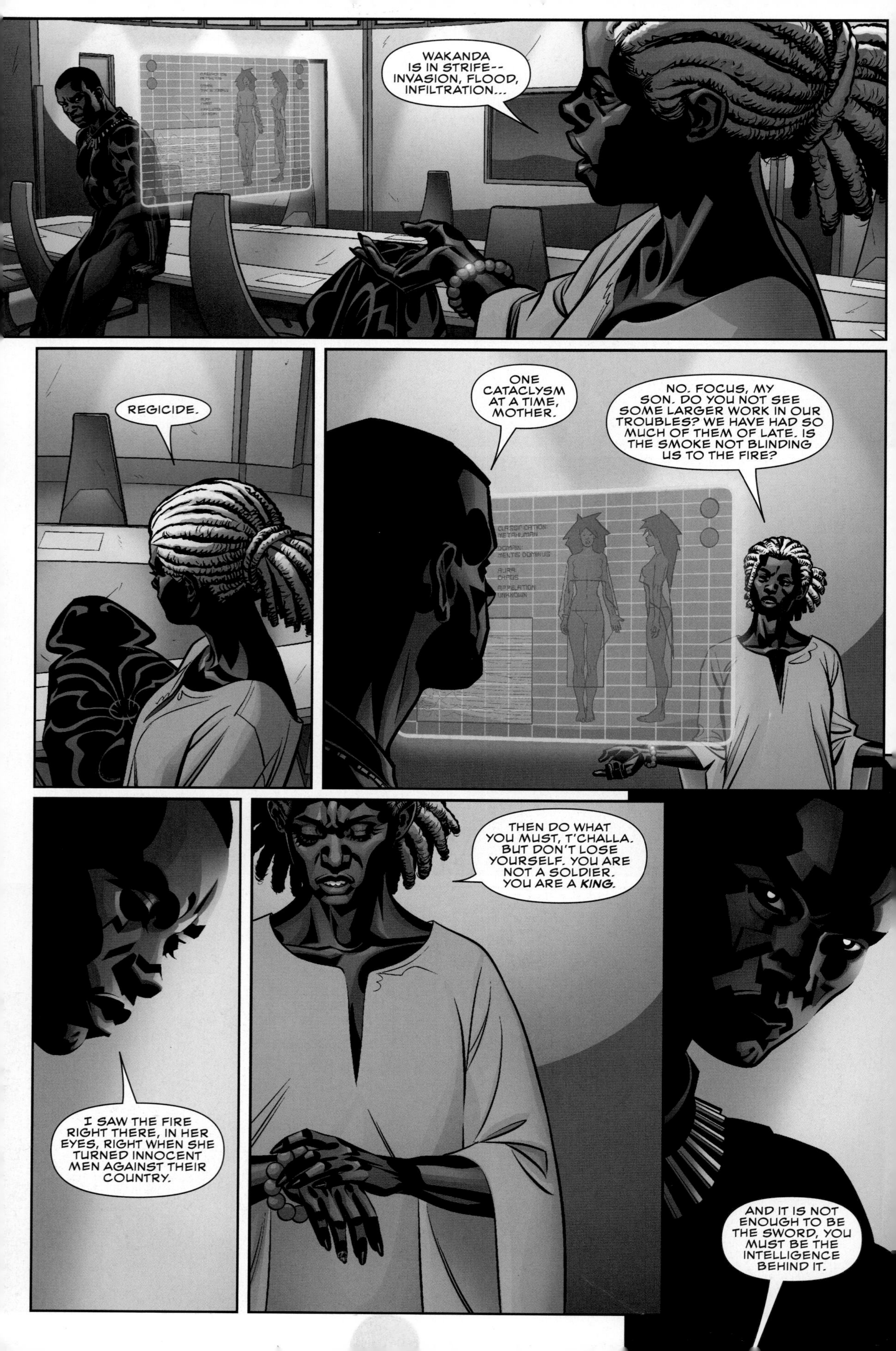
WAKANDA IS IN STRIFE-- INVASION, FLOOD, INFILTRATION...
REGICIDE.
ONE CATACLYSM AT A TIME, MOTHER.
NO. FOCUS, MY SON. DO YOU NOT SEE SOME LARGER WORK IN OUR TROUBLES? WE HAVE HAD SO MUCH OF THEM OF LATE. IS THE SMOKE NOT BLINDING US TO THE FIRE?
CLASSIFICATION: METAHUMAN
DOMAIN: MENTIS DOMINUS
AURA: CHAOS
APPELATION: UNKNOWN
I SAW THE FIRE RIGHT THERE, IN HER EYES, RIGHT WHEN SHE TURNED INNOCENT MEN AGAINST THEIR COUNTRY.
THEN DO WHAT YOU MUST, T'CHALLA. BUT DON'T LOSE YOURSELF. YOU ARE NOT A SOLDIER. YOU ARE A *KING*.
AND IT IS NOT ENOUGH TO BE THE SWORD, YOU MUST BE THE INTELLIGENCE BEHIND IT.

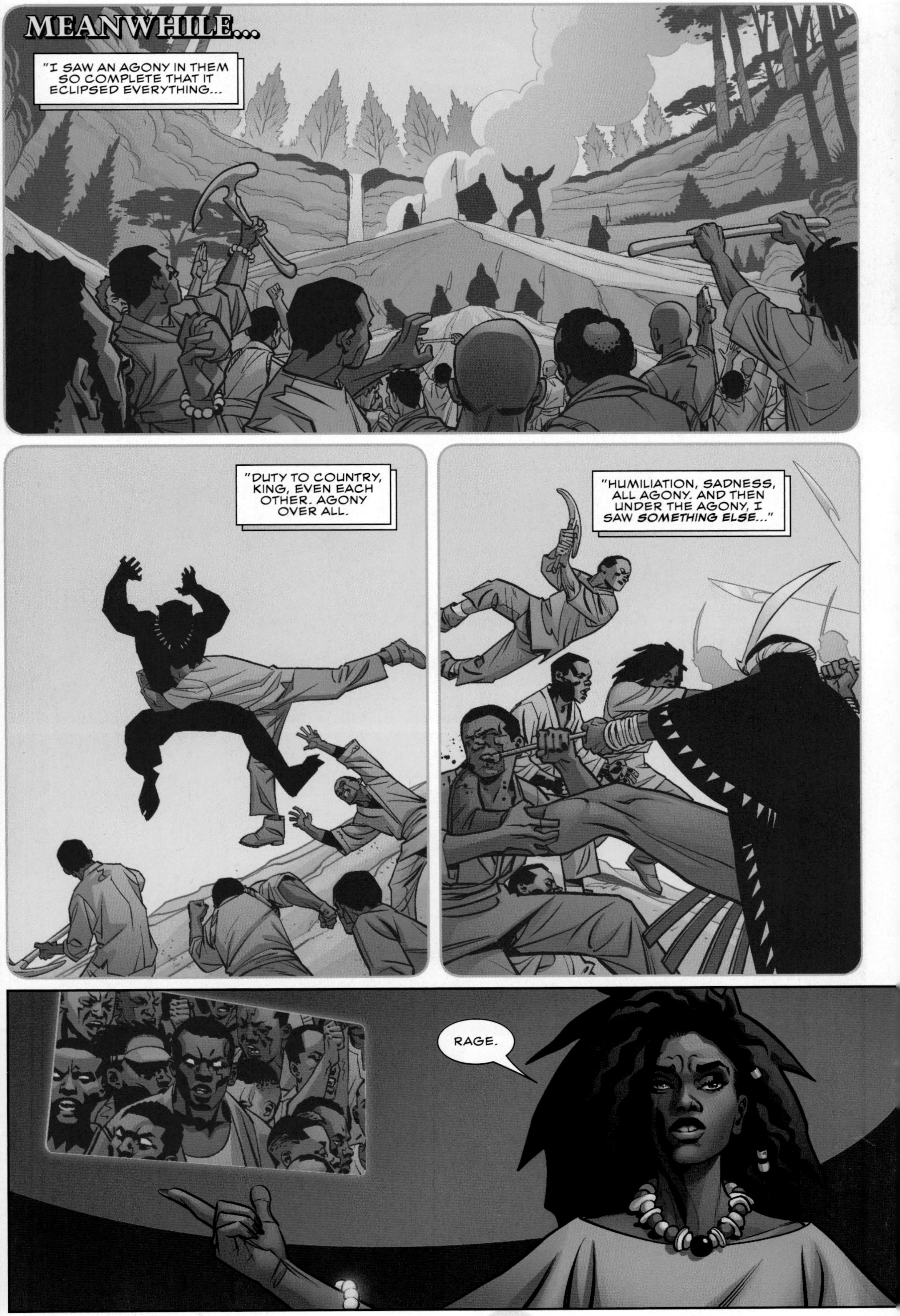
MEANWHILE...
"I SAW AN AGONY IN THEM SO COMPLETE THAT IT ECLIPSED EVERYTHING...
"DUTY TO COUNTRY, KING, EVEN EACH OTHER. AGONY OVER ALL.
"HUMILIATION, SADNESS, ALL AGONY. AND THEN UNDER THE AGONY, I SAW SOMETHING ELSE..."
RAGE.

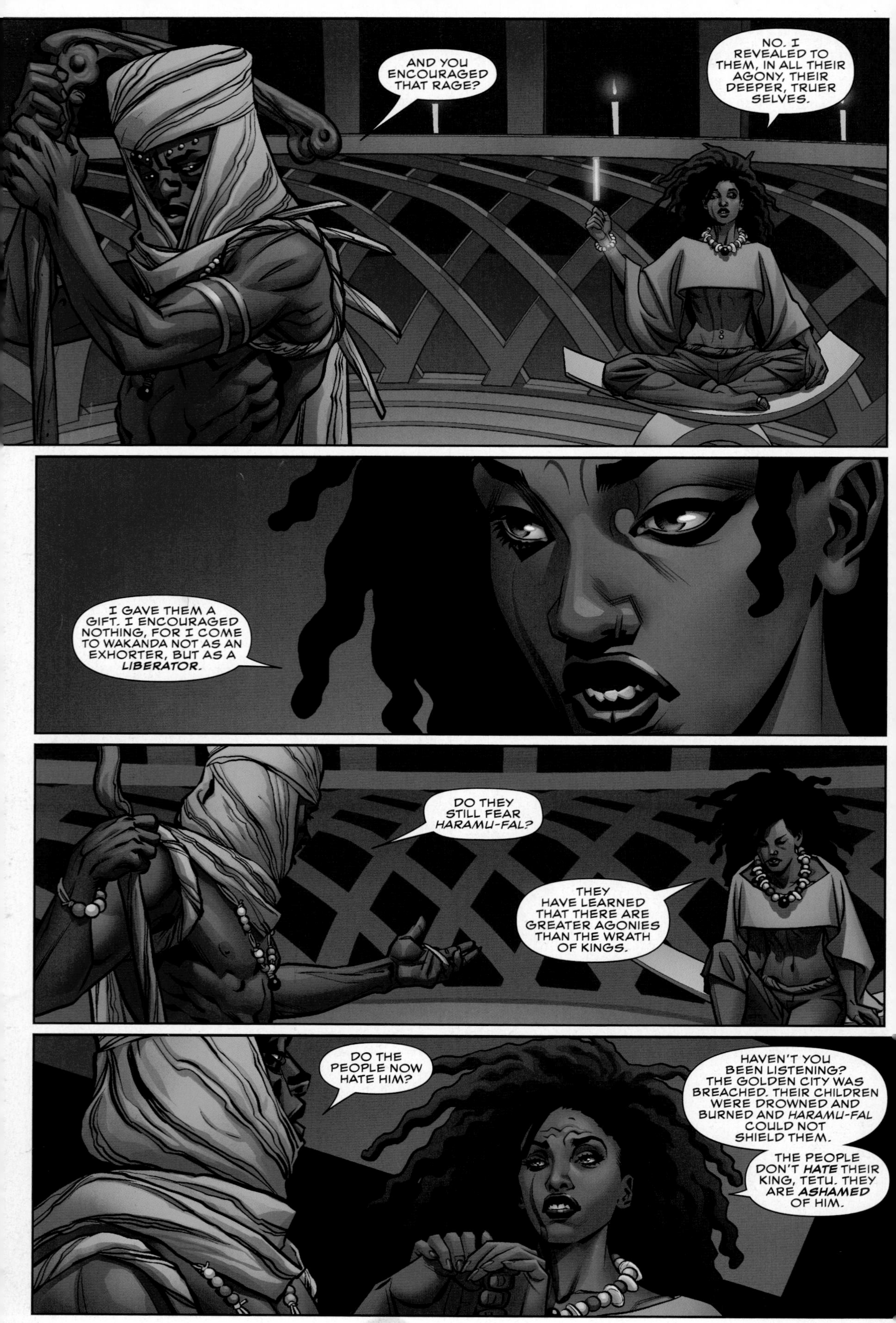
AND YOU ENCOURAGED THAT RAGE?
NO. I REVEALED TO THEM, IN ALL THEIR AGONY, THEIR DEEPER, TRUER SELVES.
I GAVE THEM A GIFT. I ENCOURAGED NOTHING, FOR I COME TO WAKANDA NOT AS AN EXHORTER, BUT AS A LIBERATOR.
DO THEY STILL FEAR HARAMU-FAL?
THEY HAVE LEARNED THAT THERE ARE GREATER AGONIES THAN THE WRATH OF KINGS.
DO THE PEOPLE NOW HATE HIM?
HAVEN'T YOU BEEN LISTENING? THE GOLDEN CITY WAS BREACHED. THEIR CHILDREN WERE DROWNED AND BURNED AND HARAMU-FAL COULD NOT SHIELD THEM.
THE PEOPLE DON'T HATE THEIR KING, TETU. THEY ARE ASHAMED OF HIM.

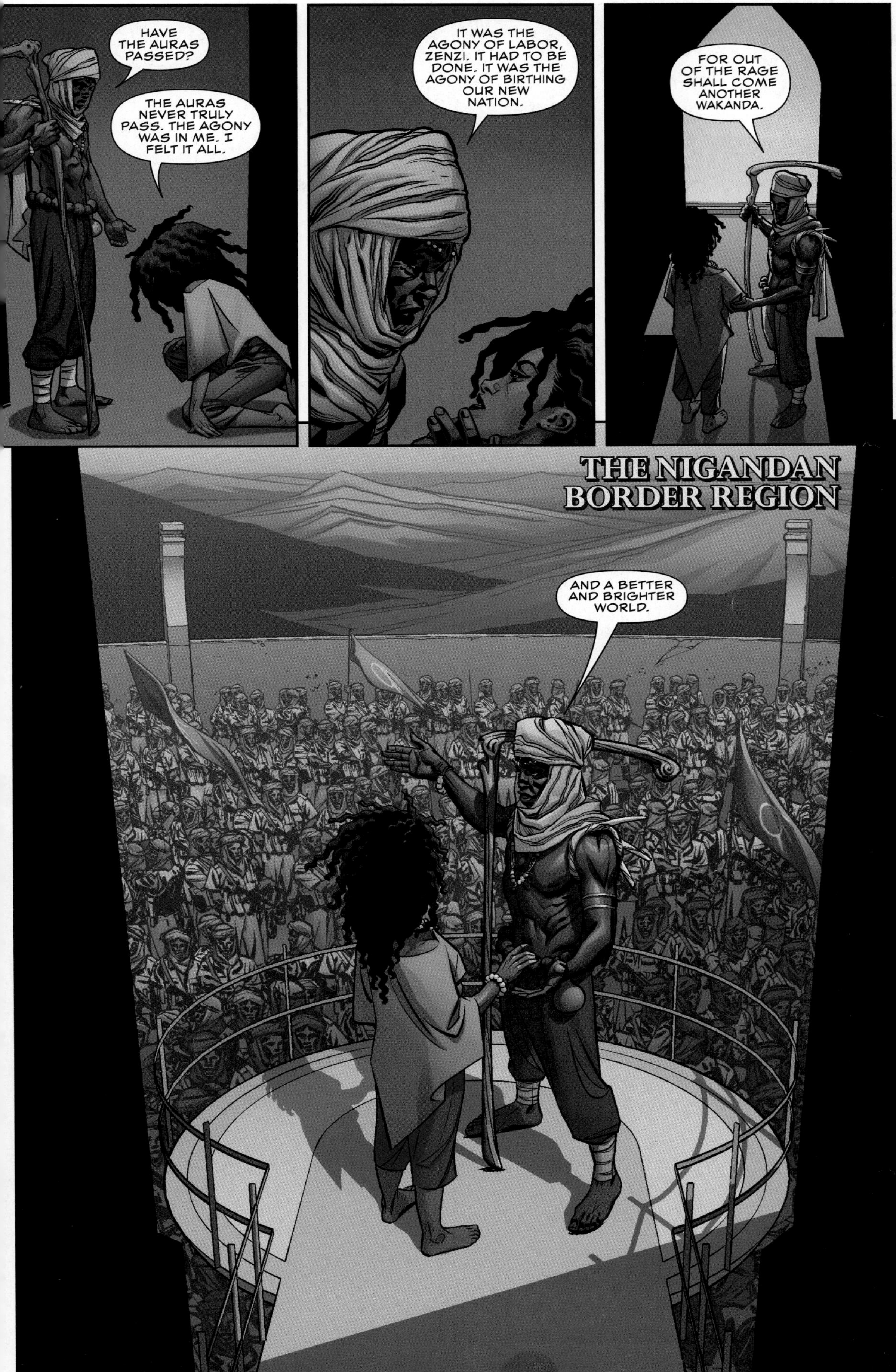
HAVE THE AURAS PASSED?
THE AURAS NEVER TRULY PASS. THE AGONY WAS IN ME. I FELT IT ALL.
IT WAS THE AGONY OF LABOR, ZENZI. IT HAD TO BE DONE. IT WAS THE AGONY OF BIRTHING OUR NEW NATION.
FOR OUT OF THE RAGE SHALL COME ANOTHER WAKANDA.
THE NIGANDAN BORDER REGION
AND A BETTER AND BRIGHTER WORLD.

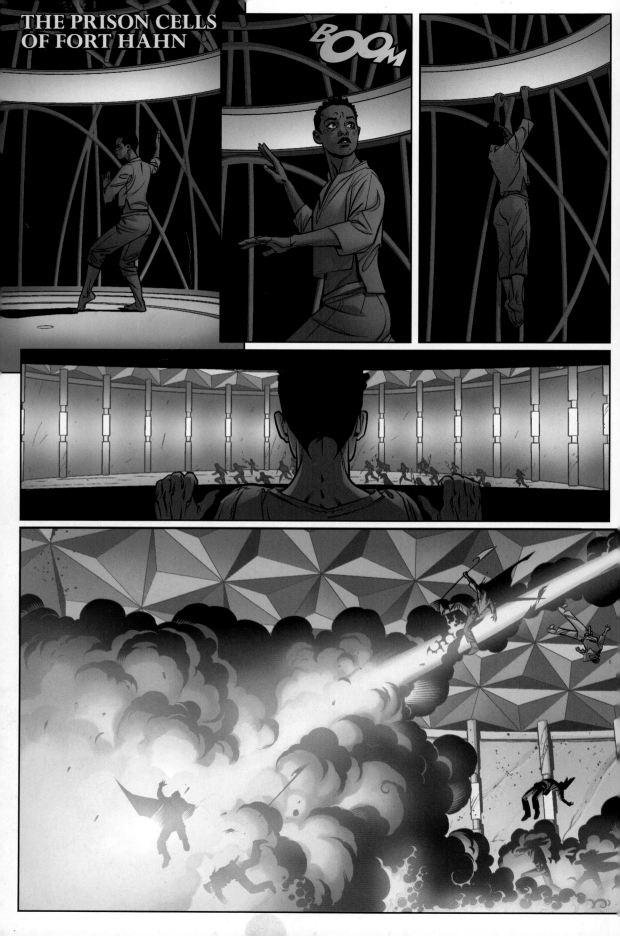

THE PRISON CELLS
OF FORT HAHN

BOOM

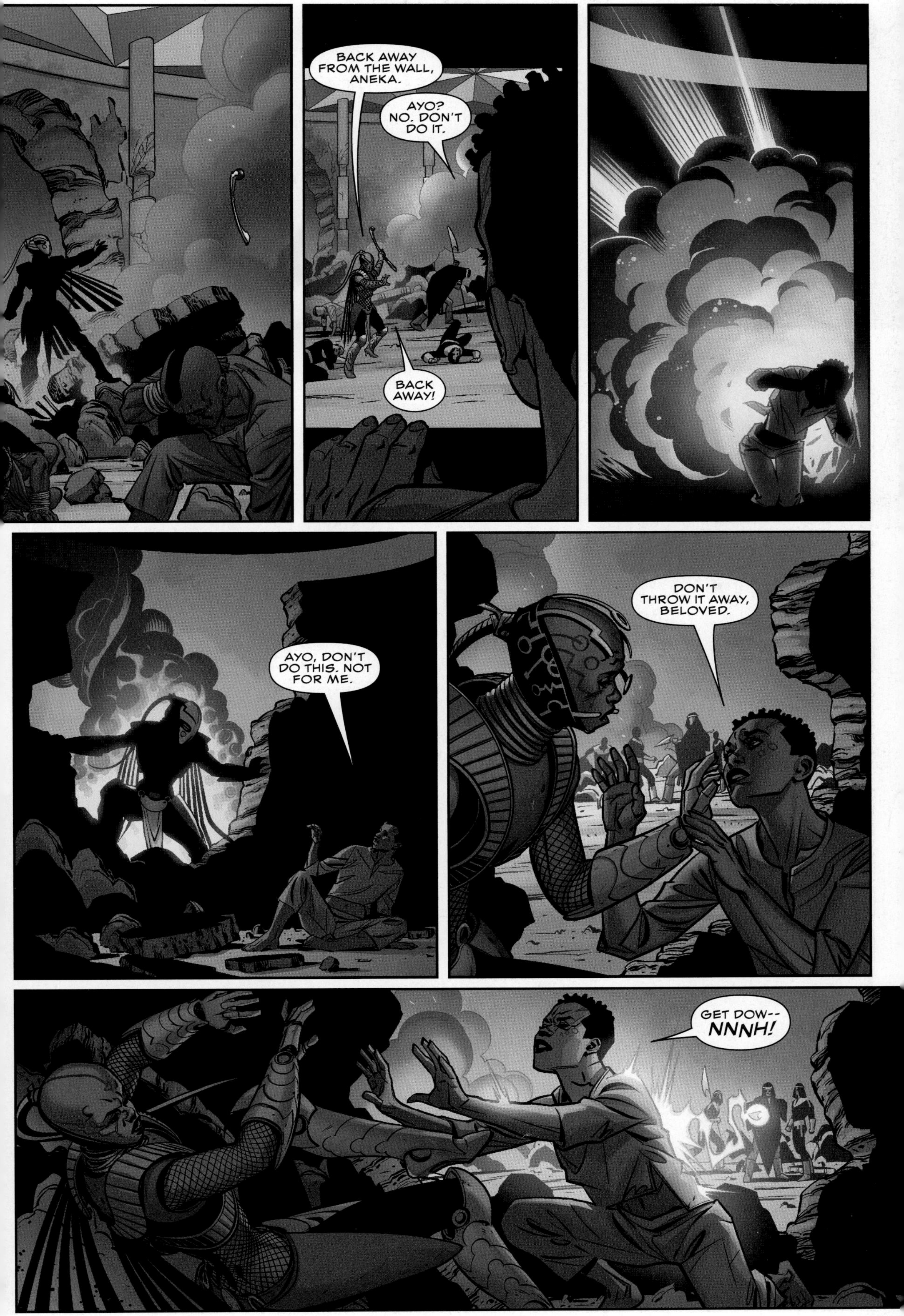
BACK AWAY FROM THE WALL, ANEKA.
AYO? NO. DON'T DO IT.
BACK AWAY!
AYO, DON'T DO THIS. NOT FOR ME.
DON'T THROW IT AWAY, BELOVED.
GET DOW-- NNNH!

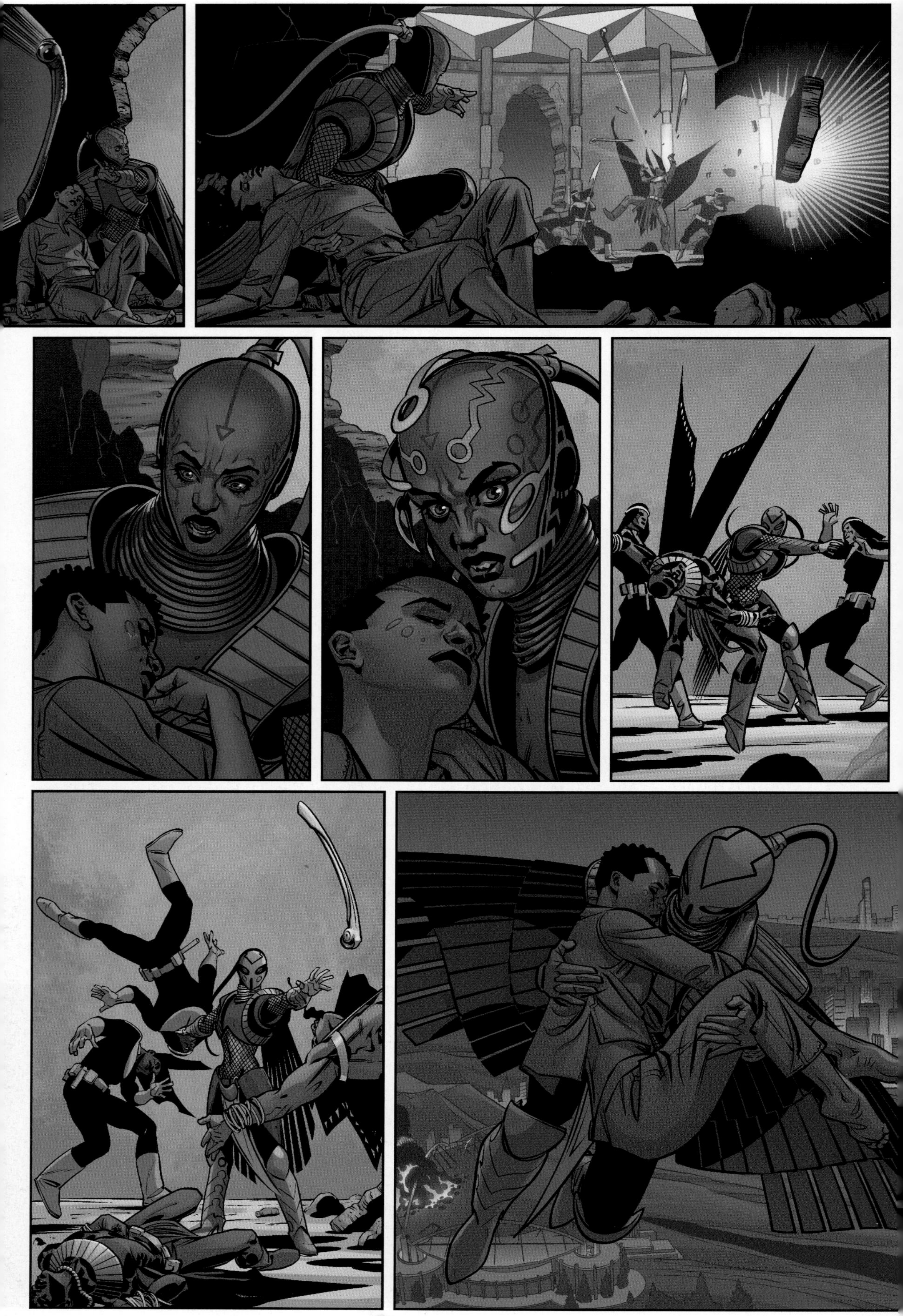

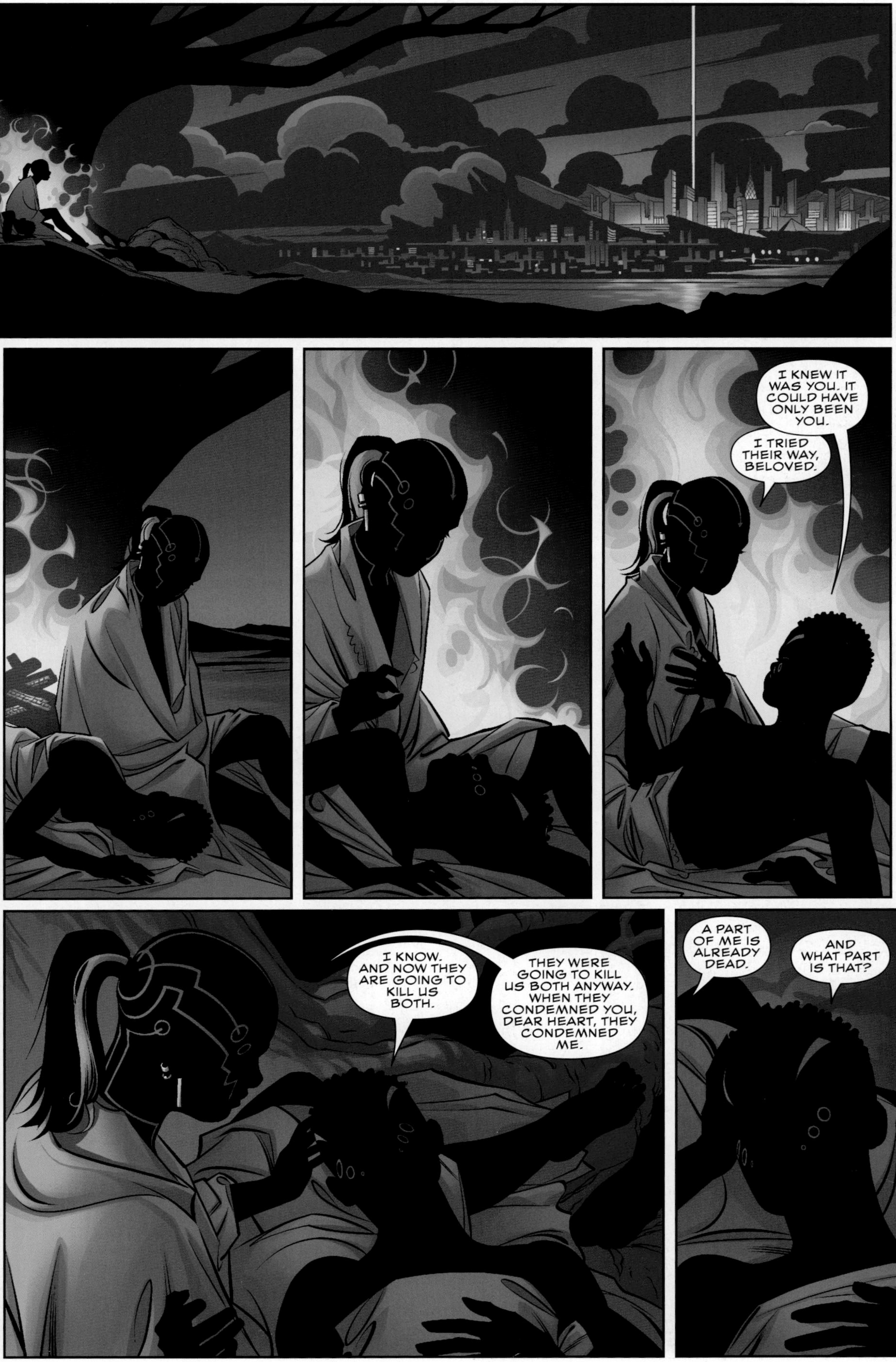
I KNEW IT WAS YOU. IT COULD HAVE ONLY BEEN YOU.
I TRIED THEIR WAY, BELOVED.
I KNOW. AND NOW THEY ARE GOING TO KILL US BOTH.
THEY WERE GOING TO KILL US BOTH ANYWAY. WHEN THEY CONDEMNED YOU, DEAR HEART, THEY CONDEMNED ME.
A PART OF ME IS ALREADY DEAD.
AND WHAT PART IS THAT?

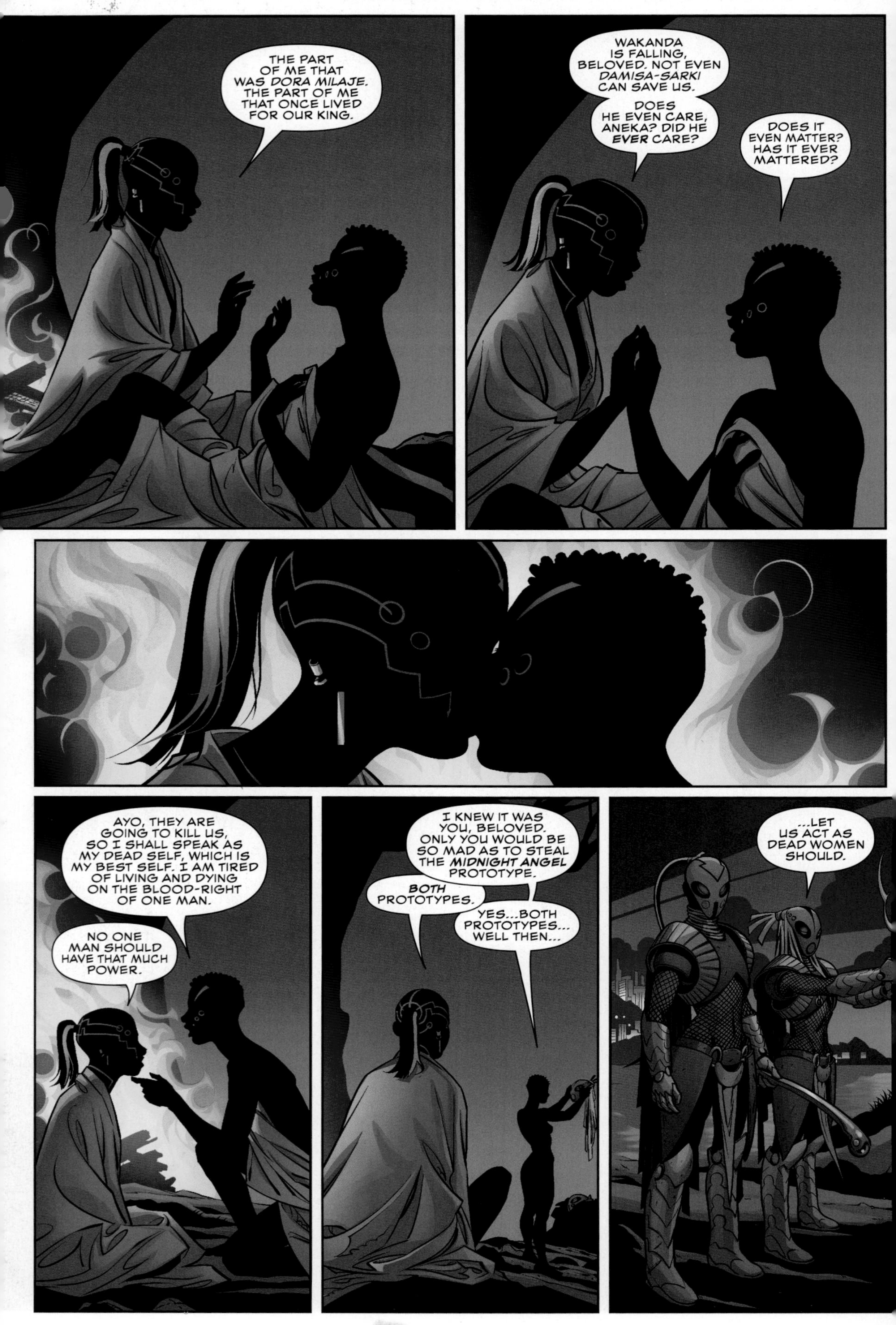
THE PART OF ME THAT WAS *DORA MILAJE.* THE PART OF ME THAT ONCE LIVED FOR OUR KING.
WAKANDA IS FALLING, BELOVED. NOT EVEN *DAMISA-SARKI* CAN SAVE US.
DOES HE EVEN CARE, ANEKA? DID HE **EVER** CARE?
DOES IT EVEN MATTER? HAS IT EVER MATTERED?
AYO, THEY ARE GOING TO KILL US, SO I SHALL SPEAK AS MY DEAD SELF, WHICH IS MY BEST SELF. I AM TIRED OF LIVING AND DYING ON THE BLOOD-RIGHT OF ONE MAN.
NO ONE MAN SHOULD HAVE THAT MUCH POWER.
I KNEW IT WAS YOU, BELOVED. ONLY YOU WOULD BE SO MAD AS TO STEAL THE ***MIDNIGHT ANGEL*** PROTOTYPE.
BOTH PROTOTYPES.
YES...BOTH PROTOTYPES... WELL THEN...
...LET US ACT AS DEAD WOMEN SHOULD.

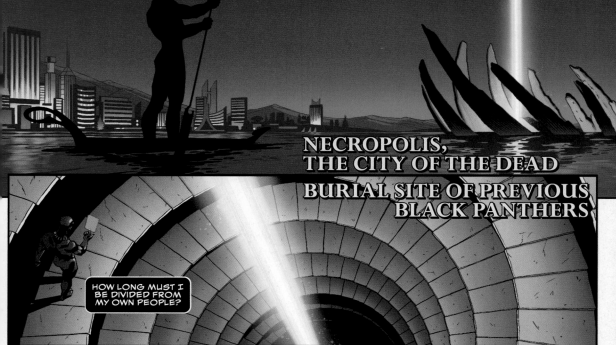

NECROPOLIS, THE CITY OF THE DEAD
BURIAL SITE OF PREVIOUS BLACK PANTHERS
HOW LONG MUST I BE DIVIDED FROM MY OWN PEOPLE?
FROM MY COUNTRY...
FROM MY OWN BLOOD?
RESUSCITATION FAILURE
SHURI...

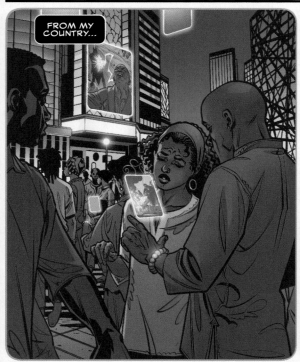

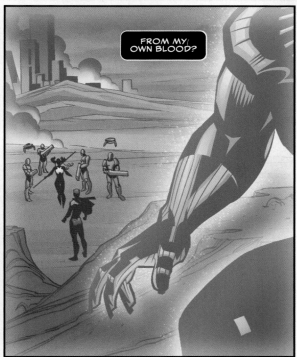

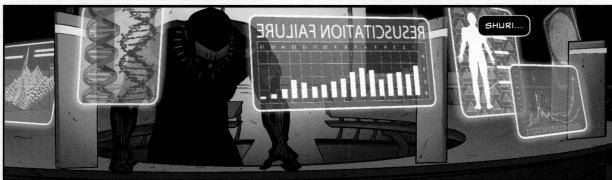

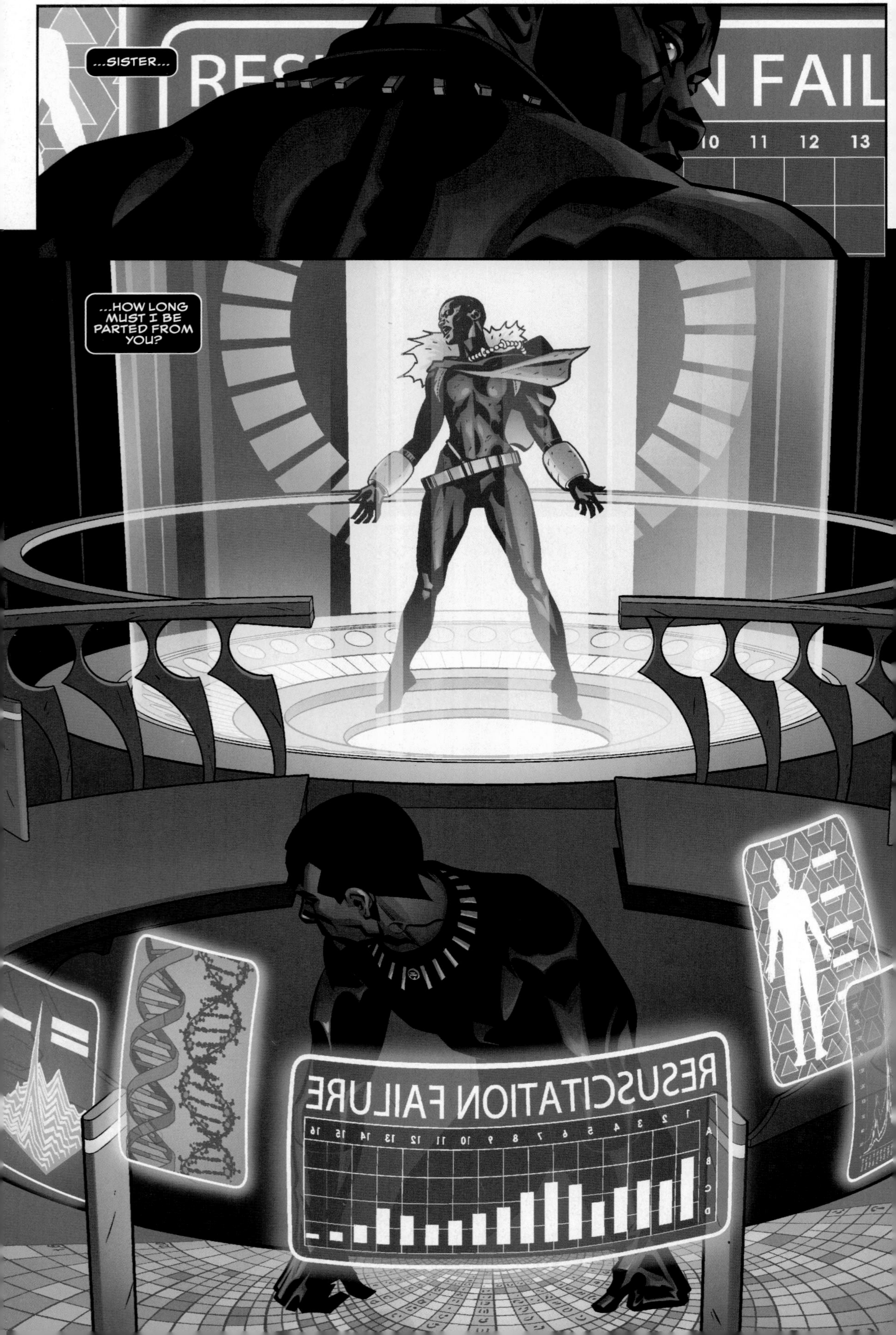
...SISTER...
...HOW LONG MUST I BE PARTED FROM YOU?
RESUSCITATION FAILURE

#1 VARIANT BY **OLIVIER COIPEL**

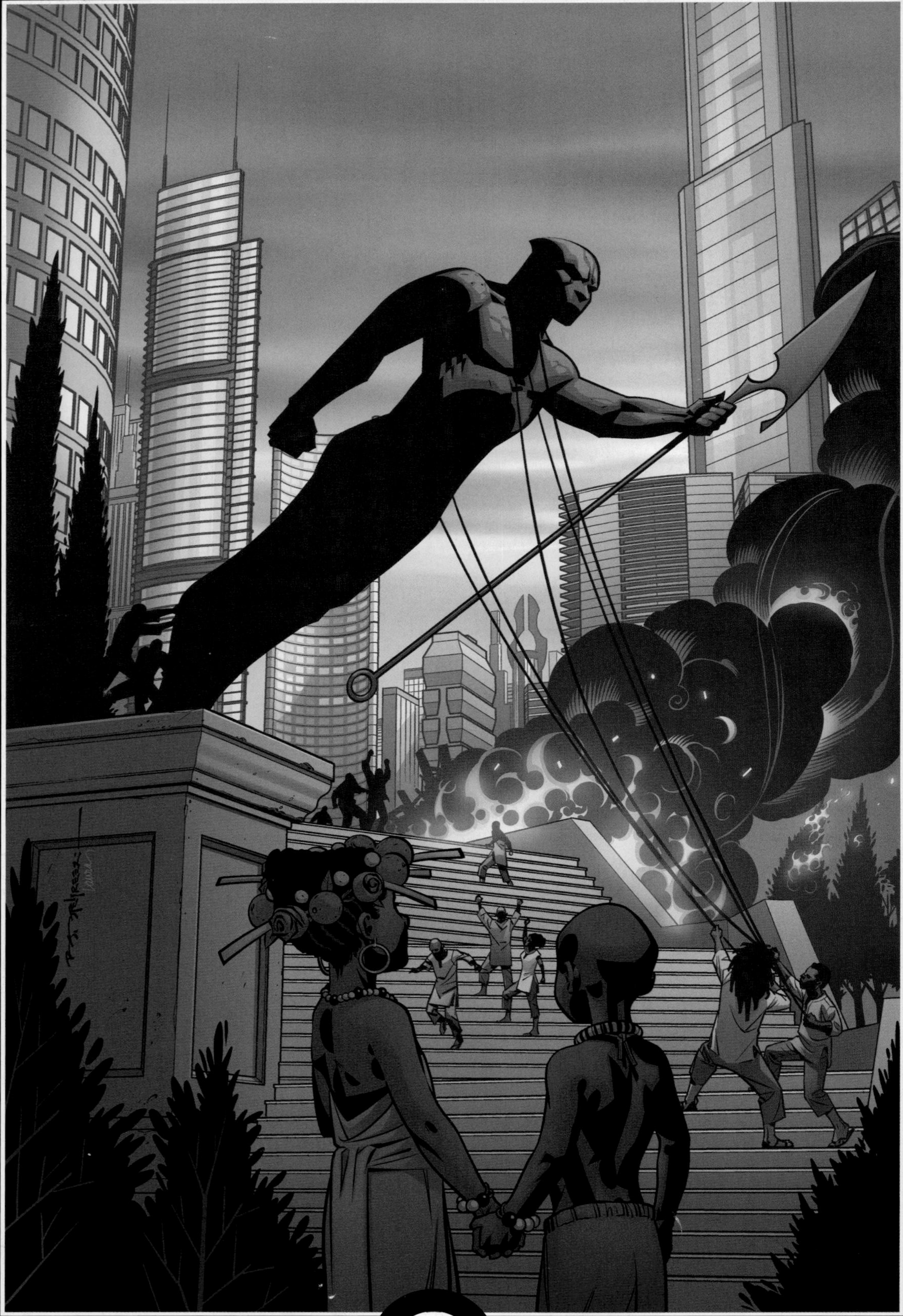

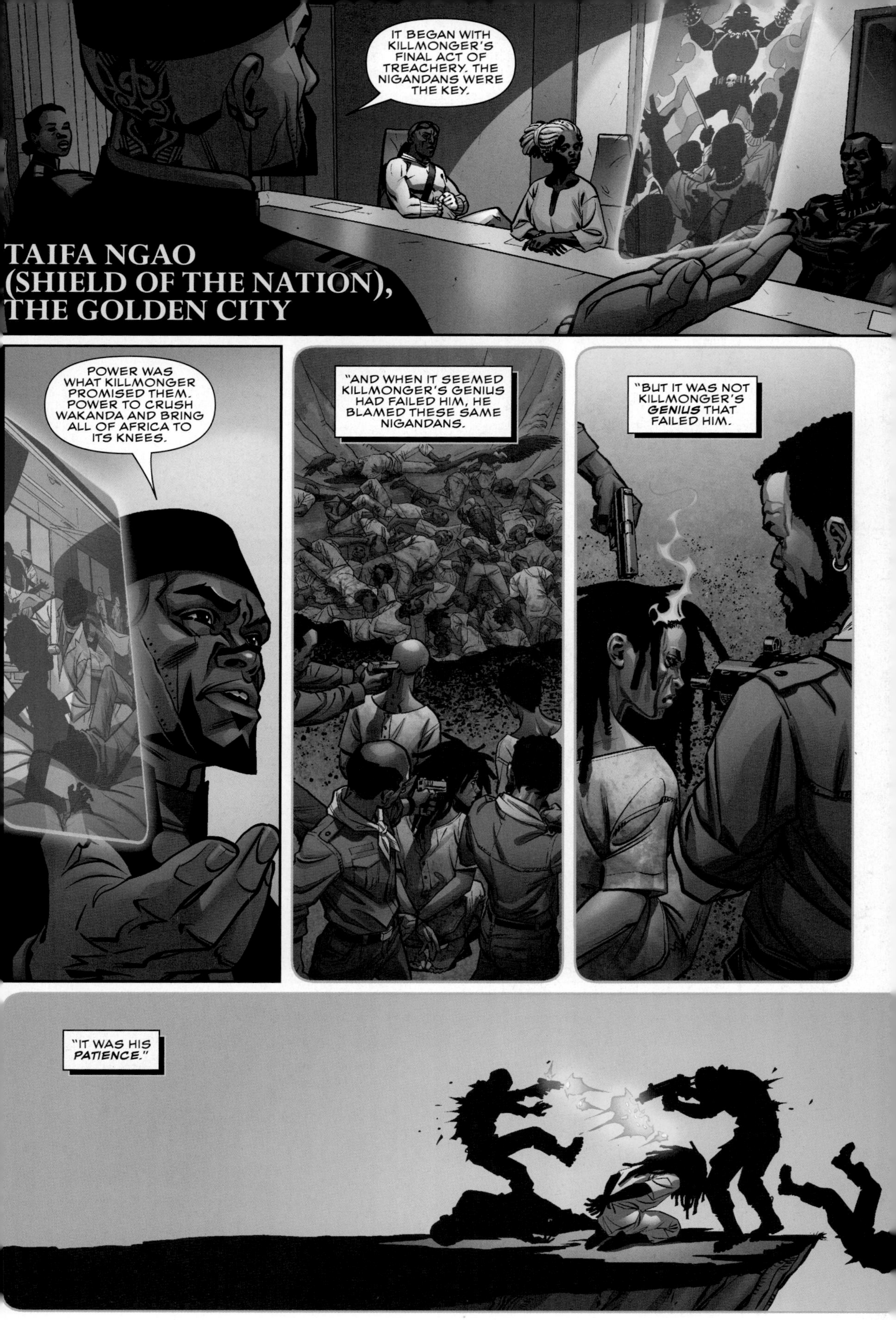

IT BEGAN WITH KILLMONGER'S FINAL ACT OF TREACHERY. THE NIGANDANS WERE THE KEY.
TAIFA NGAO (SHIELD OF THE NATION), THE GOLDEN CITY
POWER WAS WHAT KILLMONGER PROMISED THEM. POWER TO CRUSH WAKANDA AND BRING ALL OF AFRICA TO ITS KNEES.
"AND WHEN IT SEEMED KILLMONGER'S GENIUS HAD FAILED HIM, HE BLAMED THESE SAME NIGANDANS.
"BUT IT WAS NOT KILLMONGER'S GENIUS THAT FAILED HIM.
"IT WAS HIS PATIENCE."

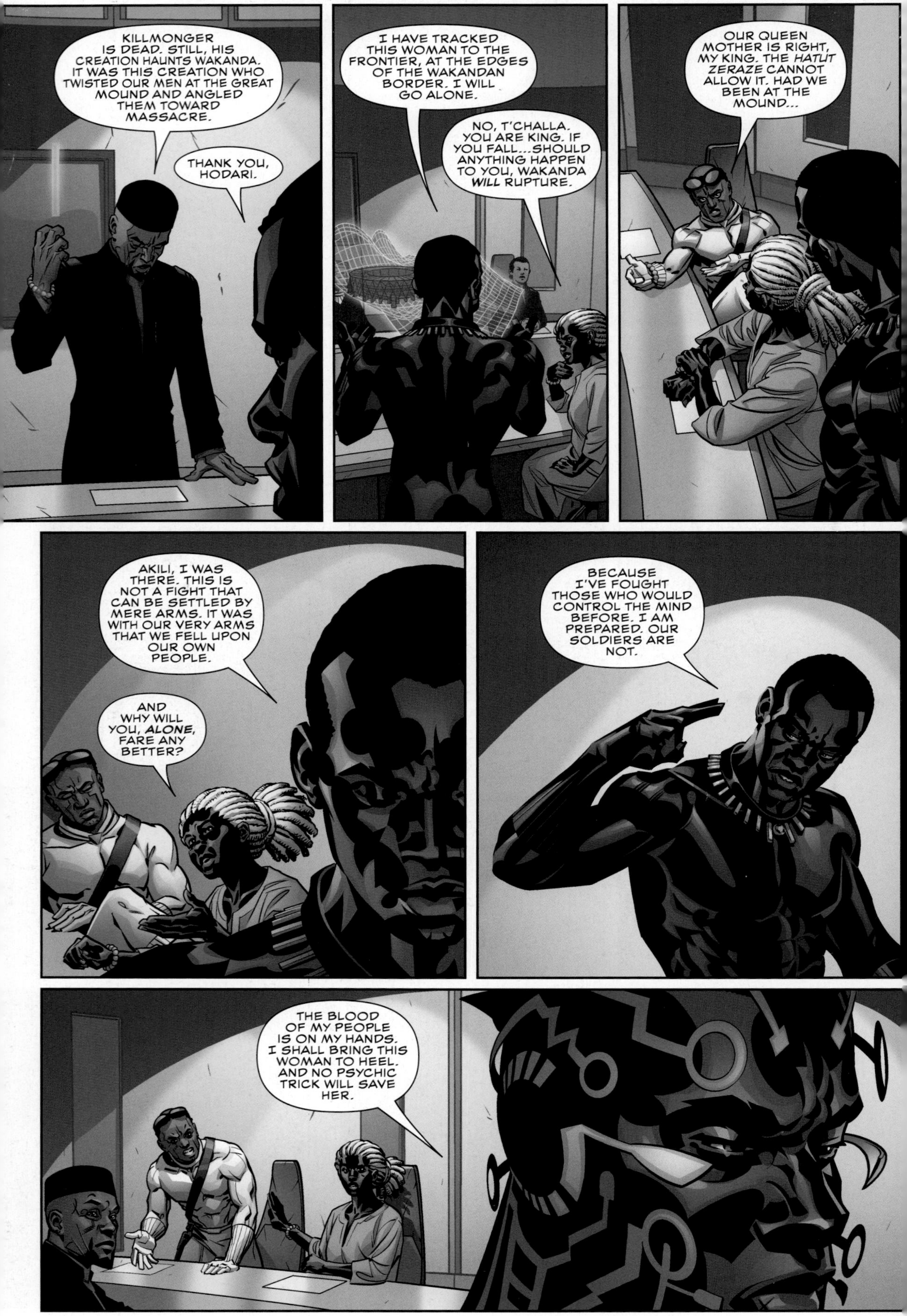
KILLMONGER IS DEAD. STILL, HIS CREATION HAUNTS WAKANDA. IT WAS THIS CREATION WHO TWISTED OUR MEN AT THE GREAT MOUND AND ANGLED THEM TOWARD MASSACRE.
THANK YOU, HODARI.
I HAVE TRACKED THIS WOMAN TO THE FRONTIER, AT THE EDGES OF THE WAKANDAN BORDER. I WILL GO ALONE.
NO, T'CHALLA. YOU ARE KING. IF YOU FALL...SHOULD ANYTHING HAPPEN TO YOU, WAKANDA *WILL* RUPTURE.
OUR QUEEN MOTHER IS RIGHT, MY KING. THE *HATUT ZERAZE* CANNOT ALLOW IT. HAD WE BEEN AT THE MOUND...
AKILI, I WAS THERE. THIS IS NOT A FIGHT THAT CAN BE SETTLED BY MERE ARMS. IT WAS WITH OUR VERY ARMS THAT WE FELL UPON OUR OWN PEOPLE.
AND WHY WILL YOU, *ALONE*, FARE ANY BETTER?
BECAUSE I'VE FOUGHT THOSE WHO WOULD CONTROL THE MIND BEFORE. I AM PREPARED. OUR SOLDIERS ARE NOT.
THE BLOOD OF MY PEOPLE IS ON MY HANDS. I SHALL BRING THIS WOMAN TO HEEL. AND NO PSYCHIC TRICK WILL SAVE HER.

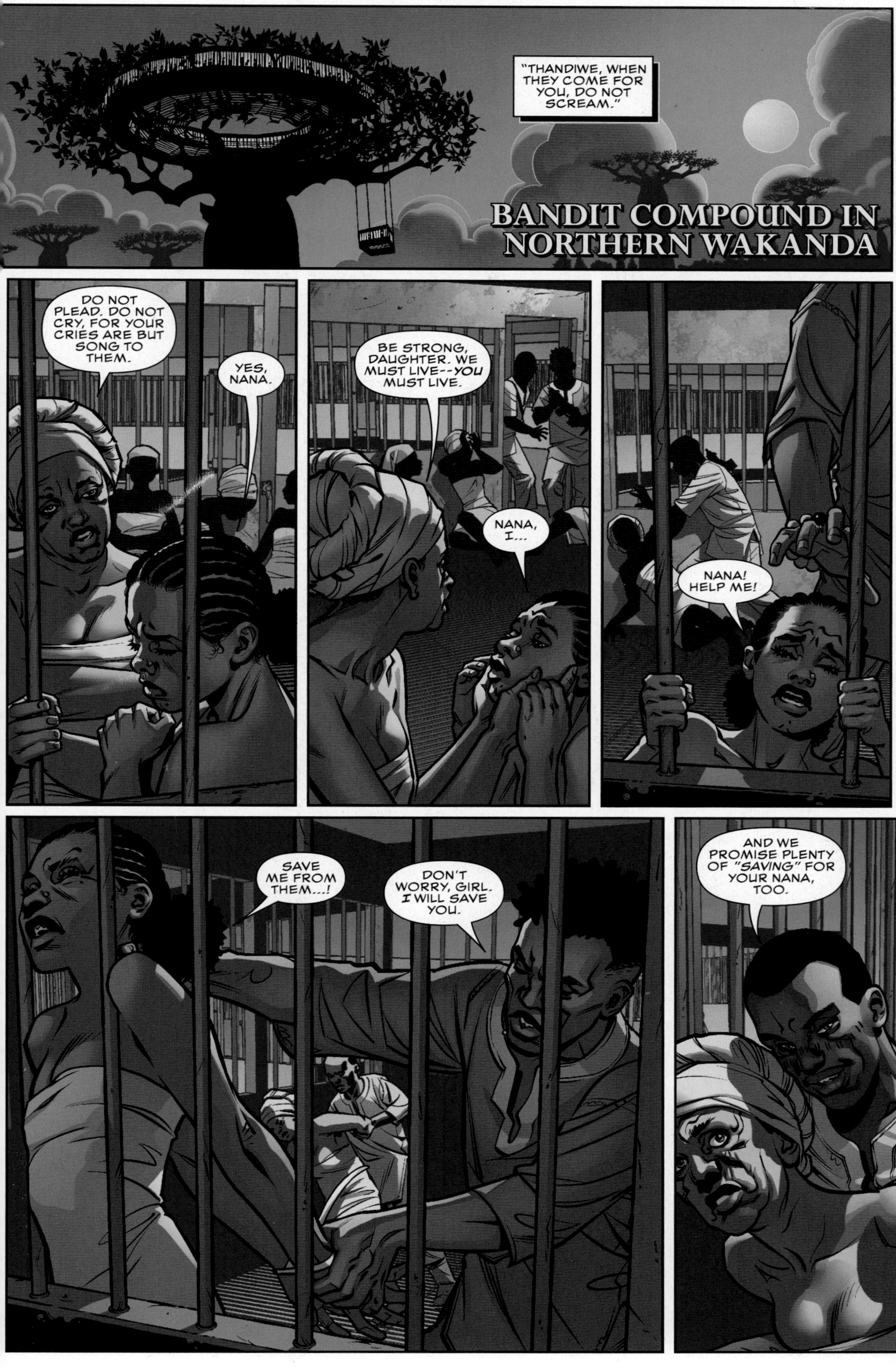
"THANDIWE, WHEN THEY COME FOR YOU, DO NOT SCREAM."
BANDIT COMPOUND IN NORTHERN WAKANDA
DO NOT PLEAD. DO NOT CRY, FOR YOUR CRIES ARE BUT SONG TO THEM.
YES, NANA.
BE STRONG, DAUGHTER. WE MUST LIVE--YOU MUST LIVE.
NANA, I...
NANA! HELP ME!
SAVE ME FROM THEM...!
DON'T WORRY, GIRL. I WILL SAVE YOU.
AND WE PROMISE PLENTY OF "SAVING" FOR YOUR NANA, TOO.

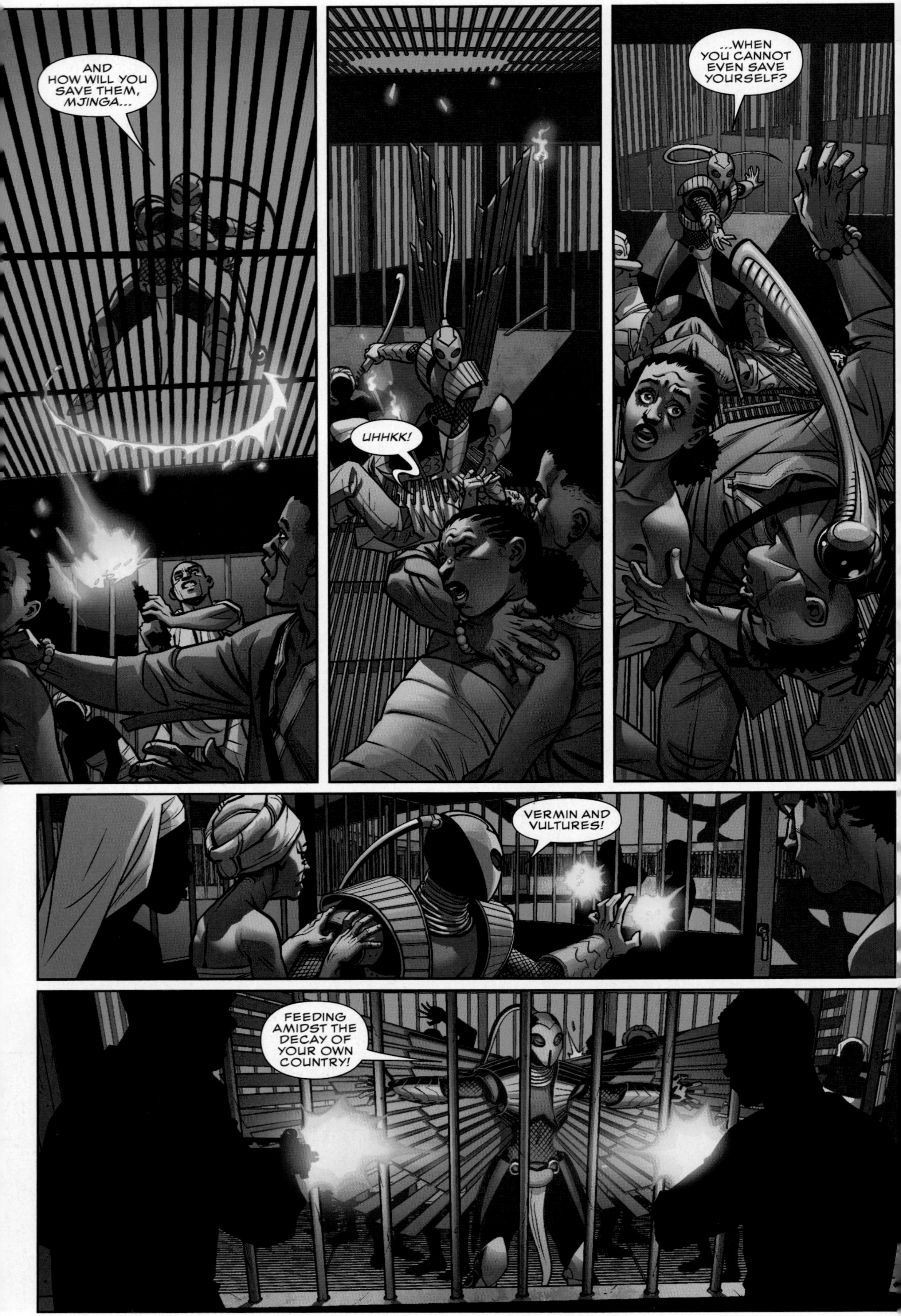
AND HOW WILL YOU SAVE THEM, MJINGA...
UHHKK!
...WHEN YOU CANNOT EVEN SAVE YOURSELF?
VERMIN AND VULTURES!
FEEDING AMIDST THE DECAY OF YOUR OWN COUNTRY!

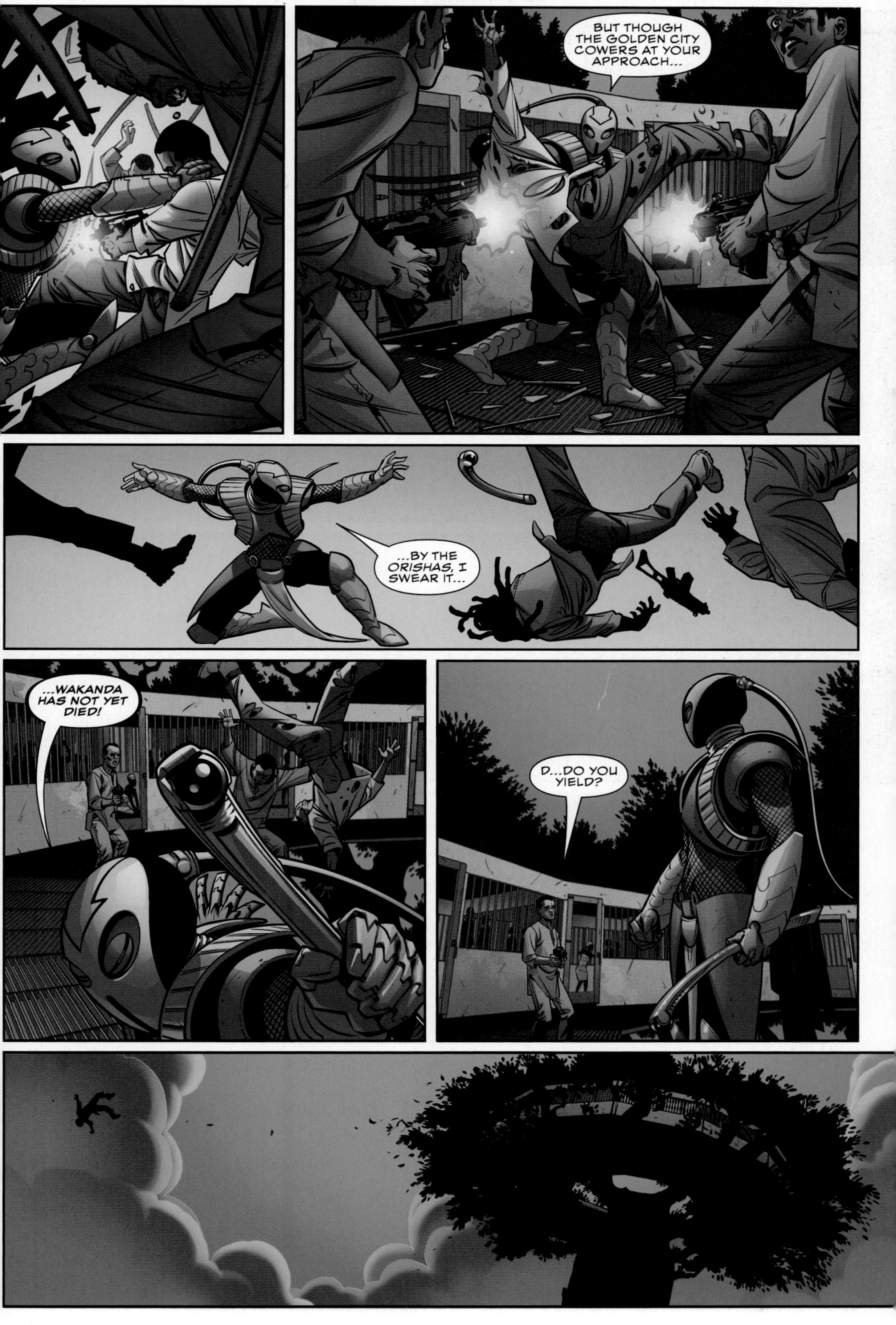
BUT THOUGH THE GOLDEN CITY COWERS AT YOUR APPROACH...
...BY THE ORISHAS, I SWEAR IT...
...WAKANDA HAS NOT YET DIED!
D...DO YOU YIELD?

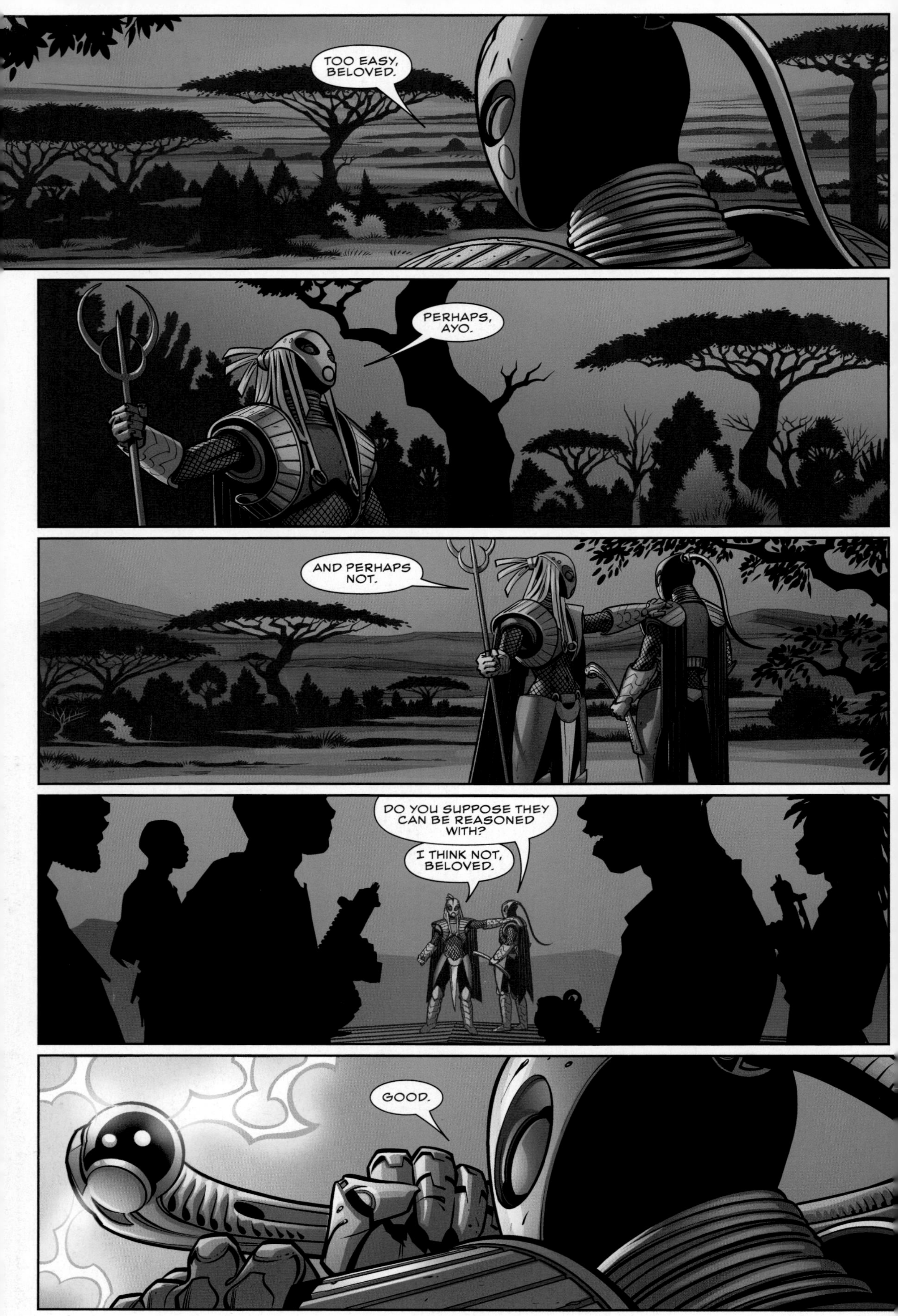
TOO EASY, BELOVED.
PERHAPS, AYO.
AND PERHAPS NOT.
DO YOU SUPPOSE THEY CAN BE REASONED WITH?
I THINK NOT, BELOVED.
GOOD.

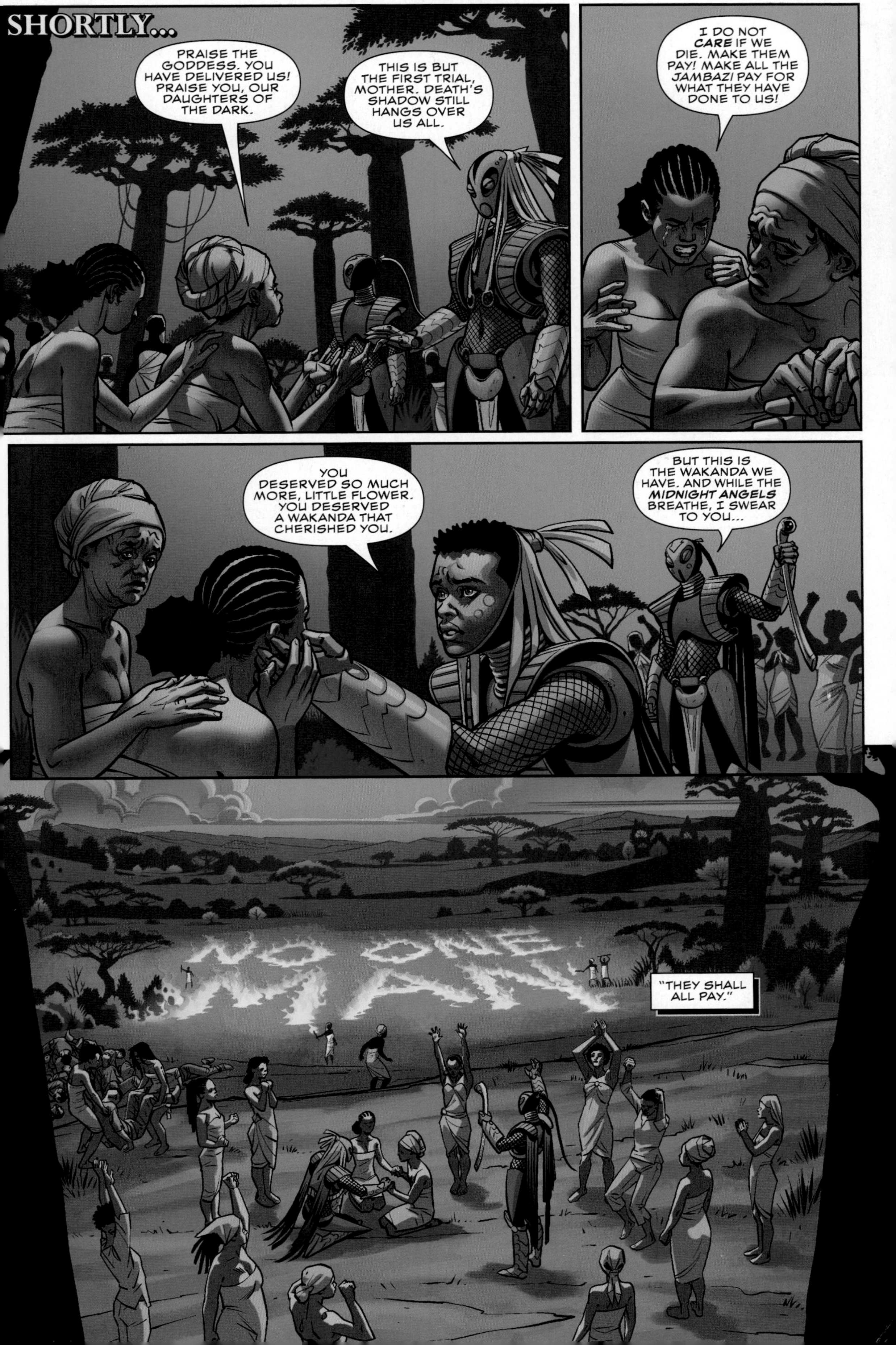
SHORTLY...
PRAISE THE GODDESS. YOU HAVE DELIVERED US! PRAISE YOU, OUR DAUGHTERS OF THE DARK.
THIS IS BUT THE FIRST TRIAL, MOTHER. DEATH'S SHADOW STILL HANGS OVER US ALL.
I DO NOT CARE IF WE DIE. MAKE THEM PAY! MAKE ALL THE JAMBAZI PAY FOR WHAT THEY HAVE DONE TO US!
YOU DESERVED SO MUCH MORE, LITTLE FLOWER. YOU DESERVED A WAKANDA THAT CHERISHED YOU.
BUT THIS IS THE WAKANDA WE HAVE. AND WHILE THE MIDNIGHT ANGELS BREATHE, I SWEAR TO YOU...
NO ONE
"THEY SHALL ALL PAY."

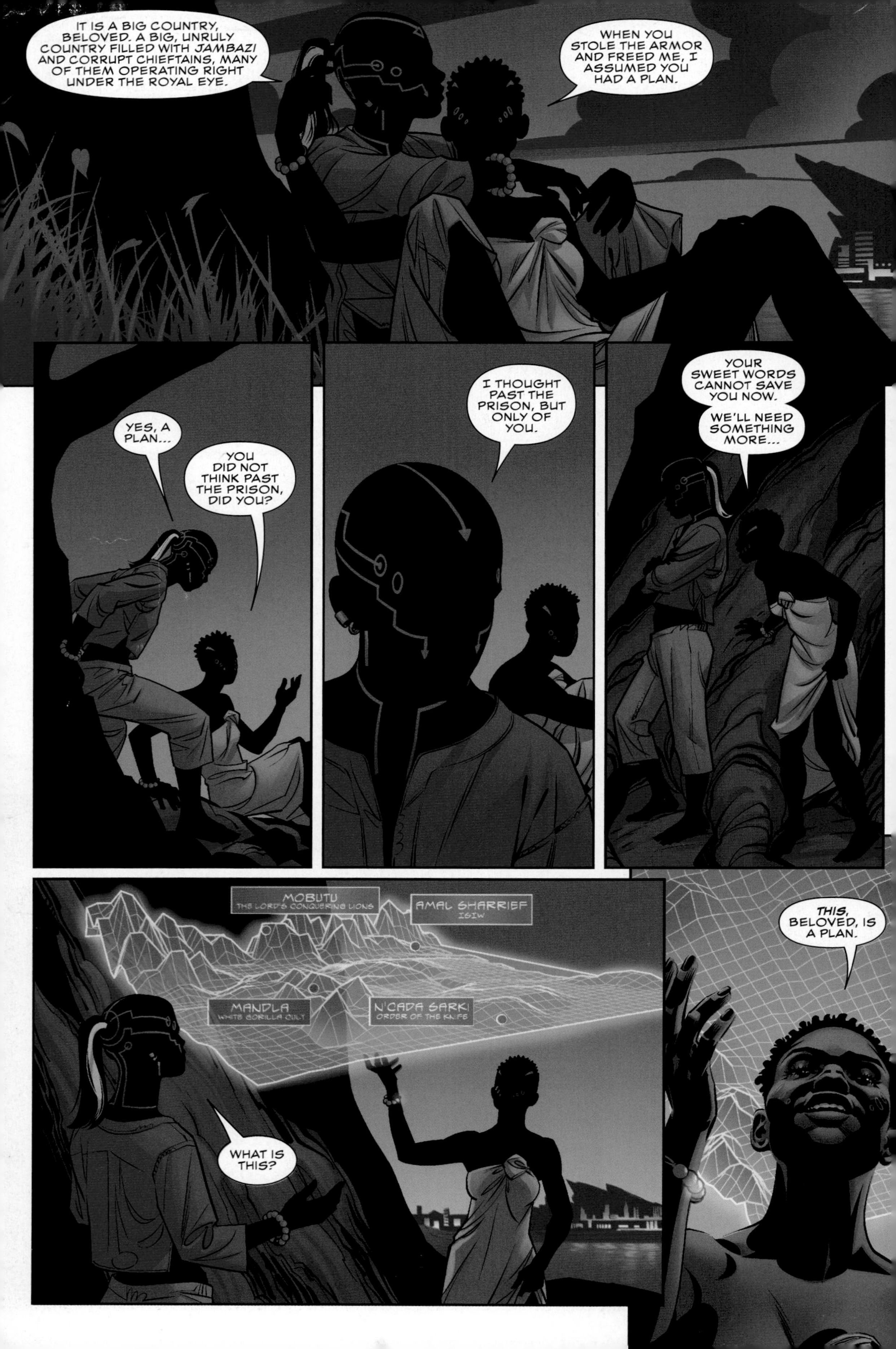
IT IS A BIG COUNTRY, BELOVED. A BIG, UNRULY COUNTRY FILLED WITH *JAMBAZI* AND CORRUPT CHIEFTAINS, MANY OF THEM OPERATING RIGHT UNDER THE ROYAL EYE.
WHEN YOU STOLE THE ARMOR AND FREED ME, I ASSUMED YOU HAD A PLAN.
YES, A PLAN...
YOU DID NOT THINK PAST THE PRISON, DID YOU?
I THOUGHT PAST THE PRISON, BUT ONLY OF YOU.
YOUR SWEET WORDS CANNOT SAVE YOU NOW.
WE'LL NEED SOMETHING MORE...
MOBUTU
THE LORD'S CONQUERING LIONS
AMAL SHARRIEF
IGIW
MANDLA
WHITE GORILLA CULT
N'CADA SARKI
ORDER OF THE KNIFE
WHAT IS THIS?
THIS, BELOVED, IS A PLAN.

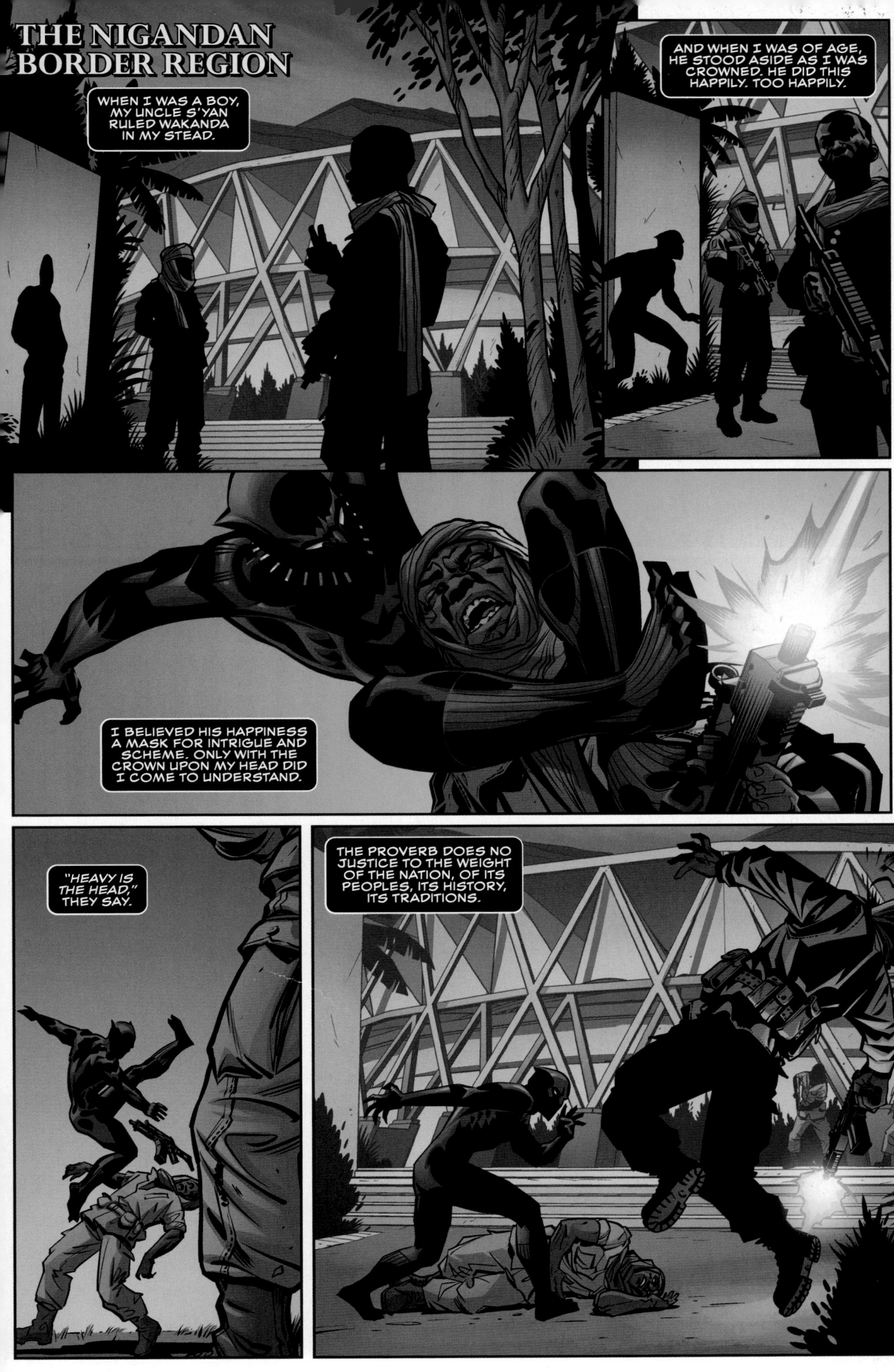
THE NIGANDAN BORDER REGION
WHEN I WAS A BOY, MY UNCLE S'YAN RULED WAKANDA IN MY STEAD.
AND WHEN I WAS OF AGE, HE STOOD ASIDE AS I WAS CROWNED. HE DID THIS HAPPILY. TOO HAPPILY.
I BELIEVED HIS HAPPINESS A MASK FOR INTRIGUE AND SCHEME. ONLY WITH THE CROWN UPON MY HEAD DID I COME TO UNDERSTAND.
"HEAVY IS THE HEAD," THEY SAY.
THE PROVERB DOES NO JUSTICE TO THE WEIGHT OF THE NATION, OF ITS PEOPLES, ITS HISTORY, ITS TRADITIONS.

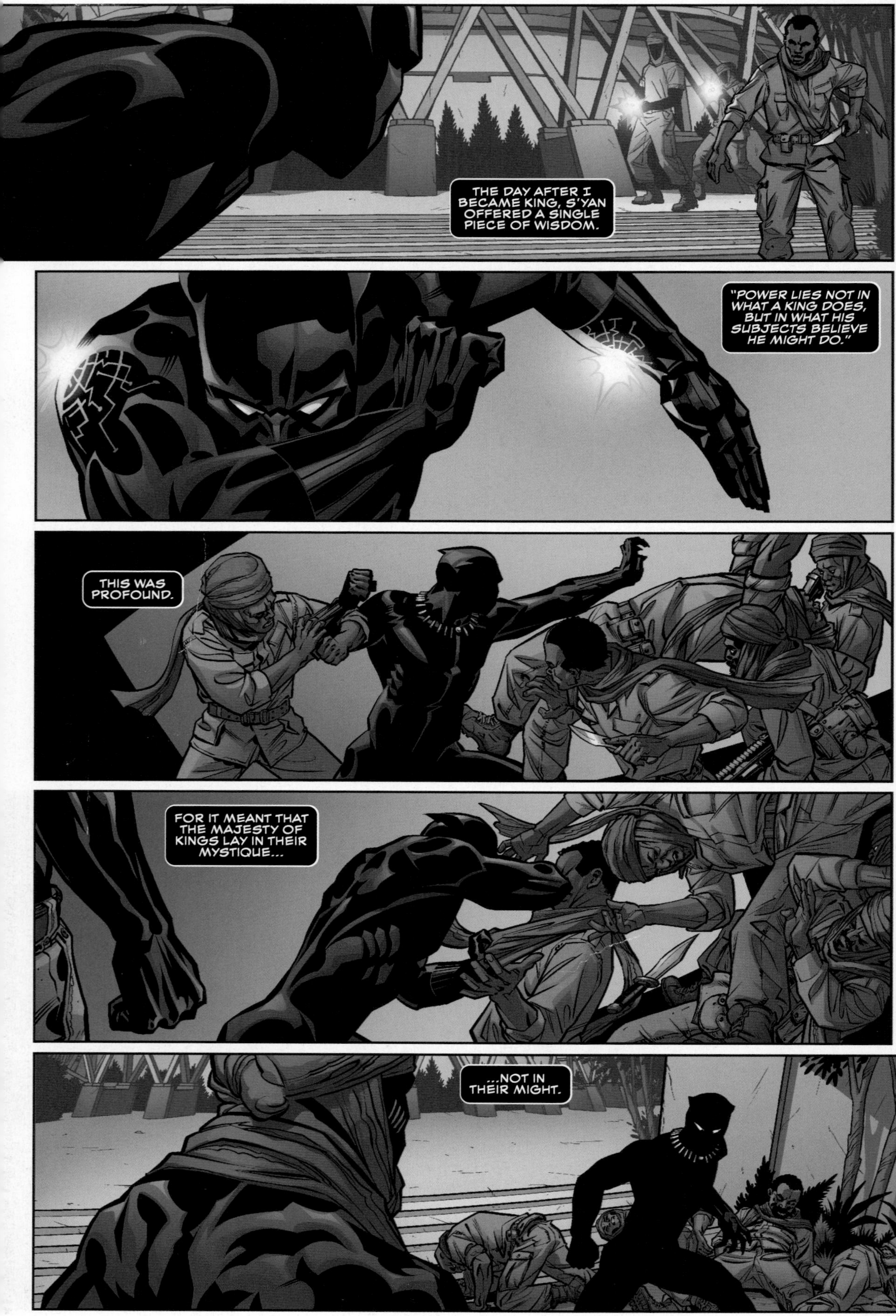
THE DAY AFTER I BECAME KING, S'YAN OFFERED A SINGLE PIECE OF WISDOM.
"POWER LIES NOT IN WHAT A KING DOES, BUT IN WHAT HIS SUBJECTS BELIEVE HE MIGHT DO."
THIS WAS PROFOUND.
FOR IT MEANT THAT THE MAJESTY OF KINGS LAY IN THEIR MYSTIQUE...
...NOT IN THEIR MIGHT.

EVERY ACT OF MIGHT DIMINISHED THE KING, FOR IT DIMINISHED HIS MYSTIQUE.

MIGHT EXPOSED THE KING'S POWERS AND THUS HIS LIMITS.

MIGHT MADE THE KING HUMAN.

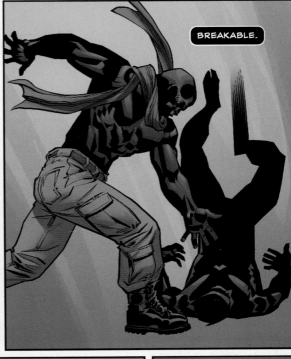

BREAKABLE.

AND SO SOME AMOUNT OF MY MIGHT I HAVE KEPT FROM THE WORLD...

...ALLOWING LEGEND AND MYTH TO FILL IN THE GAP.

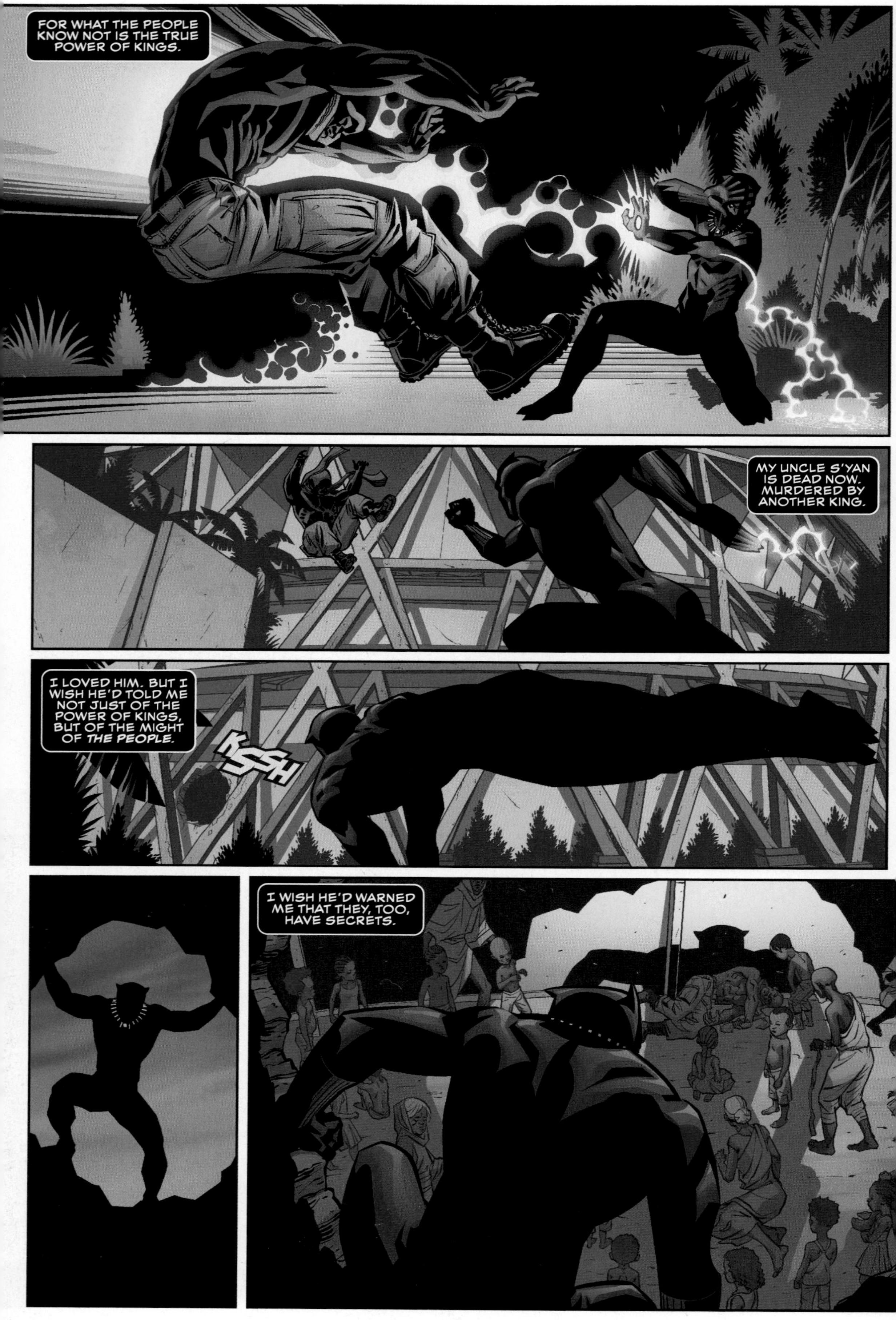
FOR WHAT THE PEOPLE KNOW NOT IS THE TRUE POWER OF KINGS.
MY UNCLE S'YAN IS DEAD NOW. MURDERED BY ANOTHER KING.
I LOVED HIM. BUT I WISH HE'D TOLD ME NOT JUST OF THE POWER OF KINGS, BUT OF THE MIGHT OF THE PEOPLE.
KSSH
I WISH HE'D WARNED ME THAT THEY, TOO, HAVE SECRETS.

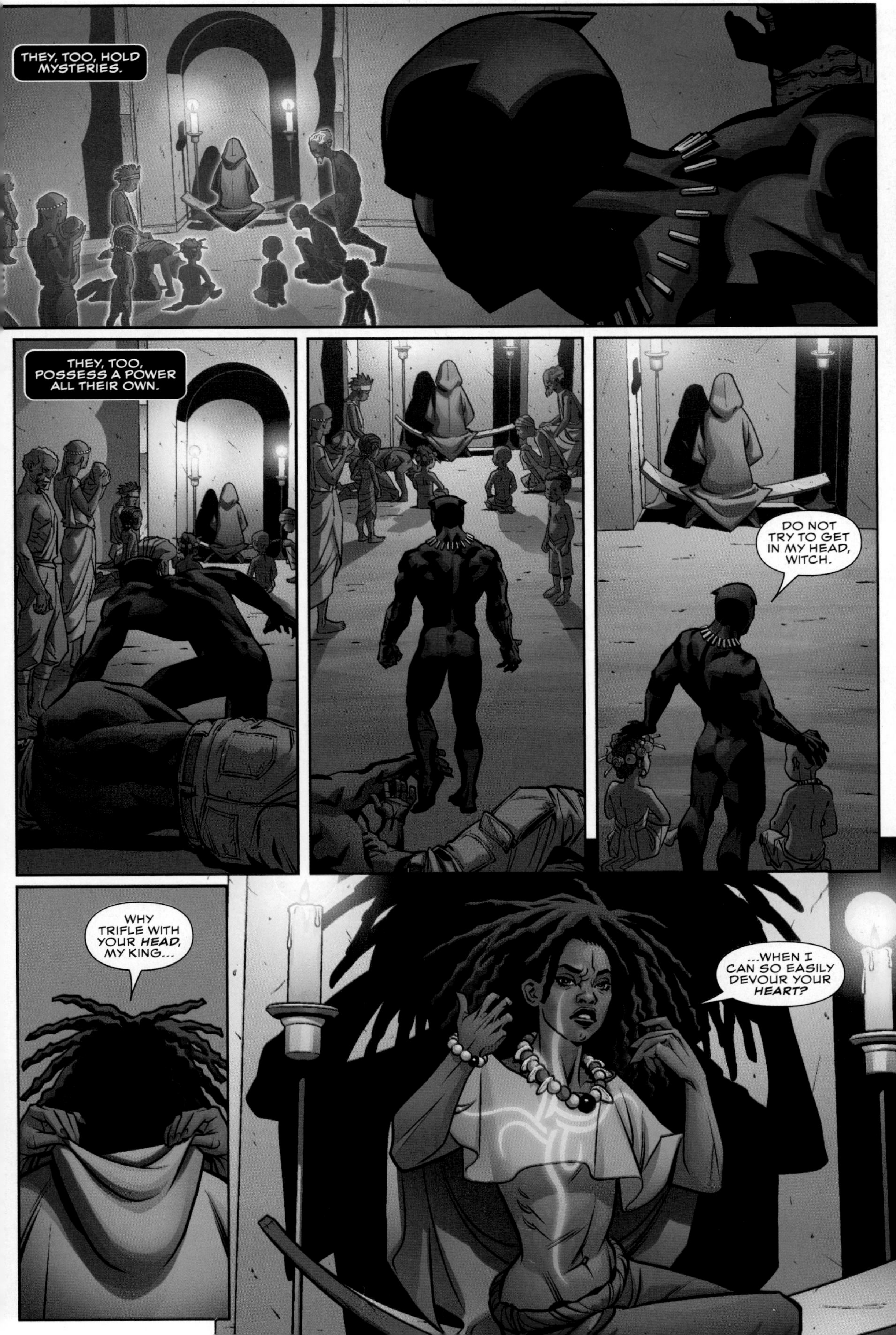
THEY, TOO, HOLD MYSTERIES.
THEY, TOO, POSSESS A POWER ALL THEIR OWN.
DO NOT TRY TO GET IN MY HEAD, WITCH.
WHY TRIFLE WITH YOUR HEAD, MY KING...
...WHEN I CAN SO EASILY DEVOUR YOUR HEART?

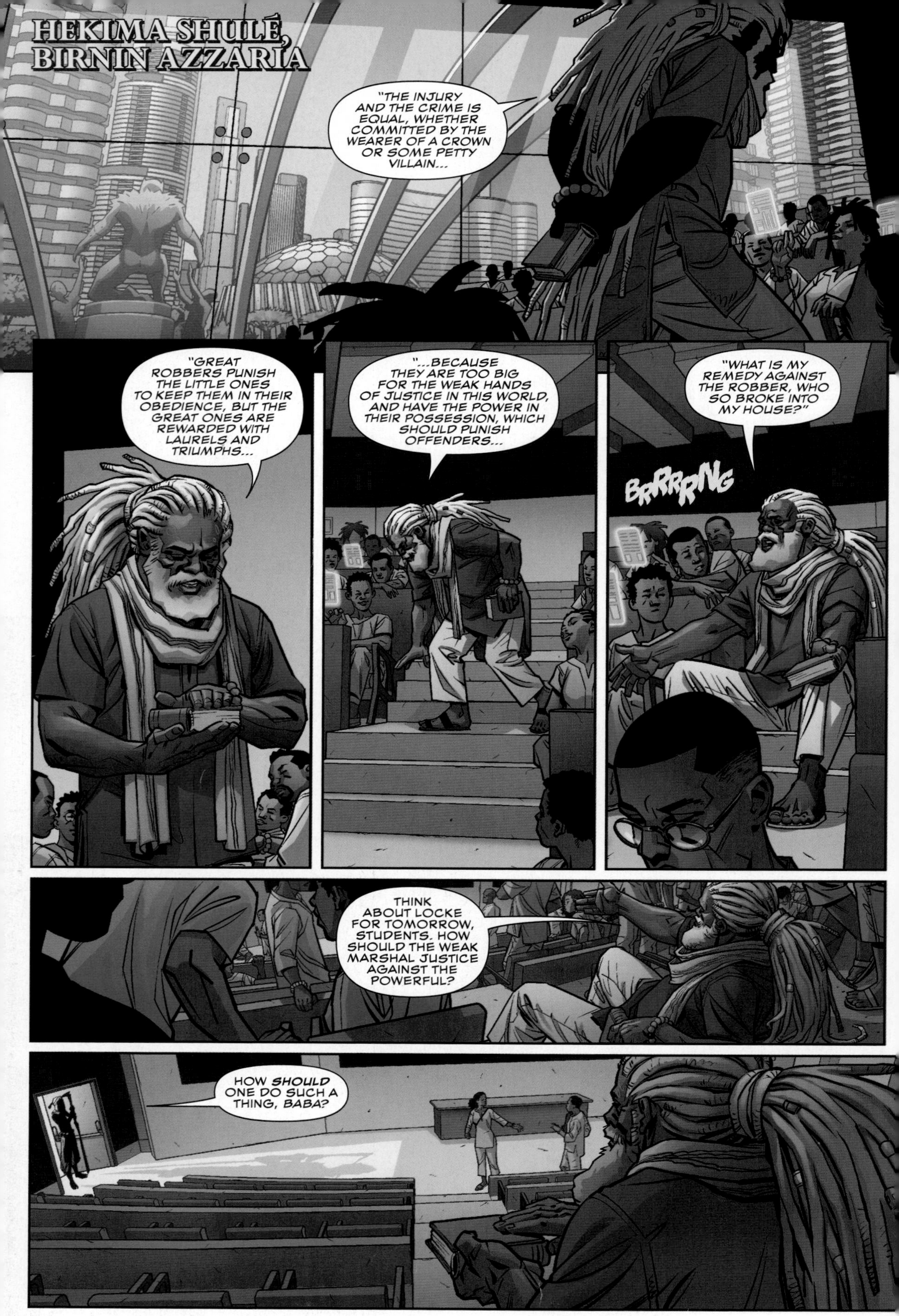
HEKIMA SHULÉ, BIRNIN AZZARIA
"THE INJURY AND THE CRIME IS EQUAL, WHETHER COMMITTED BY THE WEARER OF A CROWN OR SOME PETTY VILLAIN...
"GREAT ROBBERS PUNISH THE LITTLE ONES TO KEEP THEM IN THEIR OBEDIENCE, BUT THE GREAT ONES ARE REWARDED WITH LAURELS AND TRIUMPHS...
"...BECAUSE THEY ARE TOO BIG FOR THE WEAK HANDS OF JUSTICE IN THIS WORLD, AND HAVE THE POWER IN THEIR POSSESSION, WHICH SHOULD PUNISH OFFENDERS...
"WHAT IS MY REMEDY AGAINST THE ROBBER, WHO SO BROKE INTO MY HOUSE?"
BRRRRING
THINK ABOUT LOCKE FOR TOMORROW, STUDENTS. HOW SHOULD THE WEAK MARSHAL JUSTICE AGAINST THE POWERFUL?
HOW *SHOULD* ONE DO SUCH A THING, BABA?

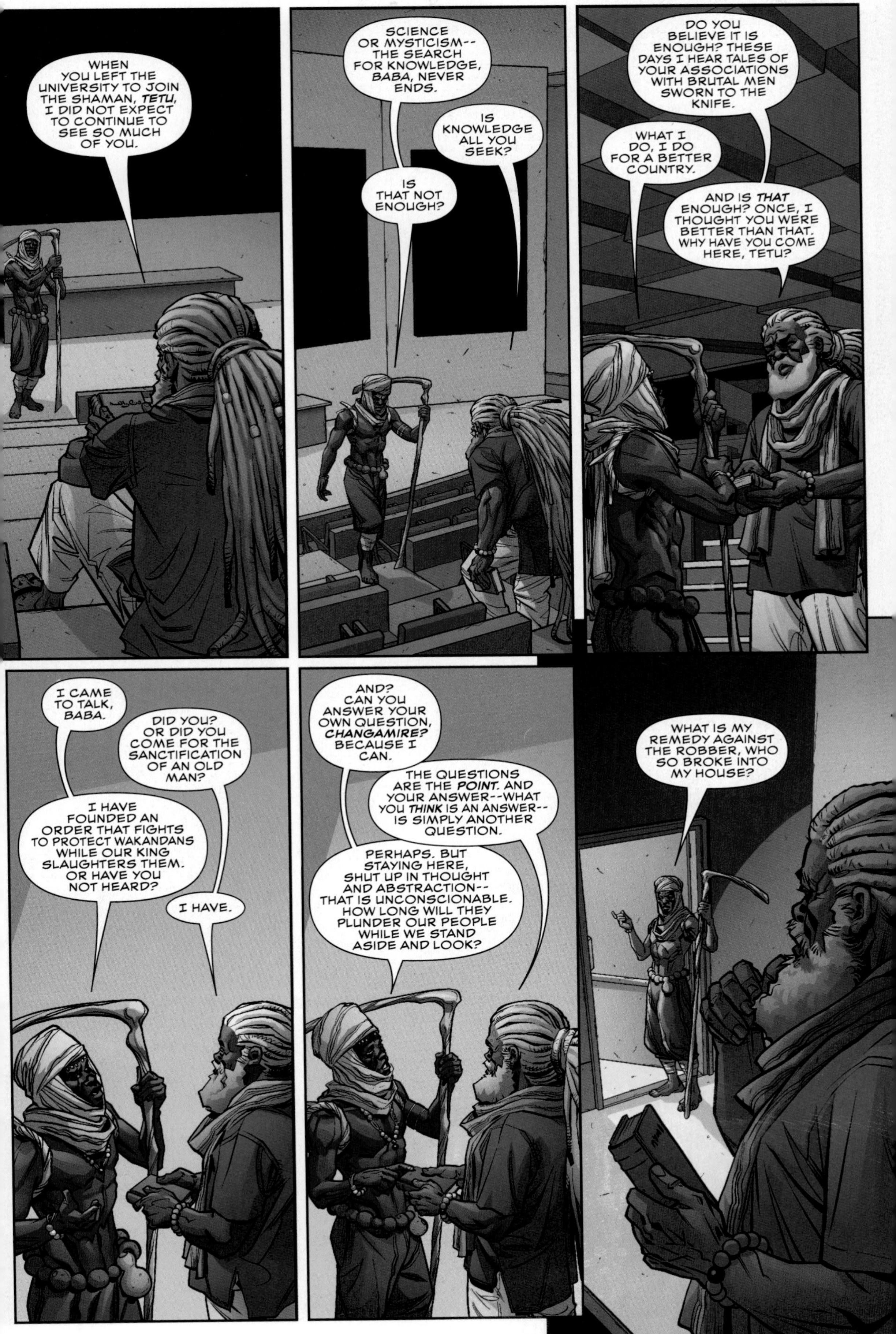
WHEN YOU LEFT THE UNIVERSITY TO JOIN THE SHAMAN, TETU, I DID NOT EXPECT TO CONTINUE TO SEE SO MUCH OF YOU.
SCIENCE OR MYSTICISM--THE SEARCH FOR KNOWLEDGE, BABA, NEVER ENDS.
IS KNOWLEDGE ALL YOU SEEK?
IS THAT NOT ENOUGH?
DO YOU BELIEVE IT IS ENOUGH? THESE DAYS I HEAR TALES OF YOUR ASSOCIATIONS WITH BRUTAL MEN SWORN TO THE KNIFE.
WHAT I DO, I DO FOR A BETTER COUNTRY.
AND IS THAT ENOUGH? ONCE, I THOUGHT YOU WERE BETTER THAN THAT. WHY HAVE YOU COME HERE, TETU?
I CAME TO TALK, BABA.
DID YOU? OR DID YOU COME FOR THE SANCTIFICATION OF AN OLD MAN?
I HAVE FOUNDED AN ORDER THAT FIGHTS TO PROTECT WAKANDANS WHILE OUR KING SLAUGHTERS THEM. OR HAVE YOU NOT HEARD?
I HAVE.
AND? CAN YOU ANSWER YOUR OWN QUESTION, CHANGAMIRE? BECAUSE I CAN.
THE QUESTIONS ARE THE POINT. AND YOUR ANSWER--WHAT YOU THINK IS AN ANSWER--IS SIMPLY ANOTHER QUESTION.
PERHAPS. BUT STAYING HERE, SHUT UP IN THOUGHT AND ABSTRACTION--THAT IS UNCONSCIONABLE. HOW LONG WILL THEY PLUNDER OUR PEOPLE WHILE WE STAND ASIDE AND LOOK?
WHAT IS MY REMEDY AGAINST THE ROBBER, WHO SO BROKE INTO MY HOUSE?

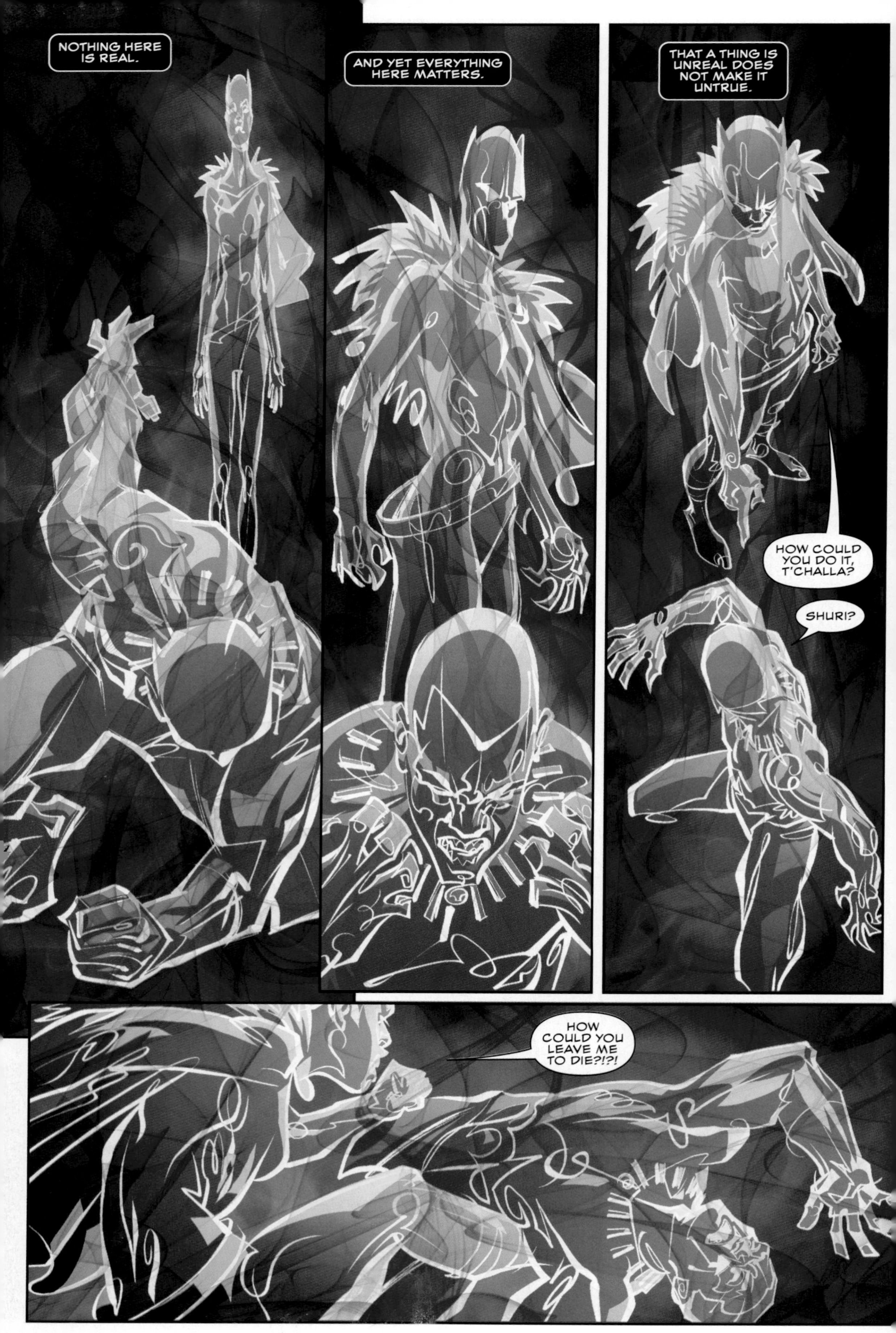
NOTHING HERE IS REAL.
AND YET EVERYTHING HERE MATTERS.
THAT A THING IS UNREAL DOES NOT MAKE IT UNTRUE.
HOW COULD YOU DO IT, T'CHALLA?
SHURI?
HOW COULD YOU LEAVE ME TO DIE?!?!

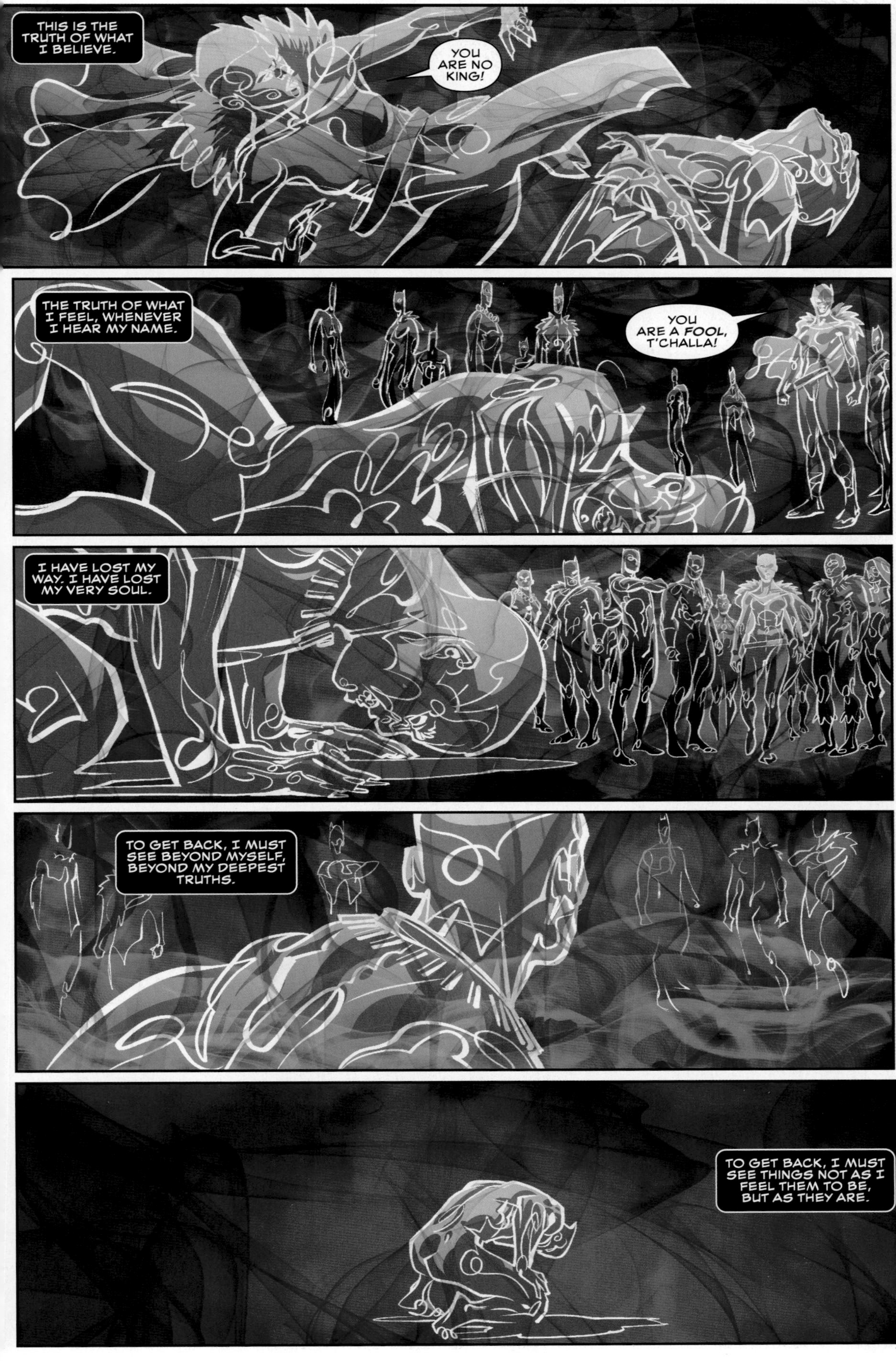
THIS IS THE TRUTH OF WHAT I BELIEVE.
YOU ARE NO KING!
THE TRUTH OF WHAT I FEEL, WHENEVER I HEAR MY NAME.
YOU ARE A FOOL, T'CHALLA!
I HAVE LOST MY WAY. I HAVE LOST MY VERY SOUL.
TO GET BACK, I MUST SEE BEYOND MYSELF, BEYOND MY DEEPEST TRUTHS.
TO GET BACK, I MUST SEE THINGS NOT AS I FEEL THEM TO BE, BUT AS THEY ARE.

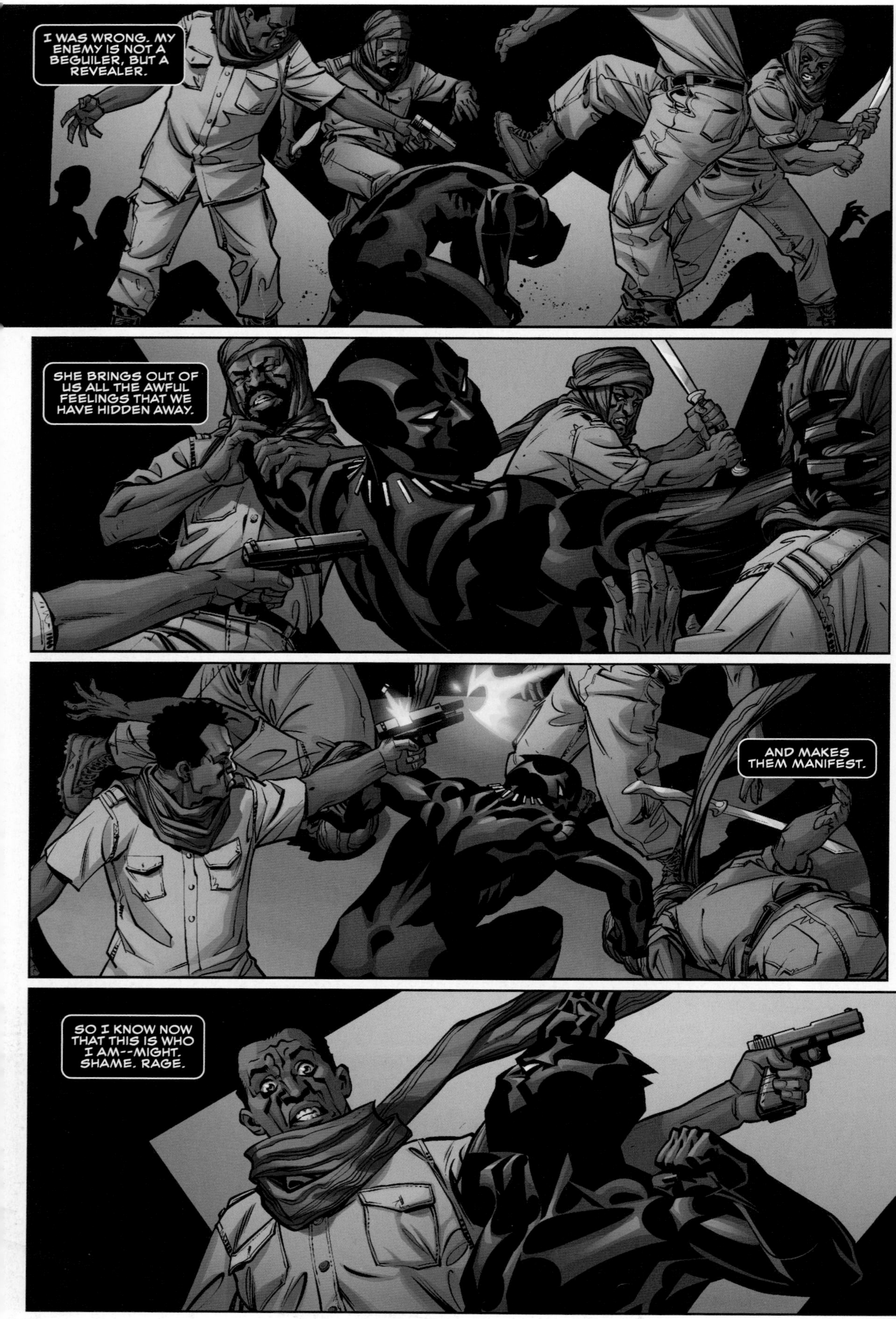
I WAS WRONG. MY ENEMY IS NOT A BEGUILER, BUT A REVEALER.
SHE BRINGS OUT OF US ALL THE AWFUL FEELINGS THAT WE HAVE HIDDEN AWAY.
AND MAKES THEM MANIFEST.
SO I KNOW NOW THAT THIS IS WHO I AM--MIGHT. SHAME. RAGE.

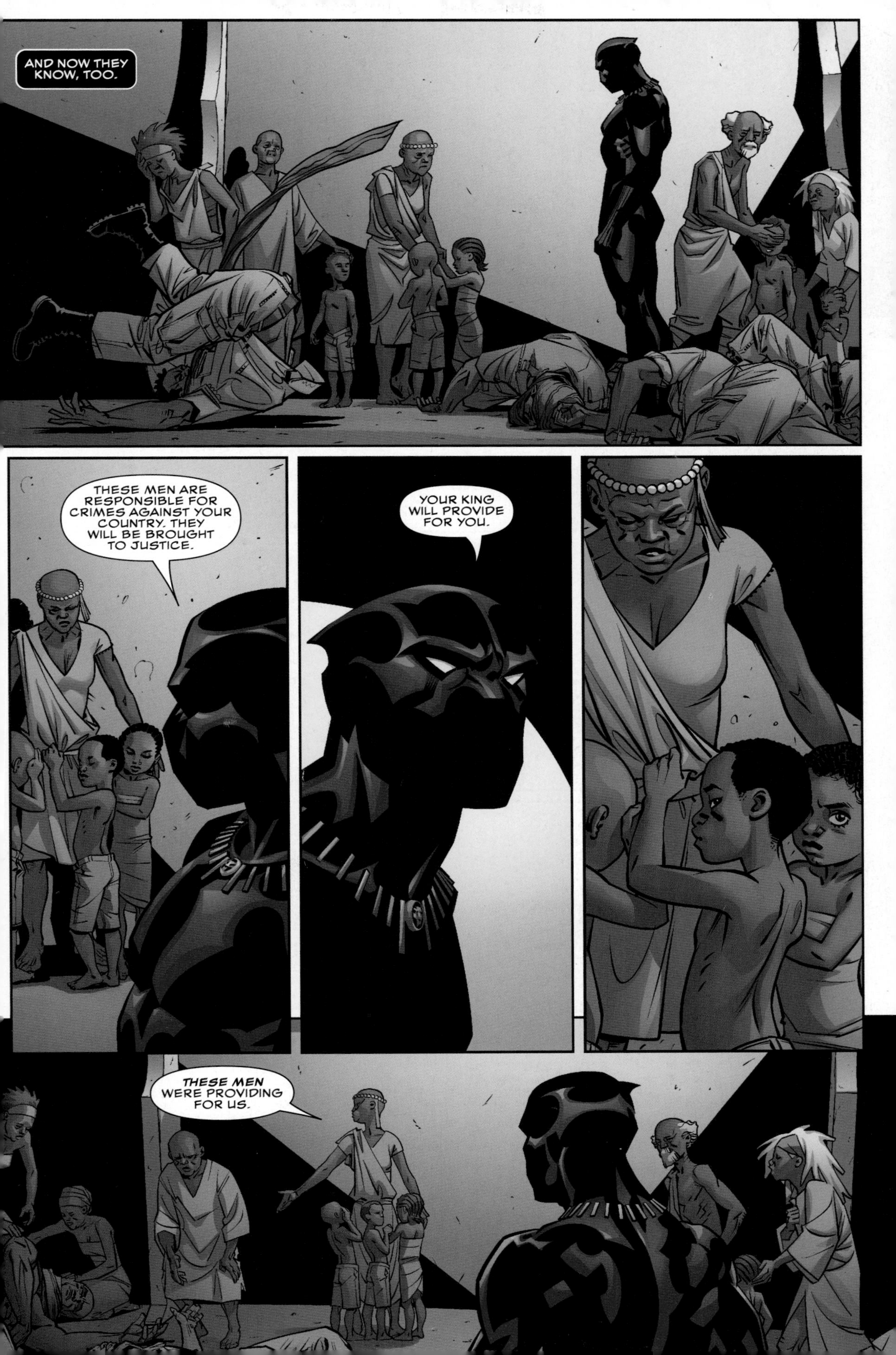
AND NOW THEY KNOW, TOO.
THESE MEN ARE RESPONSIBLE FOR CRIMES AGAINST YOUR COUNTRY. THEY WILL BE BROUGHT TO JUSTICE.
YOUR KING WILL PROVIDE FOR YOU.
THESE MEN WERE PROVIDING FOR US.

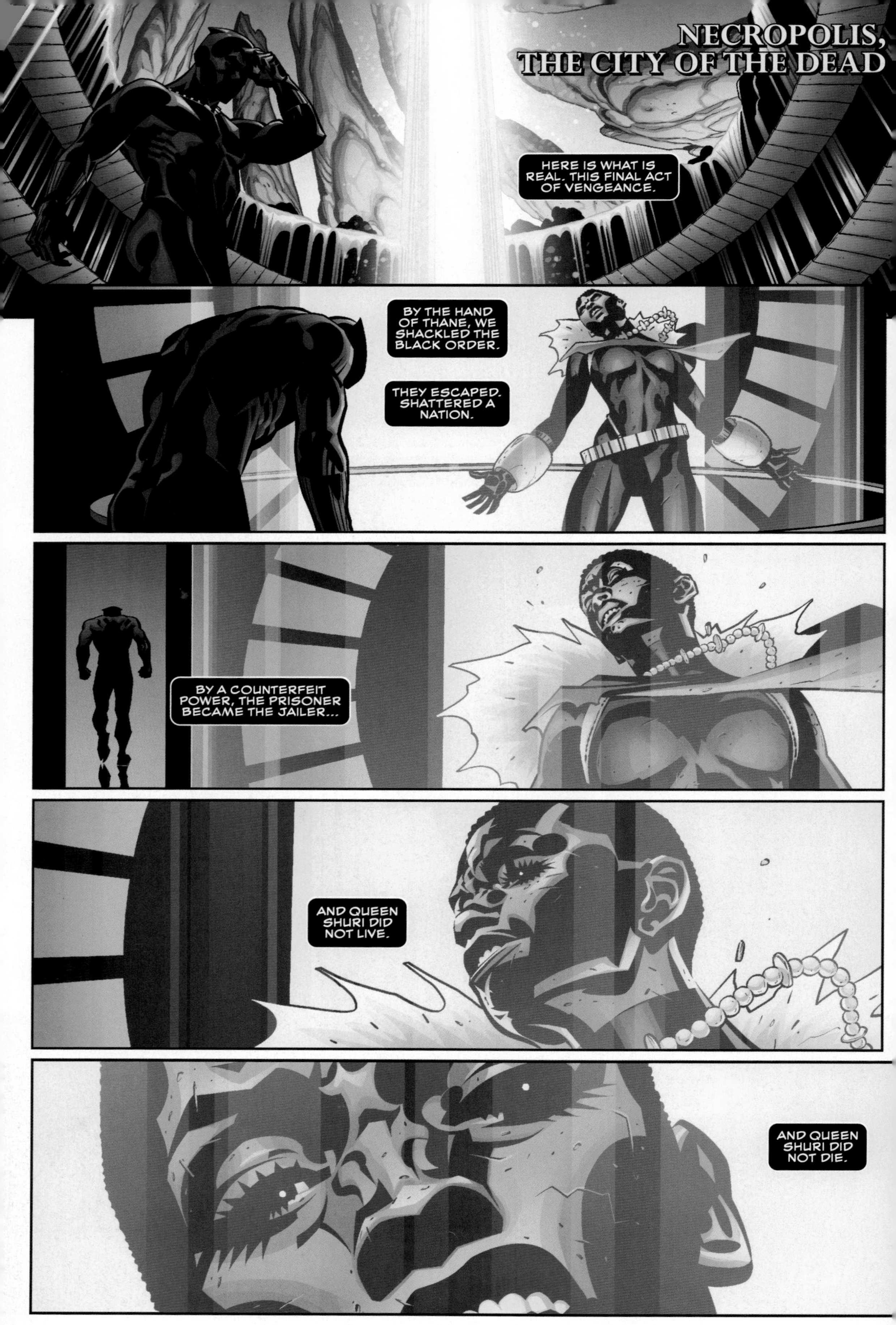
NECROPOLIS, THE CITY OF THE DEAD
HERE IS WHAT IS REAL. THIS FINAL ACT OF VENGEANCE.
BY THE HAND OF THANE, WE SHACKLED THE BLACK ORDER.
THEY ESCAPED. SHATTERED A NATION.
BY A COUNTERFEIT POWER, THE PRISONER BECAME THE JAILER...
AND QUEEN SHURI DID NOT LIVE.
AND QUEEN SHURI DID NOT DIE.

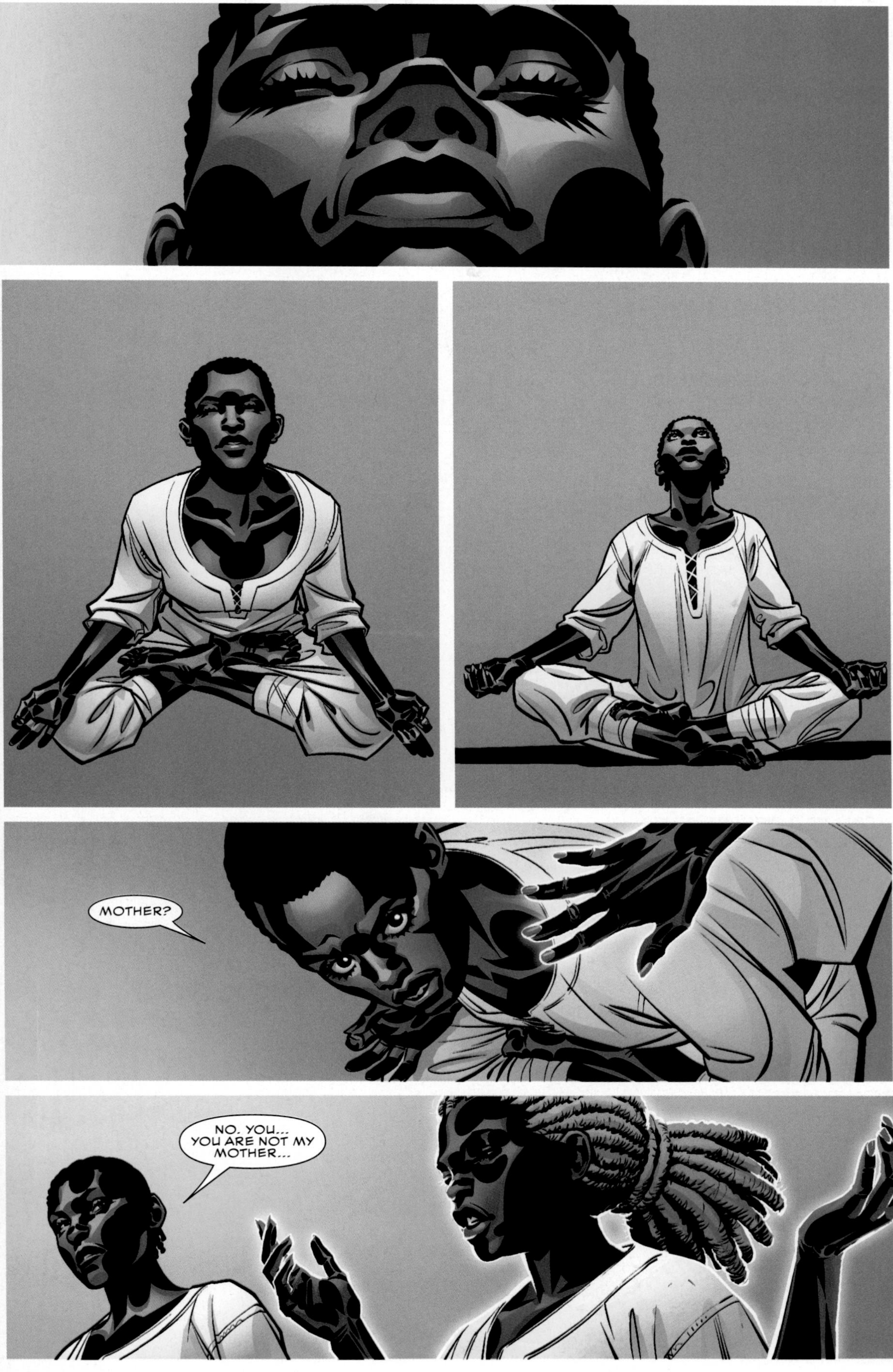
MOTHER?
NO. YOU... YOU ARE NOT MY MOTHER...

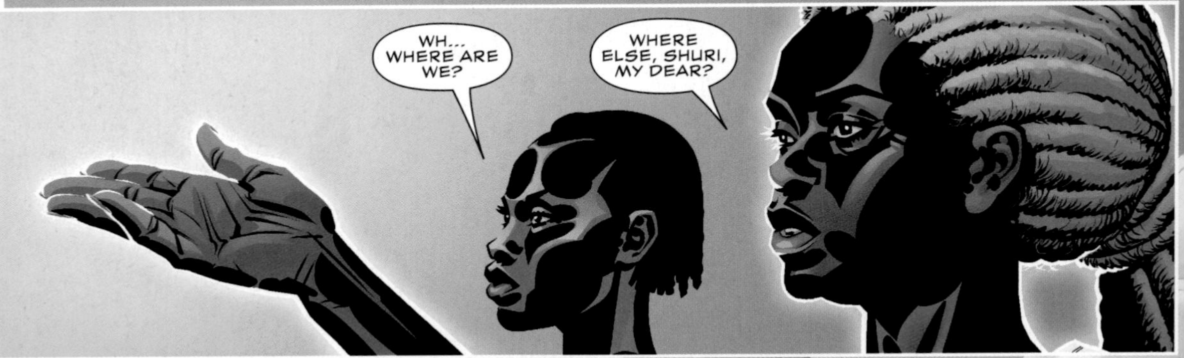
WH... WHERE ARE WE?
WHERE ELSE, SHURI, MY DEAR?

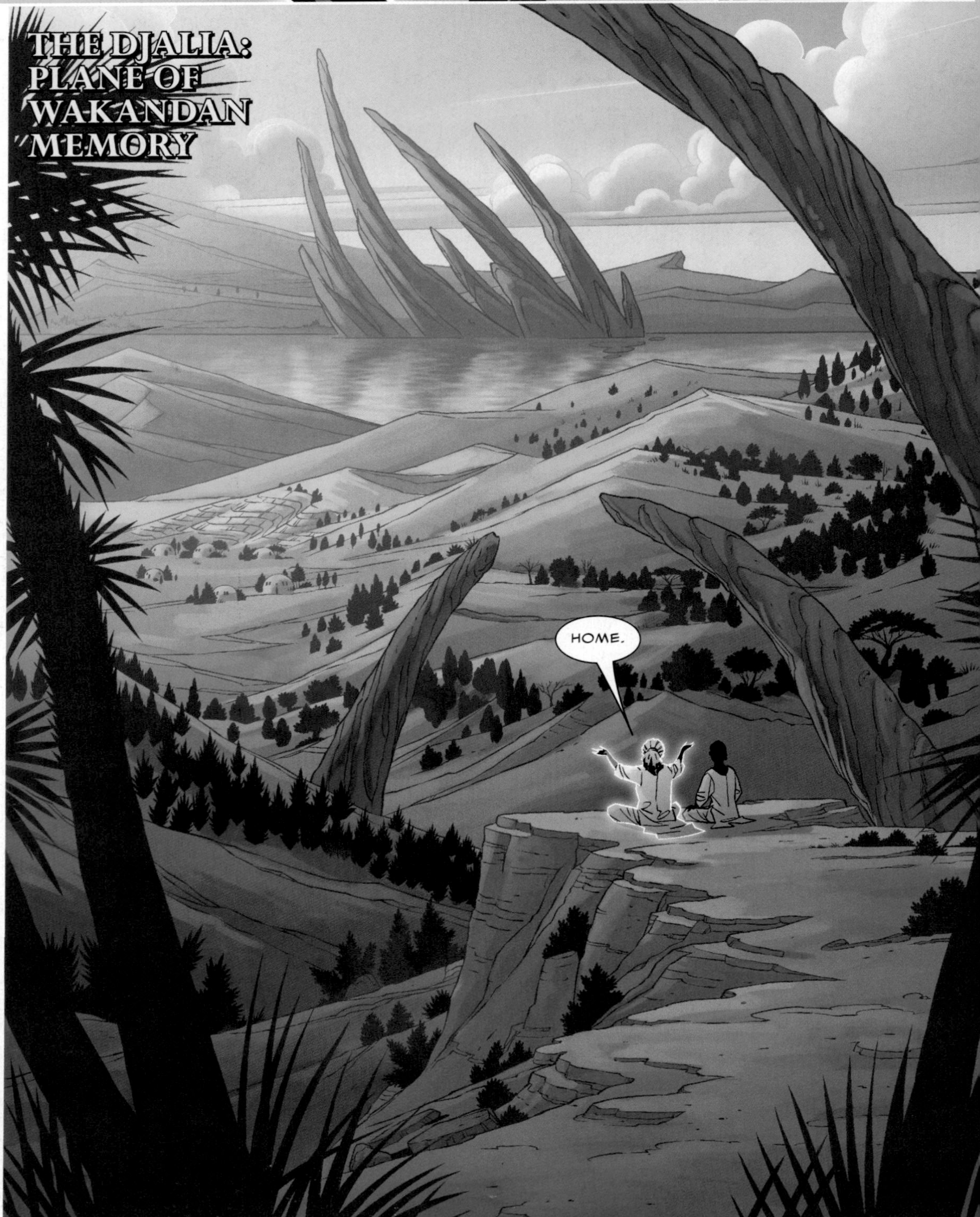
THE DJALIA: PLANE OF WAKANDAN MEMORY
HOME.

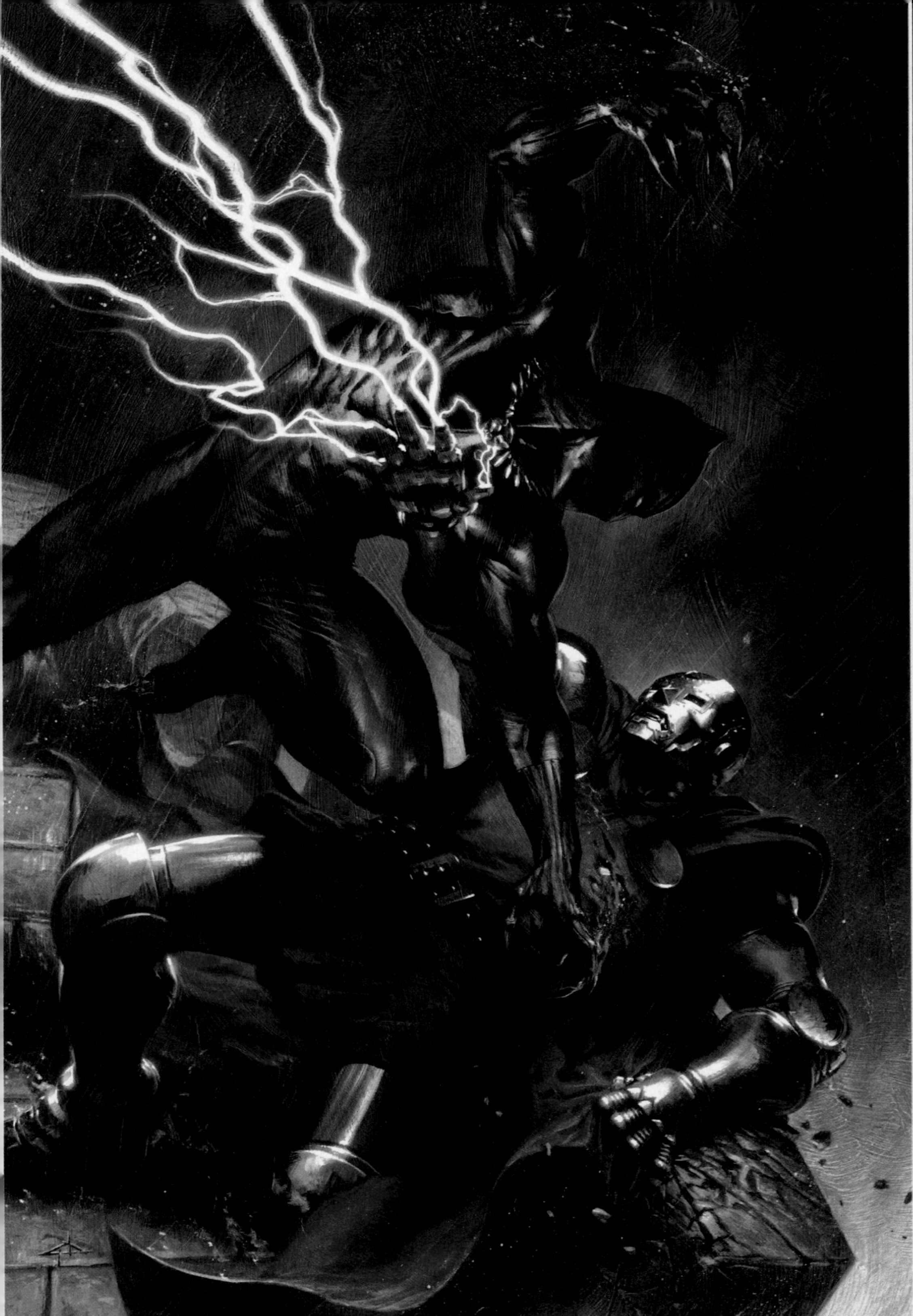

#1 VARIANT BY **GABRIELE DELL'OTTO**

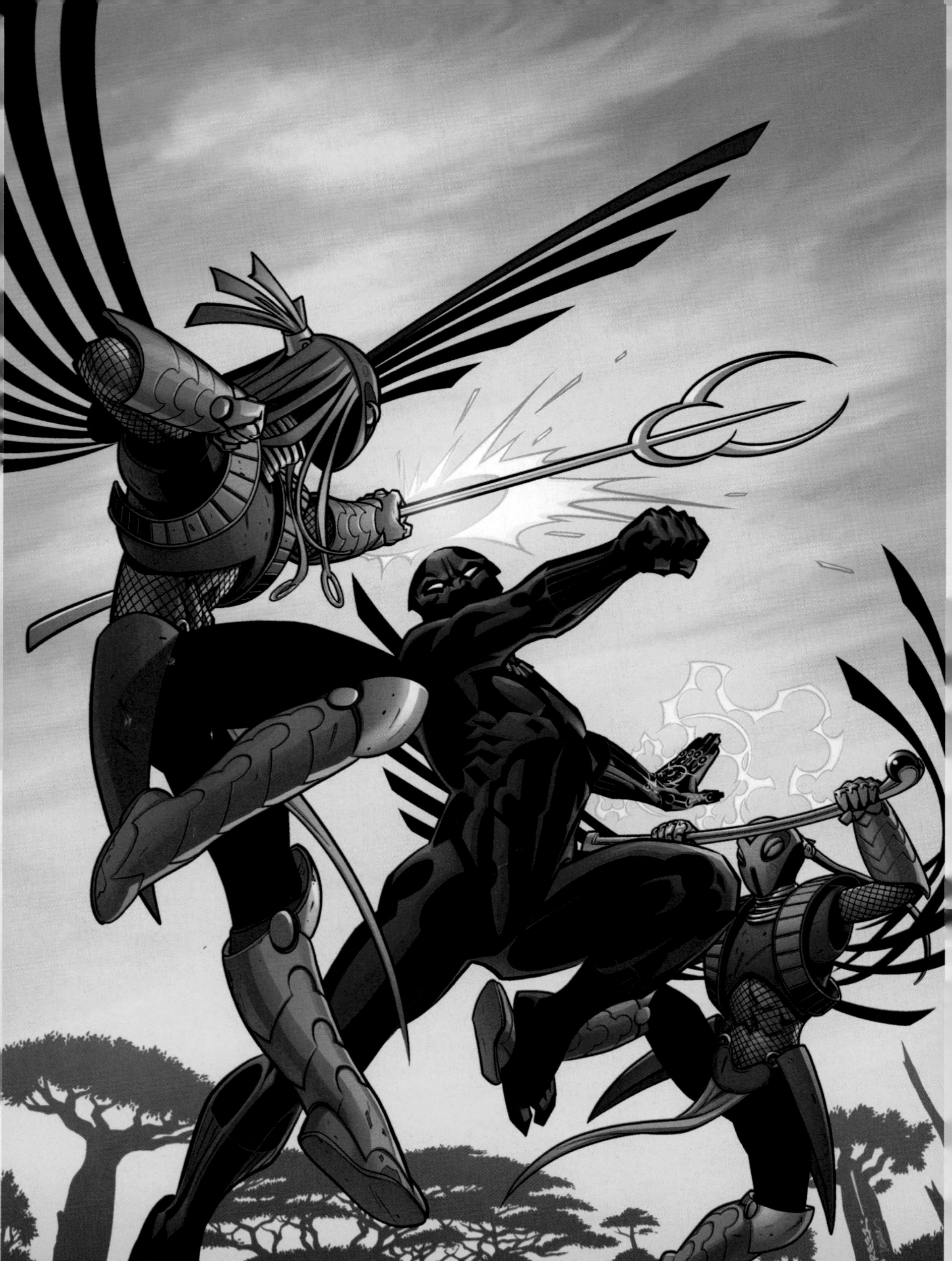

3

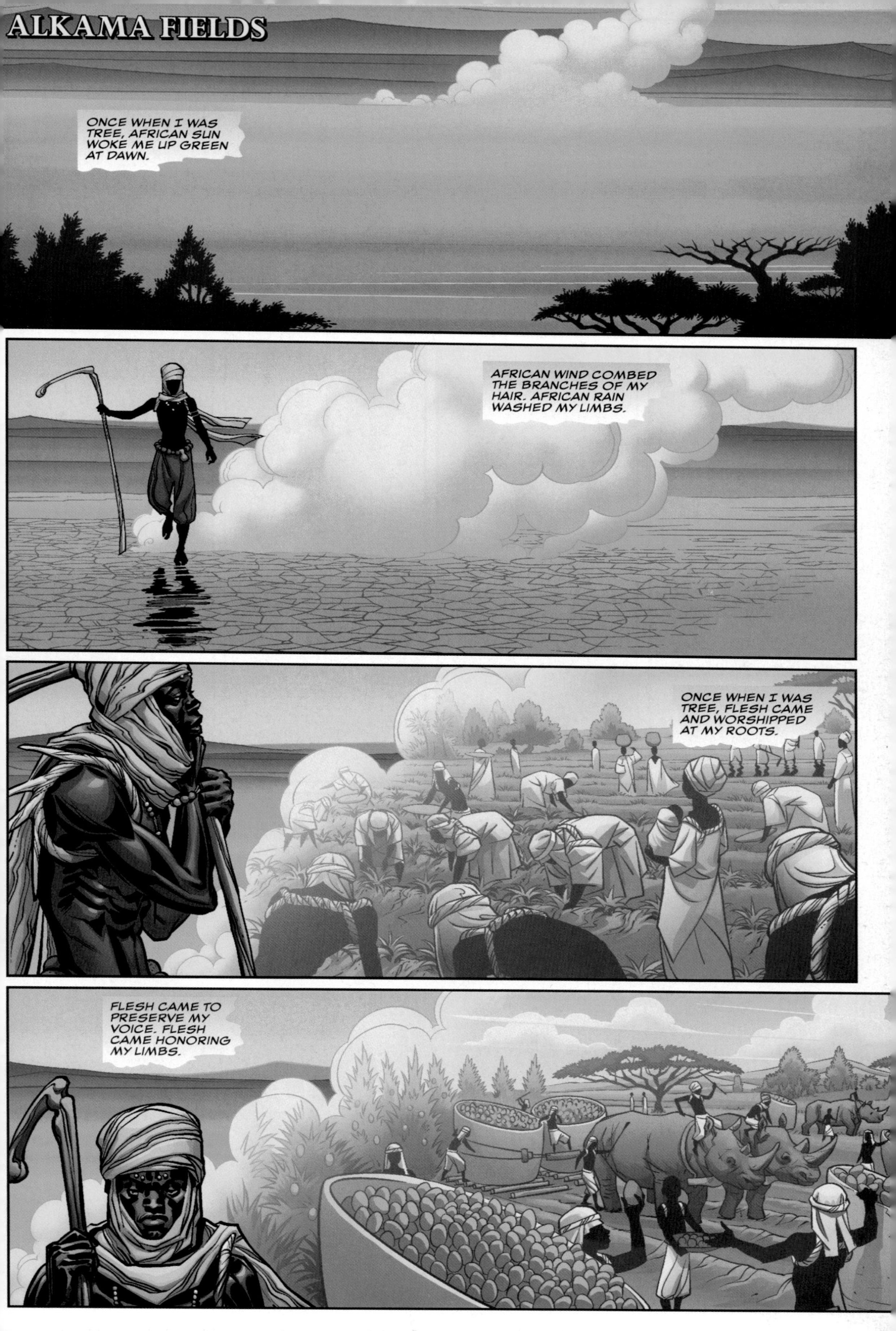
ALKAMA FIELDS
ONCE WHEN I WAS TREE, AFRICAN SUN WOKE ME UP GREEN AT DAWN.
AFRICAN WIND COMBED THE BRANCHES OF MY HAIR. AFRICAN RAIN WASHED MY LIMBS.
ONCE WHEN I WAS TREE, FLESH CAME AND WORSHIPPED AT MY ROOTS.
FLESH CAME TO PRESERVE MY VOICE. FLESH CAME HONORING MY LIMBS.

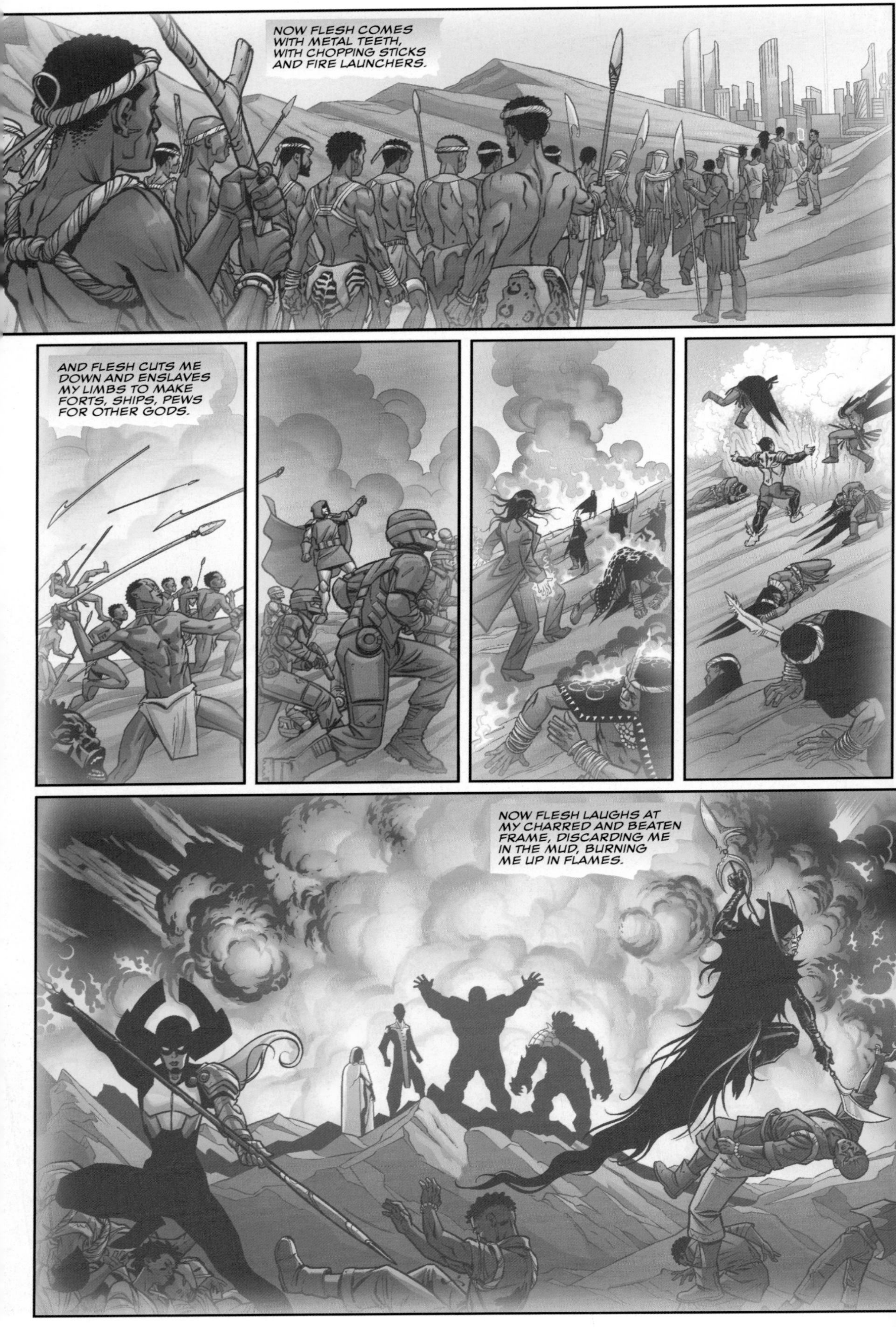
NOW FLESH COMES WITH METAL TEETH, WITH CHOPPING STICKS AND FIRE LAUNCHERS.
AND FLESH CUTS ME DOWN AND ENSLAVES MY LIMBS TO MAKE FORTS, SHIPS, PEWS FOR OTHER GODS.
NOW FLESH LAUGHS AT MY CHARRED AND BEATEN FRAME, DISCARDING ME IN THE MUD, BURNING ME UP IN FLAMES.

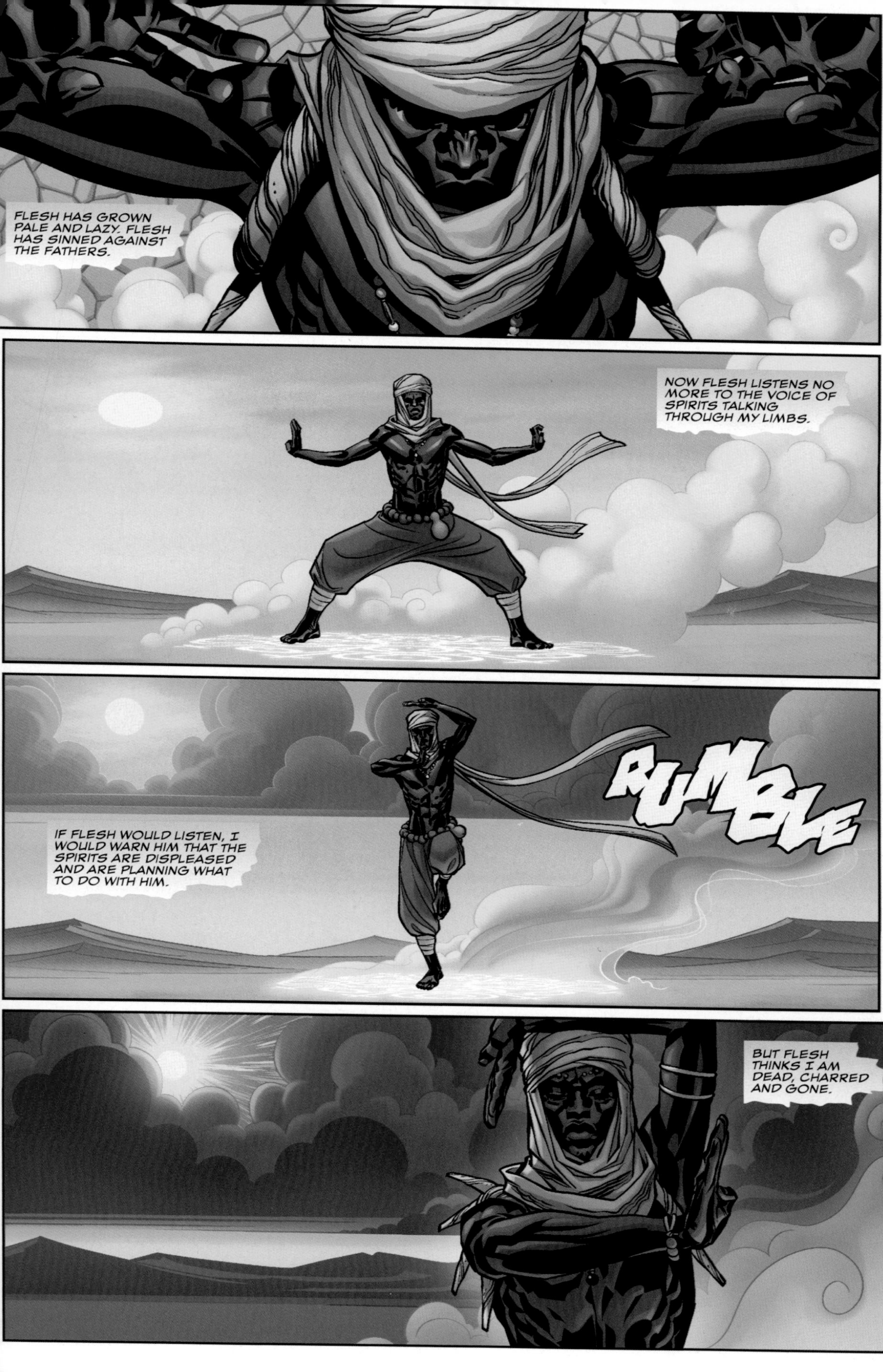
FLESH HAS GROWN PALE AND LAZY. FLESH HAS SINNED AGAINST THE FATHERS.
NOW FLESH LISTENS NO MORE TO THE VOICE OF SPIRITS TALKING THROUGH MY LIMBS.
RUMBLE
IF FLESH WOULD LISTEN, I WOULD WARN HIM THAT THE SPIRITS ARE DISPLEASED AND ARE PLANNING WHAT TO DO WITH HIM.
BUT FLESH THINKS I AM DEAD, CHARRED AND GONE.

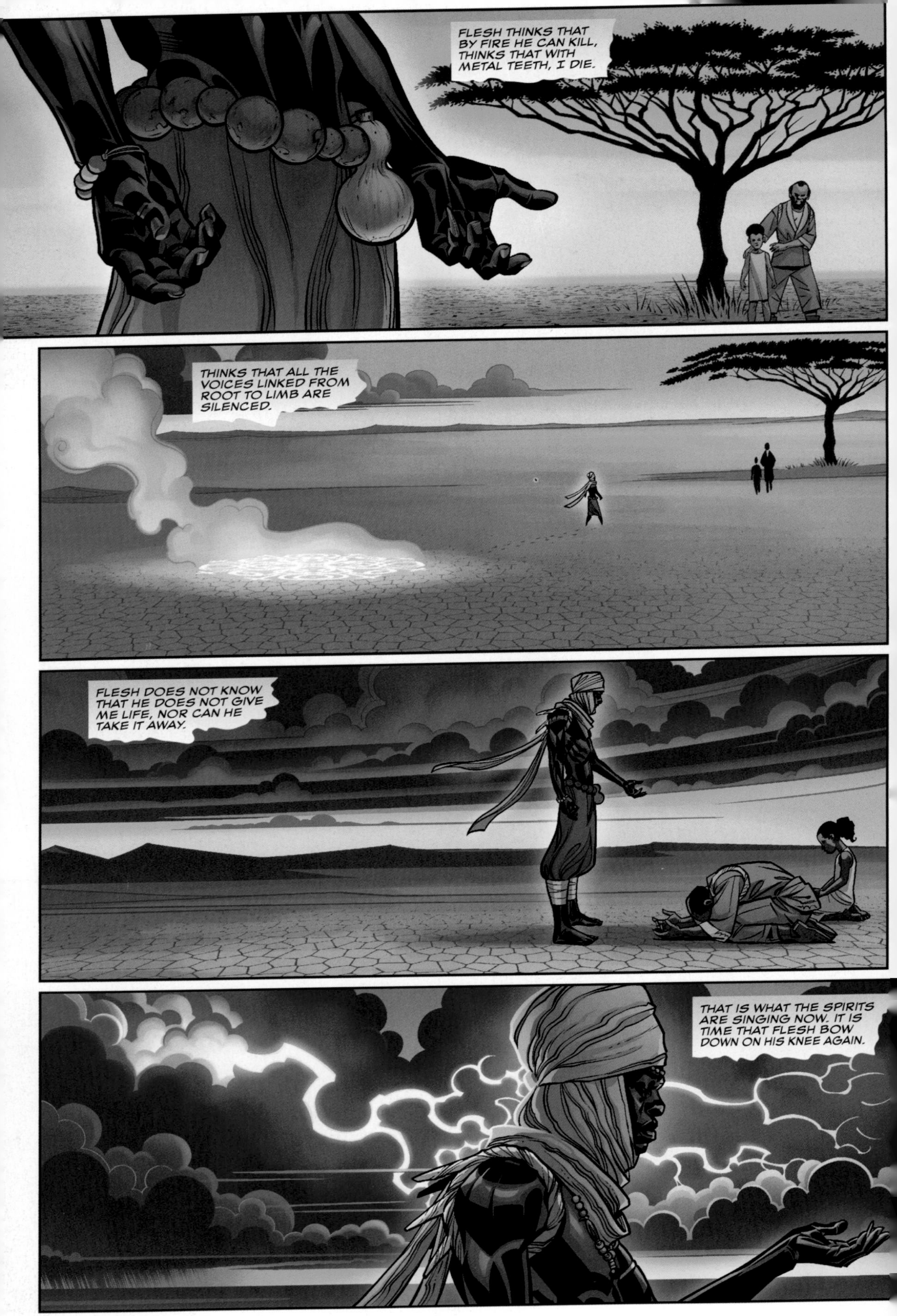
FLESH THINKS THAT BY FIRE HE CAN KILL, THINKS THAT WITH METAL TEETH, I DIE.
THINKS THAT ALL THE VOICES LINKED FROM ROOT TO LIMB ARE SILENCED.
FLESH DOES NOT KNOW THAT HE DOES NOT GIVE ME LIFE, NOR CAN HE TAKE IT AWAY.
THAT IS WHAT THE SPIRITS ARE SINGING NOW. IT IS TIME THAT FLESH BOW DOWN ON HIS KNEE AGAIN.

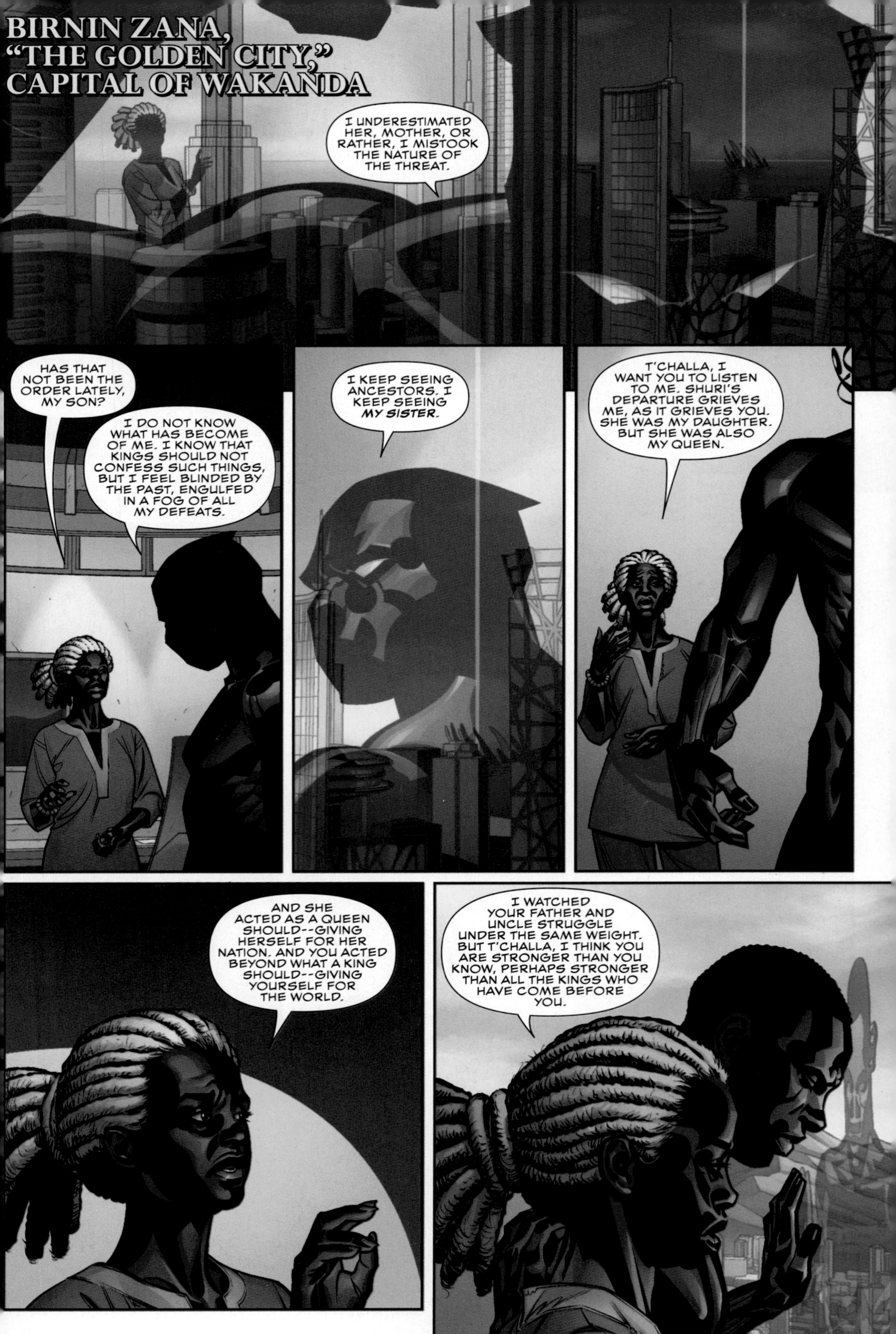
BIRNIN ZANA, "THE GOLDEN CITY," CAPITAL OF WAKANDA
I UNDERESTIMATED HER, MOTHER, OR RATHER, I MISTOOK THE NATURE OF THE THREAT.
HAS THAT NOT BEEN THE ORDER LATELY, MY SON?
I DO NOT KNOW WHAT HAS BECOME OF ME. I KNOW THAT KINGS SHOULD NOT CONFESS SUCH THINGS, BUT I FEEL BLINDED BY THE PAST, ENGULFED IN A FOG OF ALL MY DEFEATS.
I KEEP SEEING ANCESTORS. I KEEP SEEING *MY SISTER.*
T'CHALLA, I WANT YOU TO LISTEN TO ME. SHURI'S DEPARTURE GRIEVES ME, AS IT GRIEVES YOU. SHE WAS MY DAUGHTER. BUT SHE WAS ALSO MY QUEEN.
AND SHE ACTED AS A QUEEN SHOULD--GIVING HERSELF FOR HER NATION. AND YOU ACTED BEYOND WHAT A KING SHOULD--GIVING YOURSELF FOR THE WORLD.
I WATCHED YOUR FATHER AND UNCLE STRUGGLE UNDER THE SAME WEIGHT. BUT T'CHALLA, I THINK YOU ARE STRONGER THAN YOU KNOW, PERHAPS STRONGER THAN ALL THE KINGS WHO HAVE COME BEFORE YOU.

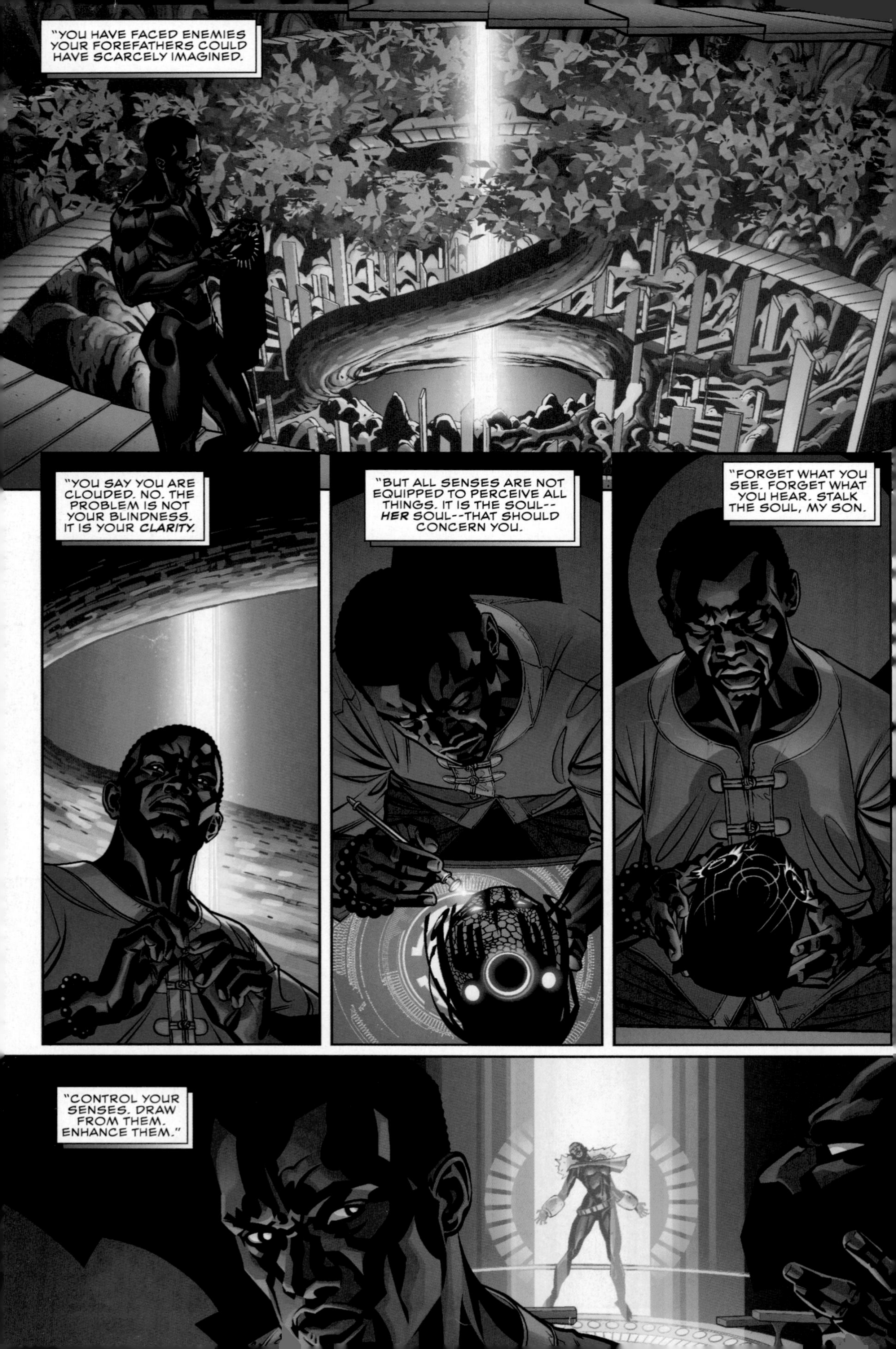
"YOU HAVE FACED ENEMIES YOUR FOREFATHERS COULD HAVE SCARCELY IMAGINED.
"YOU SAY YOU ARE CLOUDED. NO. THE PROBLEM IS NOT YOUR BLINDNESS. IT IS YOUR CLARITY.
"BUT ALL SENSES ARE NOT EQUIPPED TO PERCEIVE ALL THINGS. IT IS THE SOUL-- HER SOUL--THAT SHOULD CONCERN YOU.
"FORGET WHAT YOU SEE. FORGET WHAT YOU HEAR. STALK THE SOUL, MY SON.
"CONTROL YOUR SENSES. DRAW FROM THEM. ENHANCE THEM."

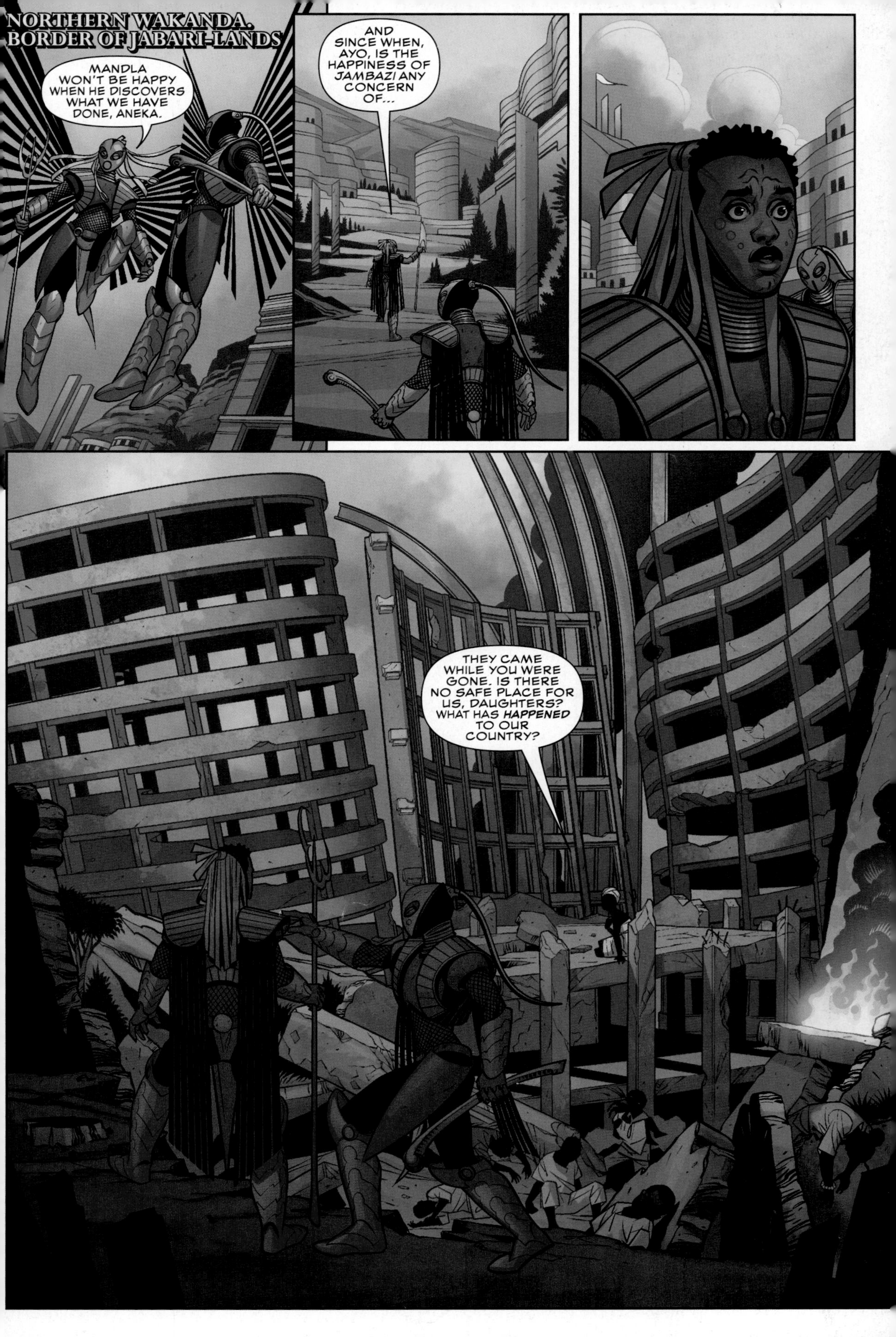
NORTHERN WAKANDA.
BORDER OF JABARI-LANDS
MANDLA WON'T BE HAPPY WHEN HE DISCOVERS WHAT WE HAVE DONE, ANEKA.
AND SINCE WHEN, AYO, IS THE HAPPINESS OF *JAMBAZI* ANY CONCERN OF...
THEY CAME WHILE YOU WERE GONE. IS THERE NO SAFE PLACE FOR US, DAUGHTERS? WHAT HAS *HAPPENED* TO OUR COUNTRY?

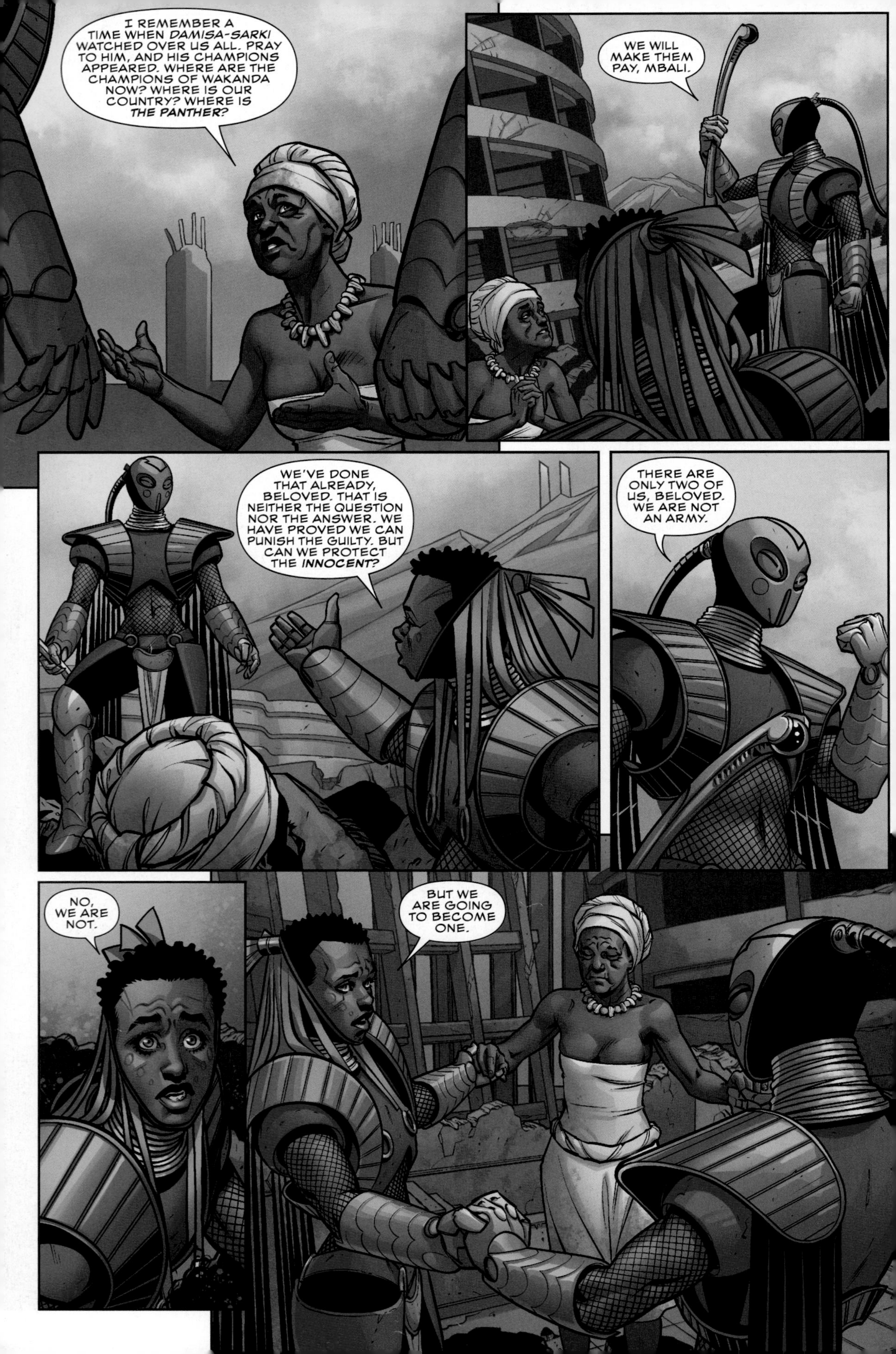
I REMEMBER A TIME WHEN DAMISA-SARKI WATCHED OVER US ALL. PRAY TO HIM, AND HIS CHAMPIONS APPEARED. WHERE ARE THE CHAMPIONS OF WAKANDA NOW? WHERE IS OUR COUNTRY? WHERE IS THE PANTHER?
WE WILL MAKE THEM PAY, MBALI.
WE'VE DONE THAT ALREADY, BELOVED. THAT IS NEITHER THE QUESTION NOR THE ANSWER. WE HAVE PROVED WE CAN PUNISH THE GUILTY. BUT CAN WE PROTECT THE INNOCENT?
THERE ARE ONLY TWO OF US, BELOVED. WE ARE NOT AN ARMY.
NO, WE ARE NOT.
BUT WE ARE GOING TO BECOME ONE.

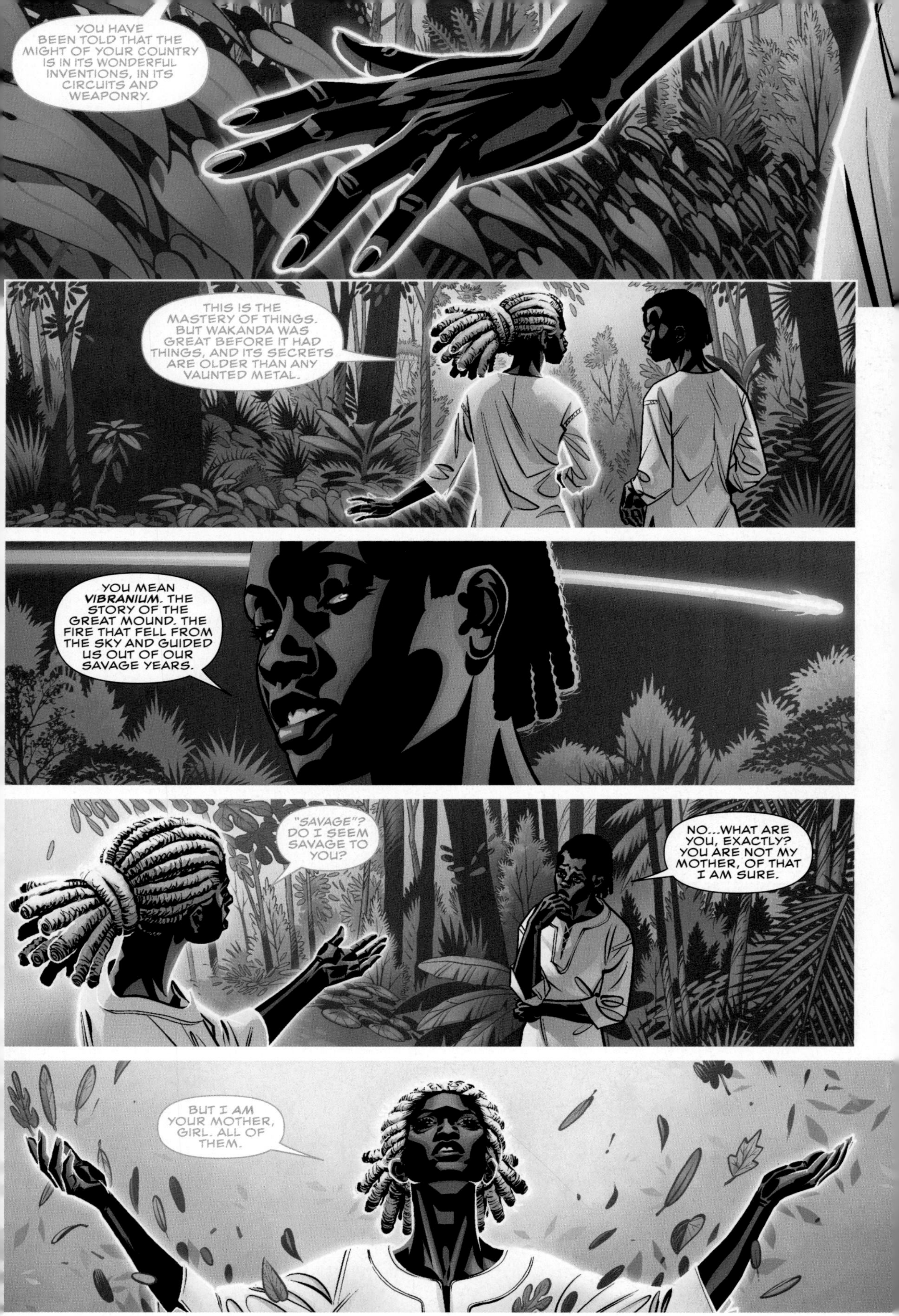
YOU HAVE BEEN TOLD THAT THE MIGHT OF YOUR COUNTRY IS IN ITS WONDERFUL INVENTIONS, IN ITS CIRCUITS AND WEAPONRY.
THIS IS THE MASTERY OF THINGS. BUT WAKANDA WAS GREAT BEFORE IT HAD THINGS, AND ITS SECRETS ARE OLDER THAN ANY VAUNTED METAL.
YOU MEAN **VIBRANIUM**. THE STORY OF THE GREAT MOUND. THE FIRE THAT FELL FROM THE SKY AND GUIDED US OUT OF OUR SAVAGE YEARS.
"SAVAGE"? DO I SEEM SAVAGE TO YOU?
NO...WHAT ARE YOU, EXACTLY? YOU ARE NOT MY MOTHER, OF THAT I AM SURE.
BUT I *AM* YOUR MOTHER, GIRL. ALL OF THEM.

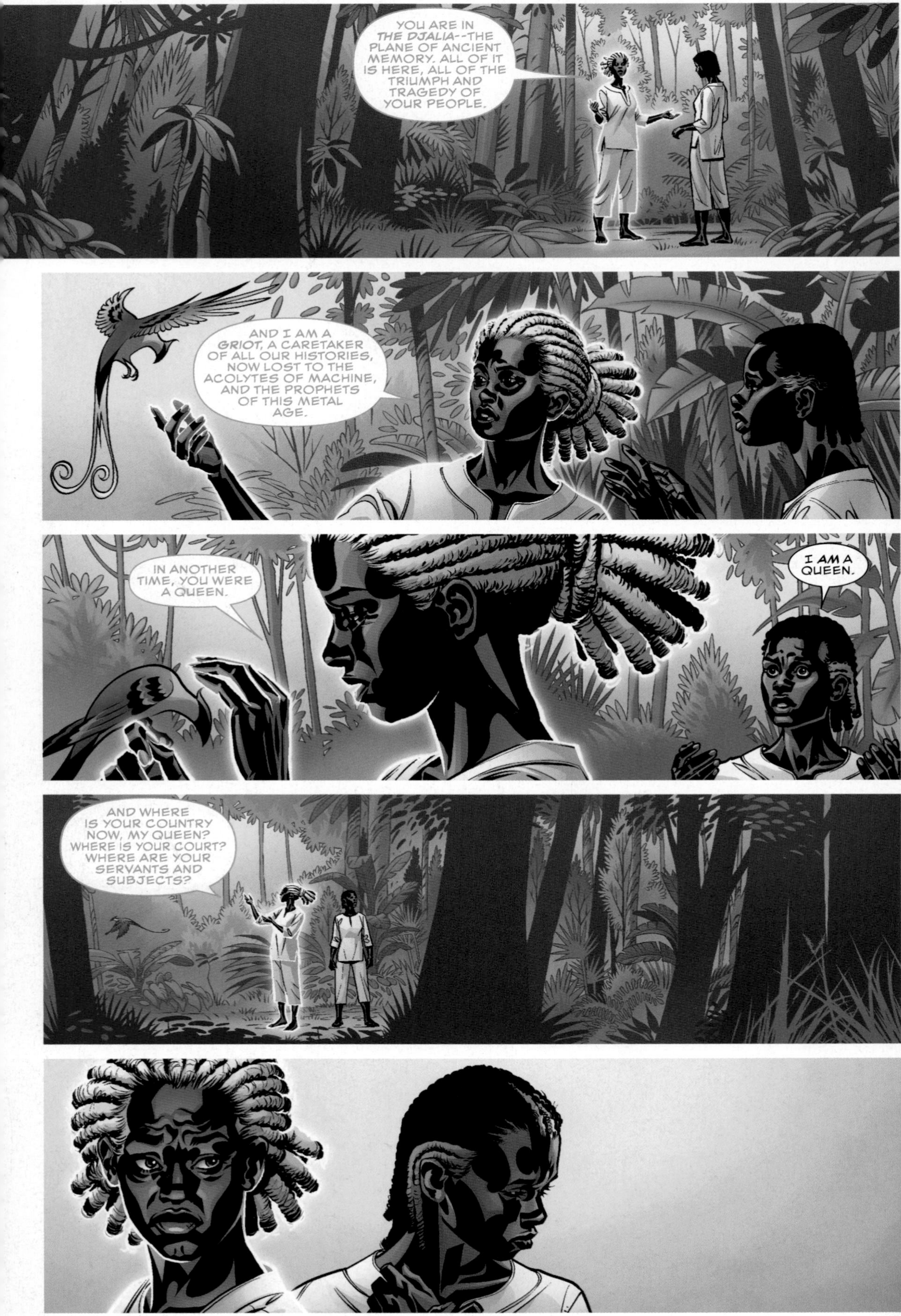
YOU ARE IN THE DJALIA--THE PLANE OF ANCIENT MEMORY. ALL OF IT IS HERE, ALL OF THE TRIUMPH AND TRAGEDY OF YOUR PEOPLE.
AND I AM A GRIOT, A CARETAKER OF ALL OUR HISTORIES, NOW LOST TO THE ACOLYTES OF MACHINE, AND THE PROPHETS OF THIS METAL AGE.
IN ANOTHER TIME, YOU WERE A QUEEN.
I AM A QUEEN.
AND WHERE IS YOUR COUNTRY NOW, MY QUEEN? WHERE IS YOUR COURT? WHERE ARE YOUR SERVANTS AND SUBJECTS?

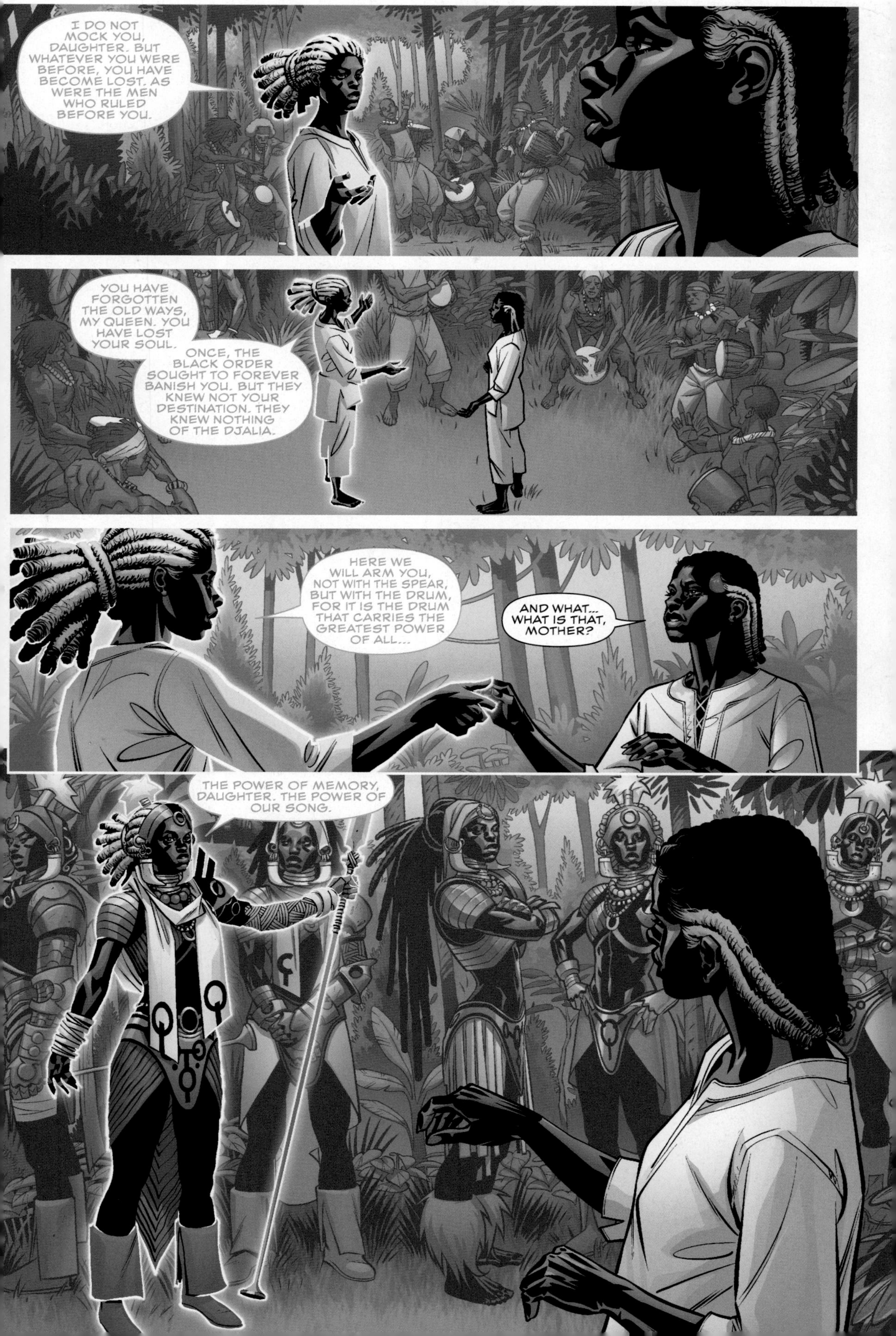
I DO NOT MOCK YOU, DAUGHTER. BUT WHATEVER YOU WERE BEFORE, YOU HAVE BECOME LOST. AS WERE THE MEN WHO RULED BEFORE YOU.
YOU HAVE FORGOTTEN THE OLD WAYS, MY QUEEN. YOU HAVE LOST YOUR SOUL.
ONCE, THE BLACK ORDER SOUGHT TO FOREVER BANISH YOU. BUT THEY KNEW NOT YOUR DESTINATION. THEY KNEW NOTHING OF THE DJALIA.
HERE WE WILL ARM YOU, NOT WITH THE SPEAR, BUT WITH THE DRUM, FOR IT IS THE DRUM THAT CARRIES THE GREATEST POWER OF ALL...
AND WHAT... WHAT IS THAT, MOTHER?
THE POWER OF MEMORY, DAUGHTER. THE POWER OF OUR SONG.

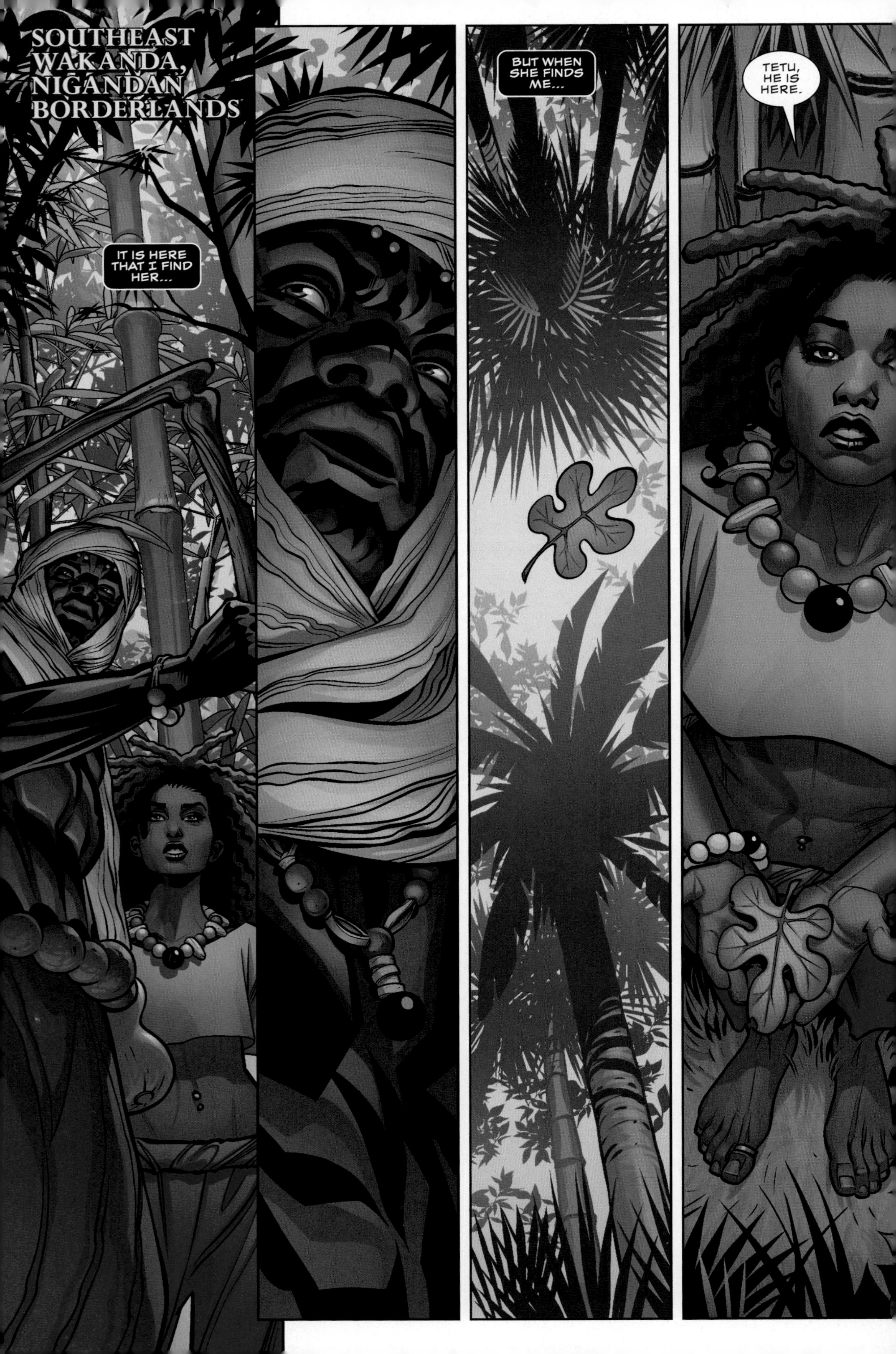
SOUTHEAST WAKANDA, NIGANDAN BORDERLANDS
IT IS HERE THAT I FIND HER...
BUT WHEN SHE FINDS ME...
TETU, HE IS HERE.

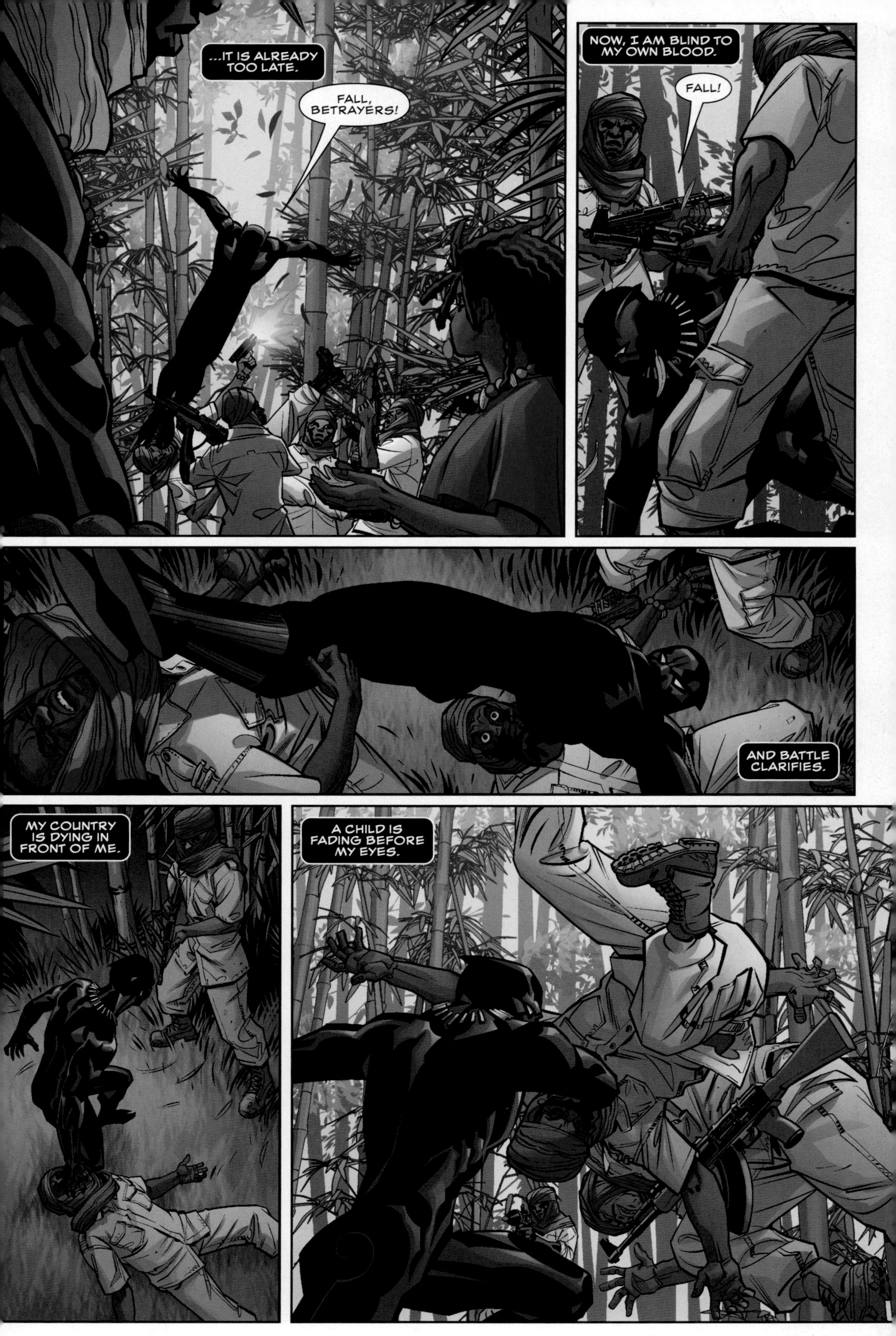

...IT IS ALREADY TOO LATE.
FALL, BETRAYERS!
NOW, I AM BLIND TO MY OWN BLOOD.
FALL!
AND BATTLE CLARIFIES.
MY COUNTRY IS DYING IN FRONT OF ME.
A CHILD IS FADING BEFORE MY EYES.

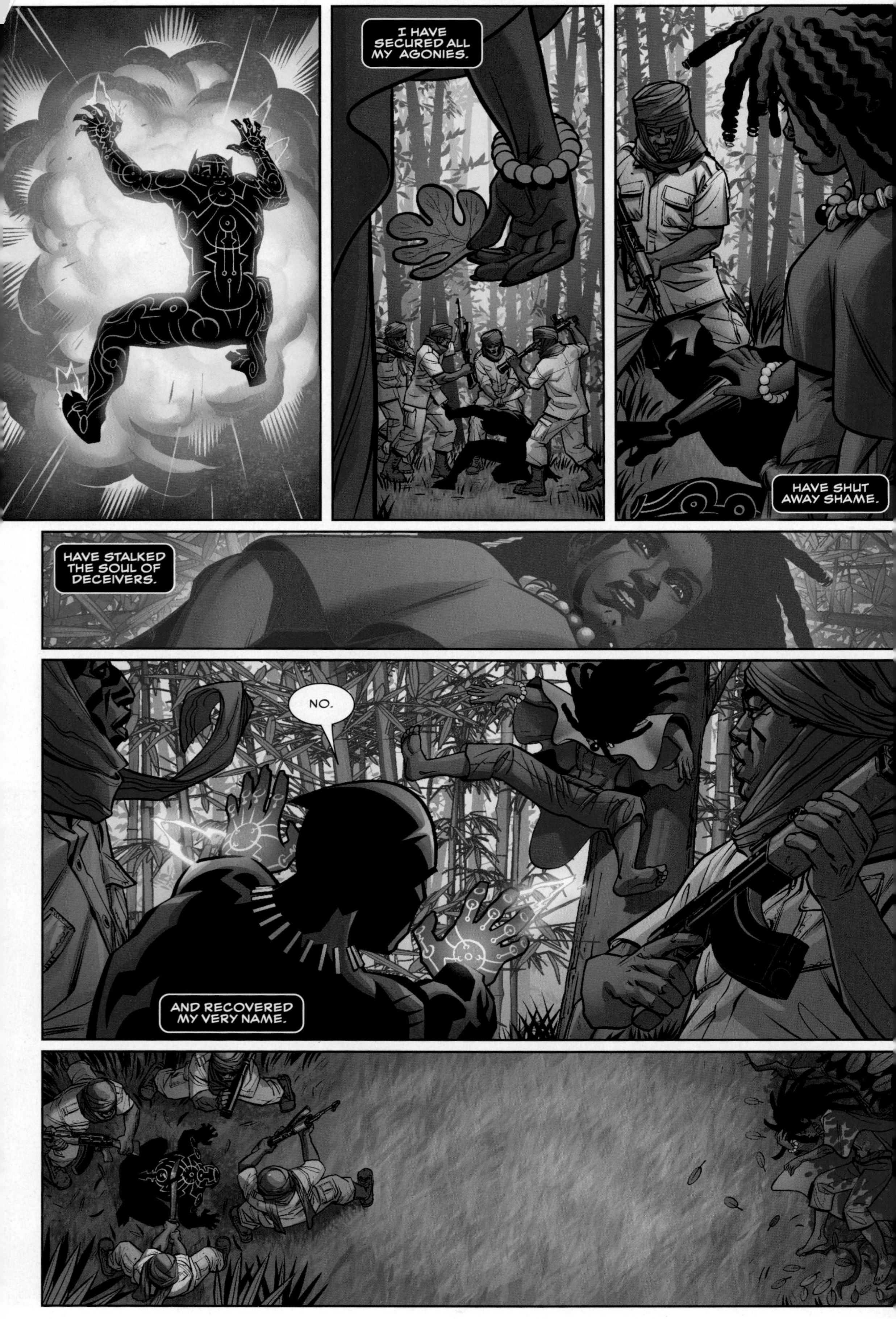
I HAVE SECURED ALL MY AGONIES.
HAVE SHUT AWAY SHAME.
HAVE STALKED THE SOUL OF DECEIVERS.
NO.
AND RECOVERED MY VERY NAME.

NOW, WAR DOGS!

WE ARE WITH YOU, MY KING!

BUT CALAMITY SURROUNDS US.

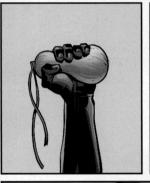

AND I AM WITH YOU, TOO.

THE PAST OVERWHELMS US.

YOU DARE ACCUSE US OF TREACHERY...

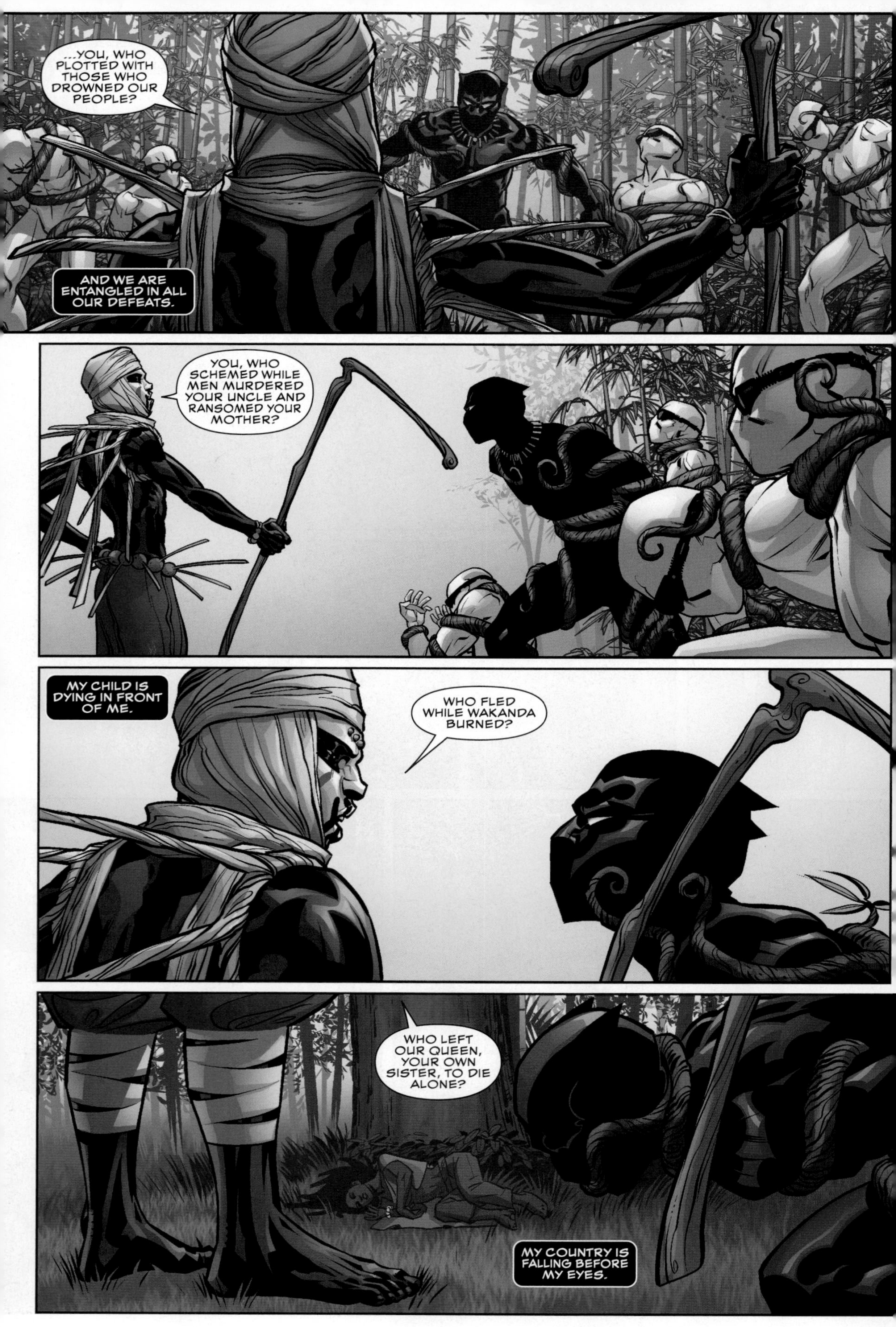
...YOU, WHO PLOTTED WITH THOSE WHO DROWNED OUR PEOPLE?
AND WE ARE ENTANGLED IN ALL OUR DEFEATS.
YOU, WHO SCHEMED WHILE MEN MURDERED YOUR UNCLE AND RANSOMED YOUR MOTHER?
MY CHILD IS DYING IN FRONT OF ME.
WHO FLED WHILE WAKANDA BURNED?
WHO LEFT OUR QUEEN, YOUR OWN SISTER, TO DIE ALONE?
MY COUNTRY IS FALLING BEFORE MY EYES.

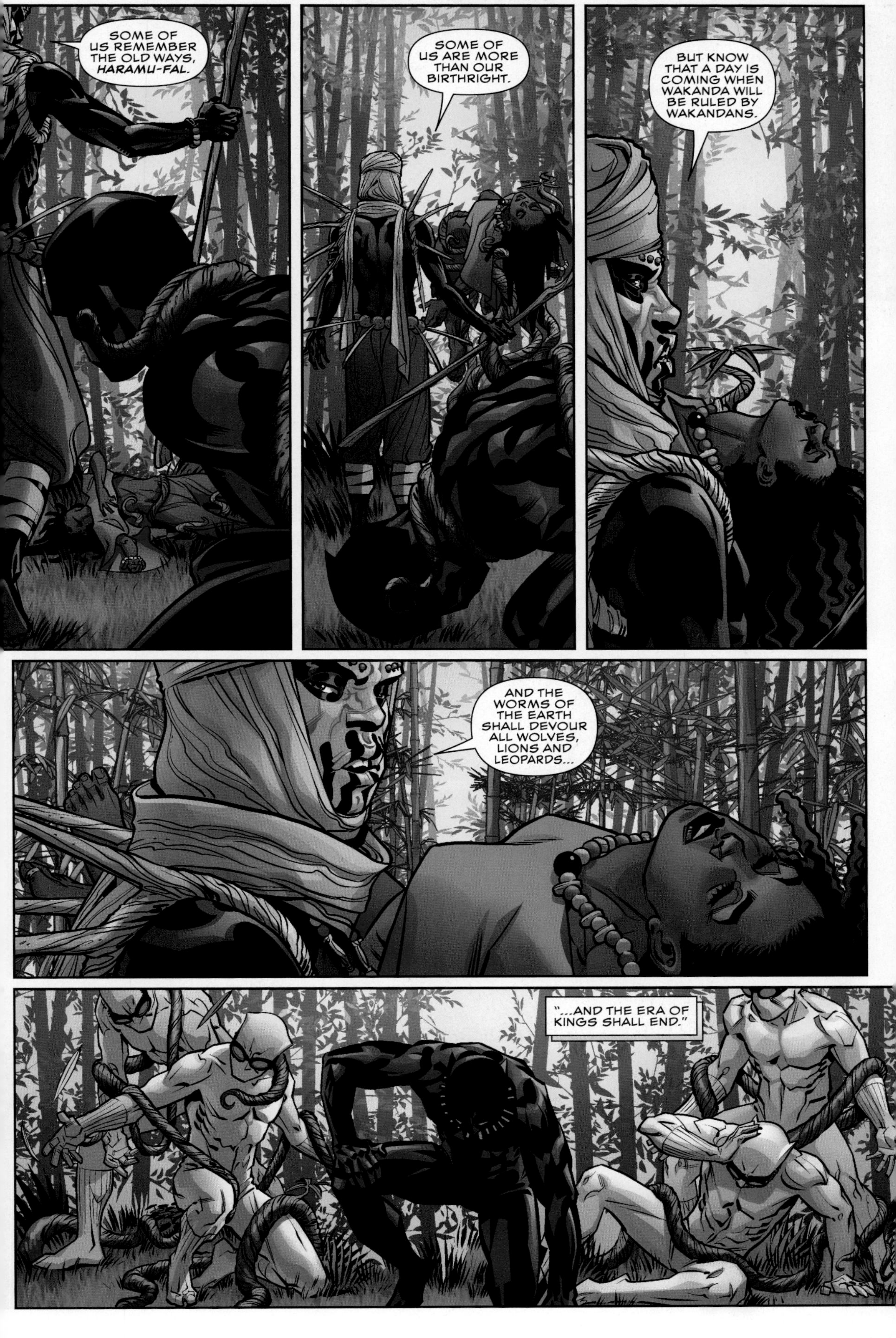
SOME OF US REMEMBER THE OLD WAYS, *HARAMU-FAL.*
SOME OF US ARE MORE THAN OUR BIRTHRIGHT.
BUT KNOW THAT A DAY IS COMING WHEN WAKANDA WILL BE RULED BY WAKANDANS.
AND THE WORMS OF THE EARTH SHALL DEVOUR ALL WOLVES, LIONS AND LEOPARDS...
"...AND THE ERA OF KINGS SHALL END."

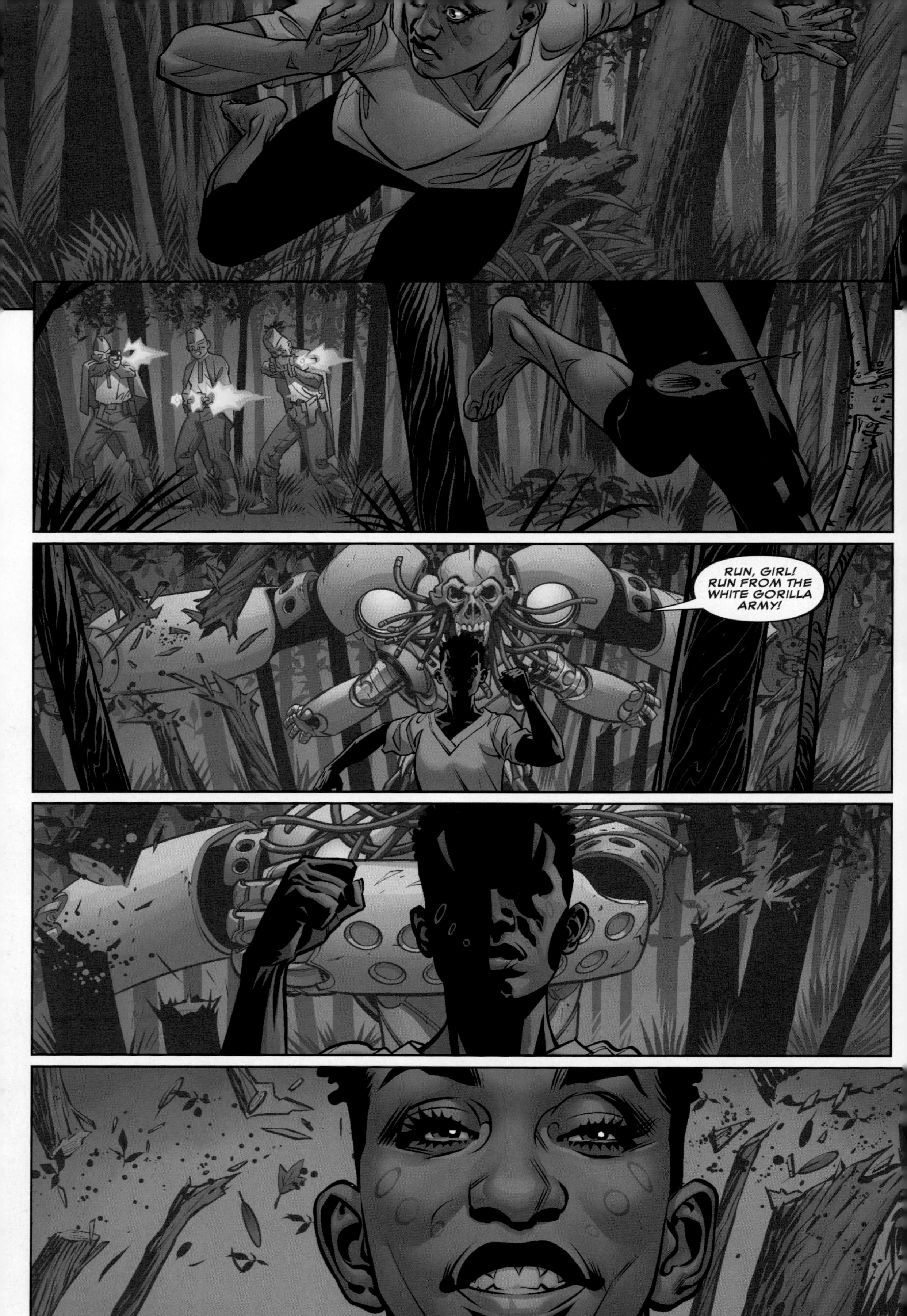
RUN, GIRL! RUN FROM THE WHITE GORILLA ARMY!

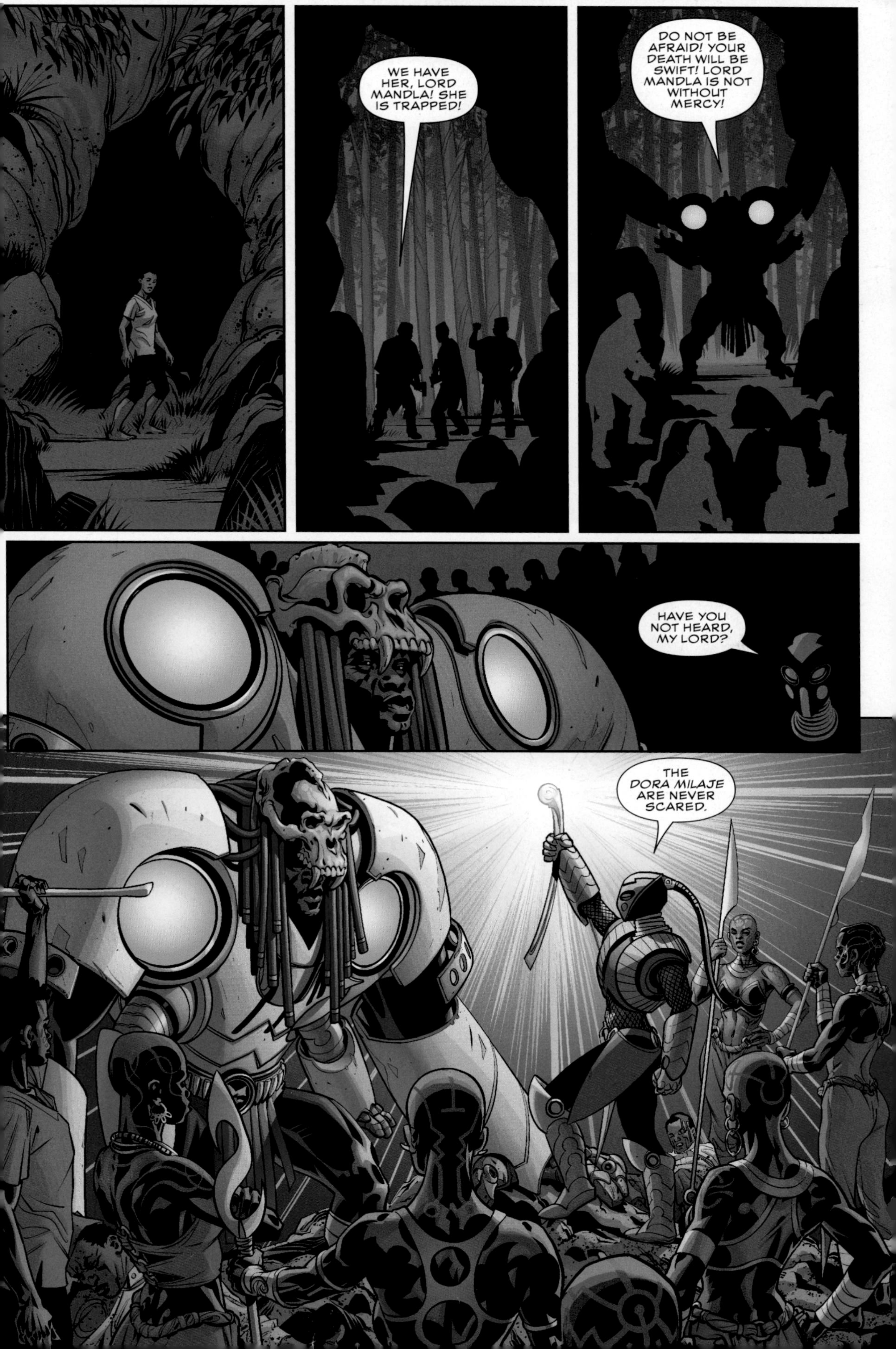
WE HAVE HER, LORD MANDLA! SHE IS TRAPPED!
DO NOT BE AFRAID! YOUR DEATH WILL BE SWIFT! LORD MANDLA IS NOT WITHOUT MERCY!
HAVE YOU NOT HEARD, MY LORD?
THE *DORA MILAJE* ARE NEVER SCARED.

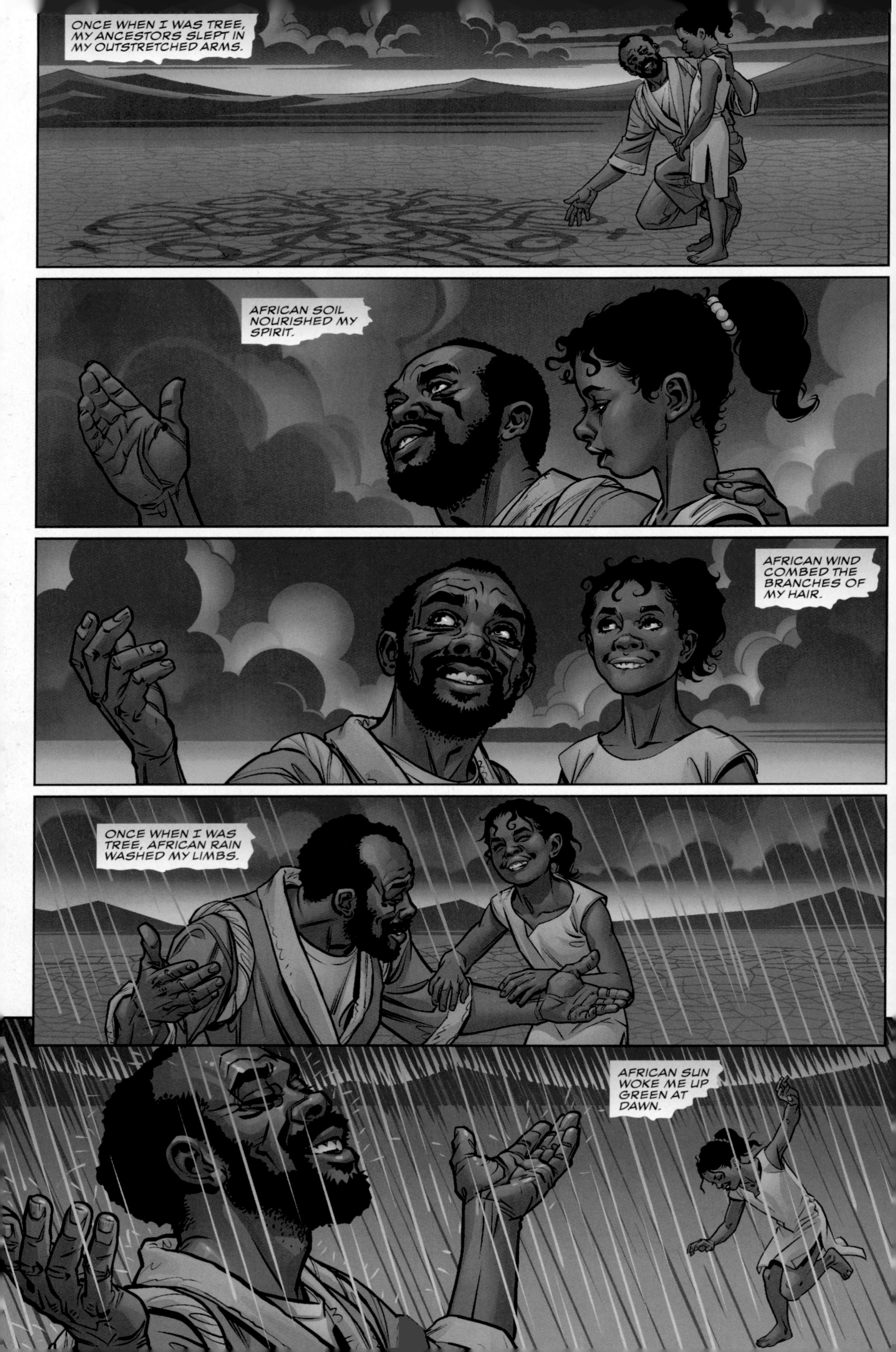
ONCE WHEN I WAS TREE, MY ANCESTORS SLEPT IN MY OUTSTRETCHED ARMS.
AFRICAN SOIL NOURISHED MY SPIRIT.
AFRICAN WIND COMBED THE BRANCHES OF MY HAIR.
ONCE WHEN I WAS TREE, AFRICAN RAIN WASHED MY LIMBS.
AFRICAN SUN WOKE ME UP GREEN AT DAWN.

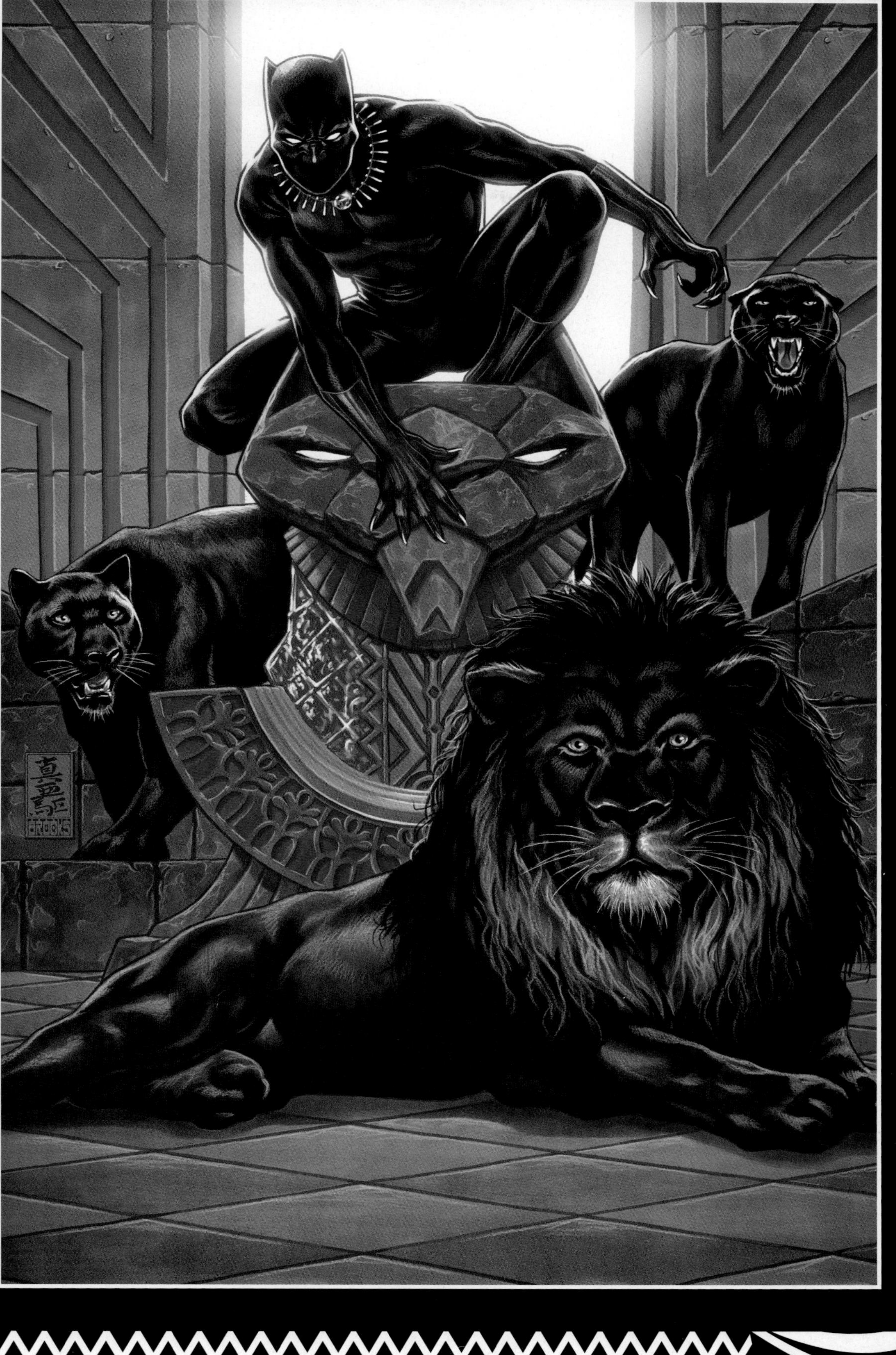
BROOKS

#1 VARIANT BY **MARK BROOKS**

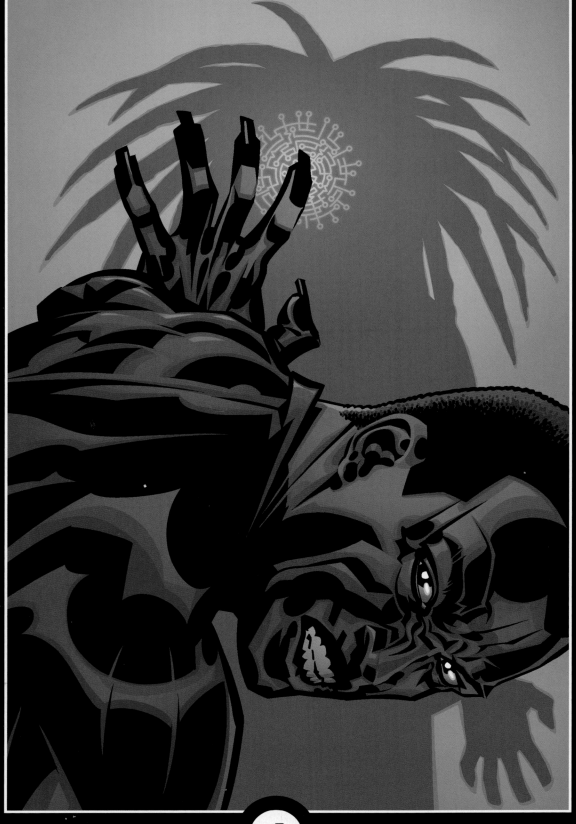

4

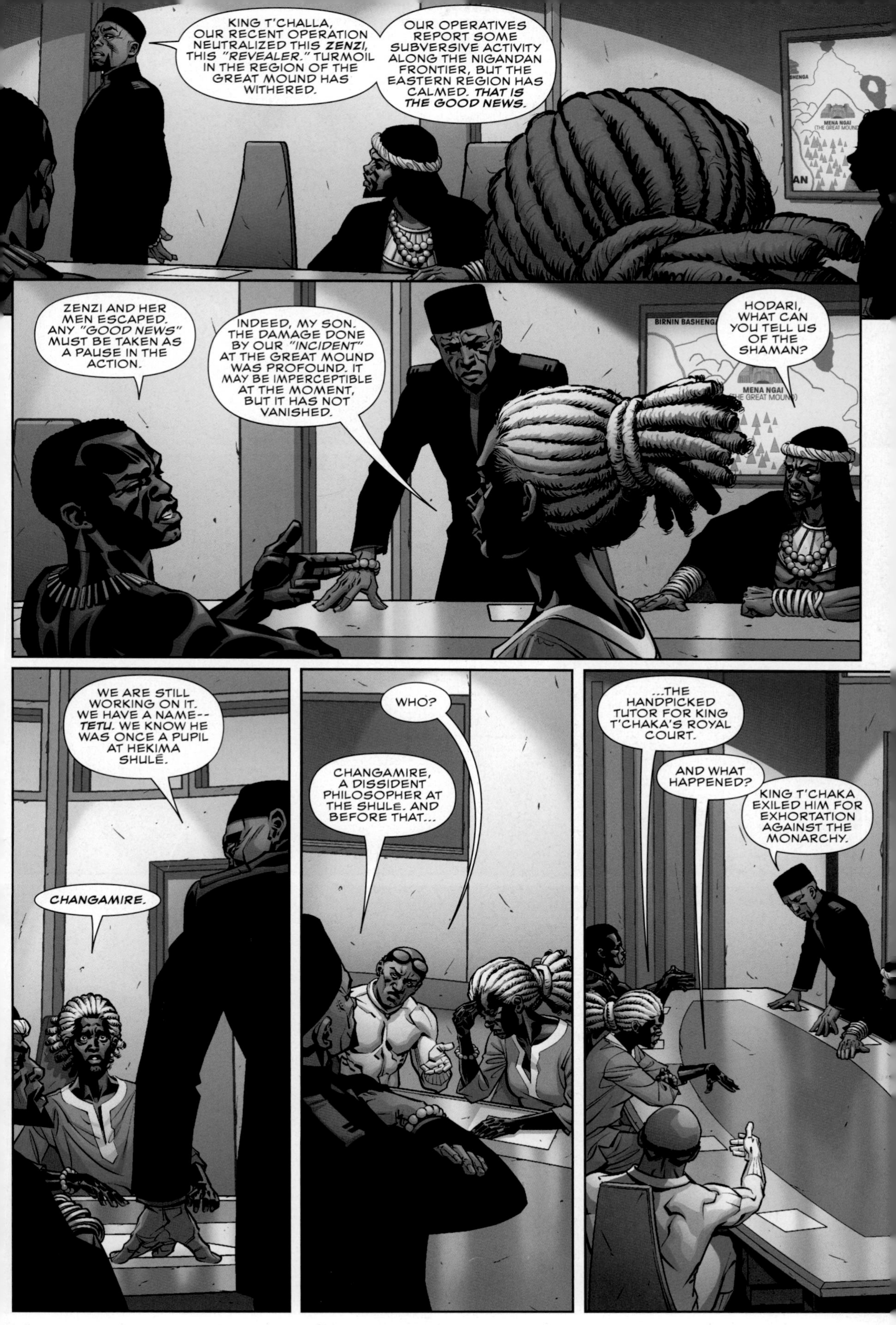
KING T'CHALLA, OUR RECENT OPERATION NEUTRALIZED THIS ZENZI, THIS "REVEALER." TURMOIL IN THE REGION OF THE GREAT MOUND HAS WITHERED.
OUR OPERATIVES REPORT SOME SUBVERSIVE ACTIVITY ALONG THE NIGANDAN FRONTIER, BUT THE EASTERN REGION HAS CALMED. THAT IS THE GOOD NEWS.
MENA NGAI (THE GREAT MOUND)
ZENZI AND HER MEN ESCAPED. ANY "GOOD NEWS" MUST BE TAKEN AS A PAUSE IN THE ACTION.
INDEED, MY SON. THE DAMAGE DONE BY OUR "INCIDENT" AT THE GREAT MOUND WAS PROFOUND. IT MAY BE IMPERCEPTIBLE AT THE MOMENT, BUT IT HAS NOT VANISHED.
BIRNIN BASHENGA
HODARI, WHAT CAN YOU TELL US OF THE SHAMAN?
WE ARE STILL WORKING ON IT. WE HAVE A NAME-- TETU. WE KNOW HE WAS ONCE A PUPIL AT HEKIMA SHULÉ.
CHANGAMIRE.
WHO?
CHANGAMIRE, A DISSIDENT PHILOSOPHER AT THE SHULÉ. AND BEFORE THAT...
...THE HANDPICKED TUTOR FOR KING T'CHAKA'S ROYAL COURT.
AND WHAT HAPPENED?
KING T'CHAKA EXILED HIM FOR EXHORTATION AGAINST THE MONARCHY.

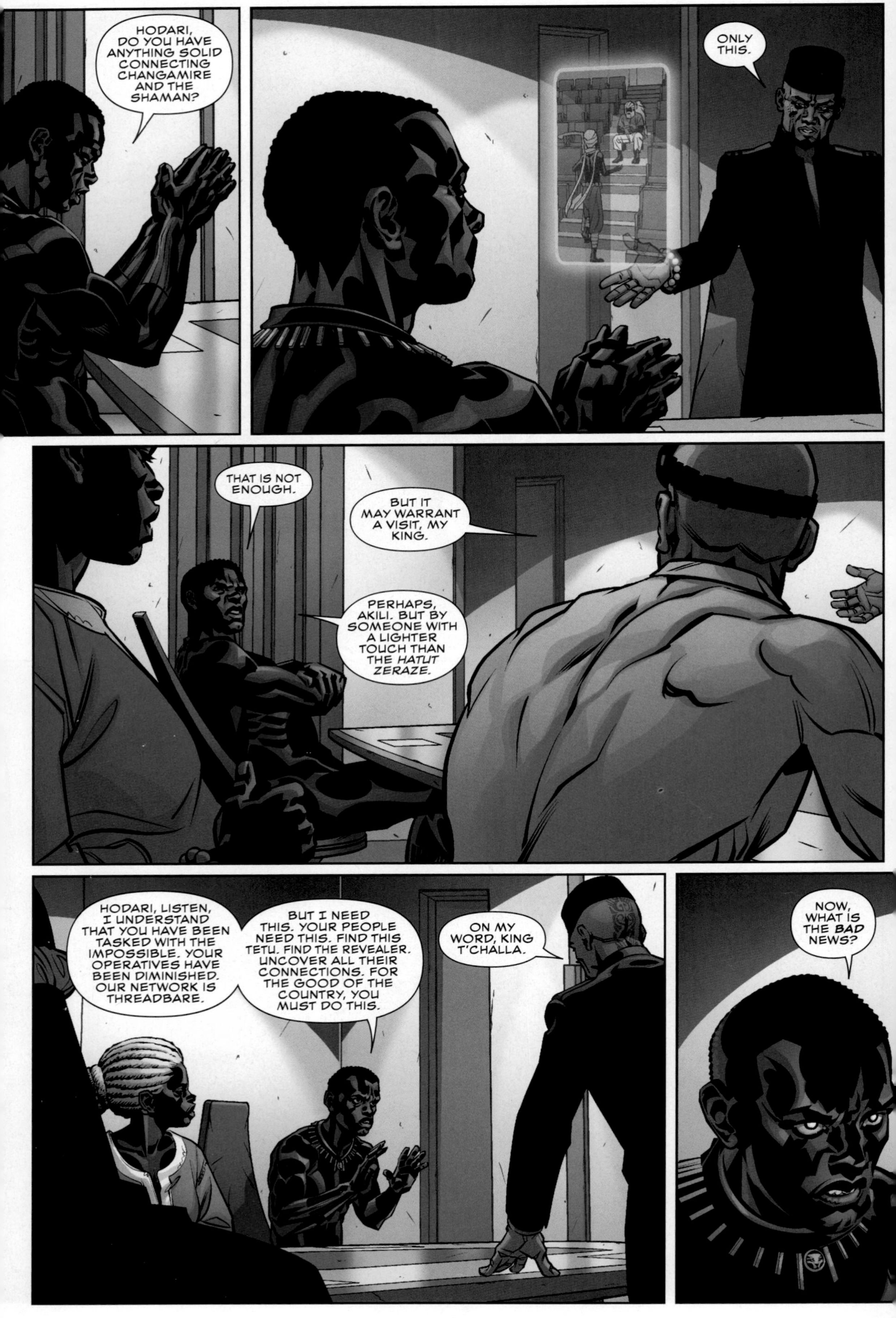
HODARI, DO YOU HAVE ANYTHING SOLID CONNECTING CHANGAMIRE AND THE SHAMAN?
ONLY THIS.
THAT IS NOT ENOUGH.
BUT IT MAY WARRANT A VISIT, MY KING.
PERHAPS, AKILI. BUT BY SOMEONE WITH A LIGHTER TOUCH THAN THE *HATUT ZERAZE*.
HODARI, LISTEN, I UNDERSTAND THAT YOU HAVE BEEN TASKED WITH THE IMPOSSIBLE. YOUR OPERATIVES HAVE BEEN DIMINISHED. OUR NETWORK IS THREADBARE.
BUT I NEED THIS. YOUR PEOPLE NEED THIS. FIND THIS TETU. FIND THE REVEALER. UNCOVER ALL THEIR CONNECTIONS. FOR THE GOOD OF THE COUNTRY, YOU MUST DO THIS.
ON MY WORD, KING T'CHALLA.
NOW, WHAT IS THE *BAD* NEWS?

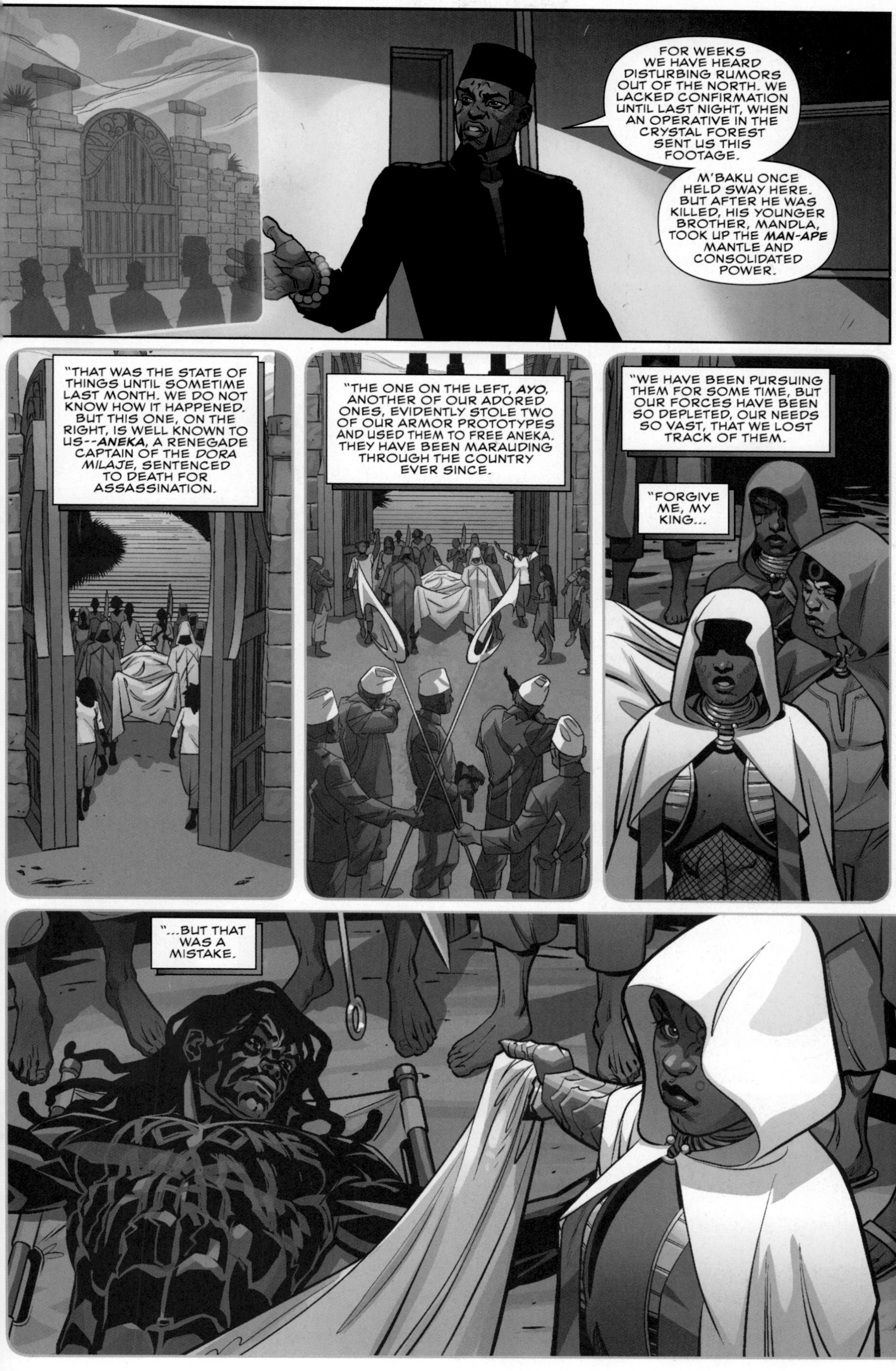
FOR WEEKS WE HAVE HEARD DISTURBING RUMORS OUT OF THE NORTH. WE LACKED CONFIRMATION UNTIL LAST NIGHT, WHEN AN OPERATIVE IN THE CRYSTAL FOREST SENT US THIS FOOTAGE.
M'BAKU ONCE HELD SWAY HERE. BUT AFTER HE WAS KILLED, HIS YOUNGER BROTHER, MANDLA, TOOK UP THE *MAN-APE* MANTLE AND CONSOLIDATED POWER.
"THAT WAS THE STATE OF THINGS UNTIL SOMETIME LAST MONTH. WE DO NOT KNOW HOW IT HAPPENED. BUT THIS ONE, ON THE RIGHT, IS WELL KNOWN TO US--*ANEKA*, A RENEGADE CAPTAIN OF THE *DORA MILAJE*, SENTENCED TO DEATH FOR ASSASSINATION.
"THE ONE ON THE LEFT, *AYO*, ANOTHER OF OUR ADORED ONES, EVIDENTLY STOLE TWO OF OUR ARMOR PROTOTYPES AND USED THEM TO FREE ANEKA. THEY HAVE BEEN MARAUDING THROUGH THE COUNTRY EVER SINCE.
"WE HAVE BEEN PURSUING THEM FOR SOME TIME, BUT OUR FORCES HAVE BEEN SO DEPLETED, OUR NEEDS SO VAST, THAT WE LOST TRACK OF THEM.
"FORGIVE ME, MY KING...
"...BUT THAT WAS A MISTAKE.

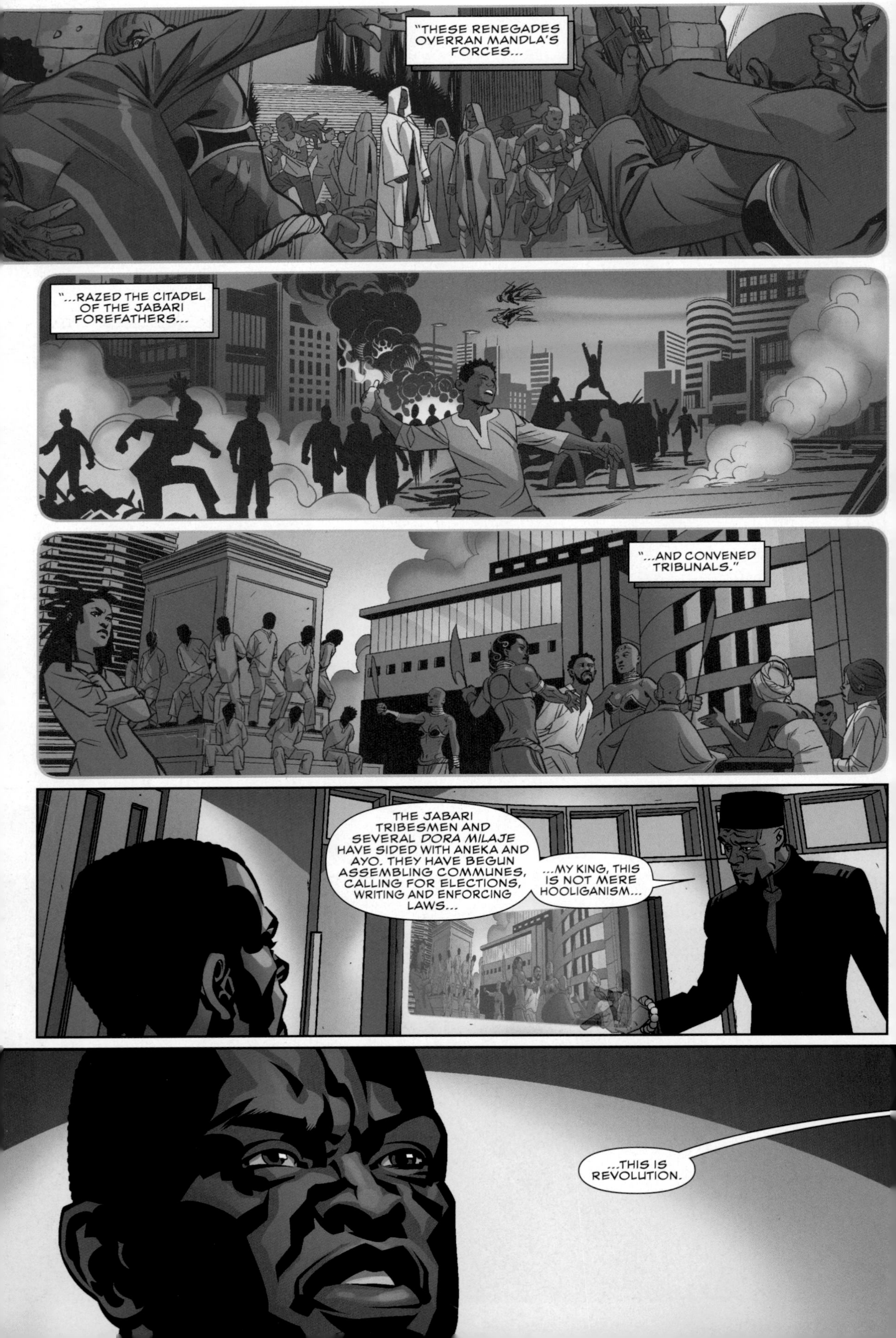
"THESE RENEGADES OVERRAN MANDLA'S FORCES...
"...RAZED THE CITADEL OF THE JABARI FOREFATHERS...
"...AND CONVENED TRIBUNALS."
THE JABARI TRIBESMEN AND SEVERAL *DORA MILAJE* HAVE SIDED WITH ANEKA AND AYO. THEY HAVE BEGUN ASSEMBLING COMMUNES, CALLING FOR ELECTIONS, WRITING AND ENFORCING LAWS...
...MY KING, THIS IS NOT MERE HOOLIGANISM...
...THIS IS REVOLUTION.

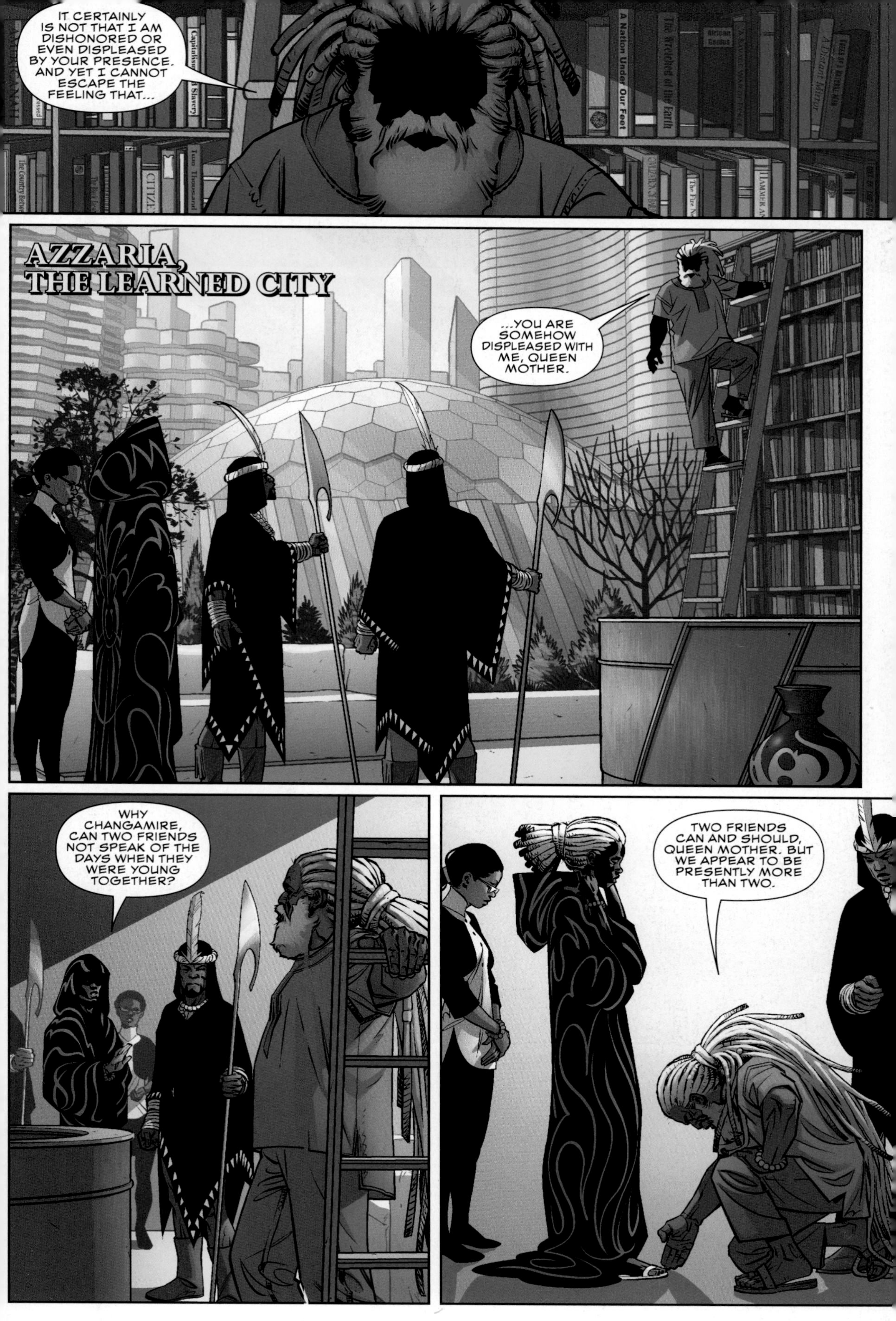
IT CERTAINLY IS NOT THAT I AM DISHONORED OR EVEN DISPLEASED BY YOUR PRESENCE. AND YET I CANNOT ESCAPE THE FEELING THAT...
AZZARIA, THE LEARNED CITY
...YOU ARE SOMEHOW DISPLEASED WITH ME, QUEEN MOTHER.
WHY CHANGAMIRE, CAN TWO FRIENDS NOT SPEAK OF THE DAYS WHEN THEY WERE YOUNG TOGETHER?
TWO FRIENDS CAN AND SHOULD, QUEEN MOTHER. BUT WE APPEAR TO BE PRESENTLY MORE THAN TWO.

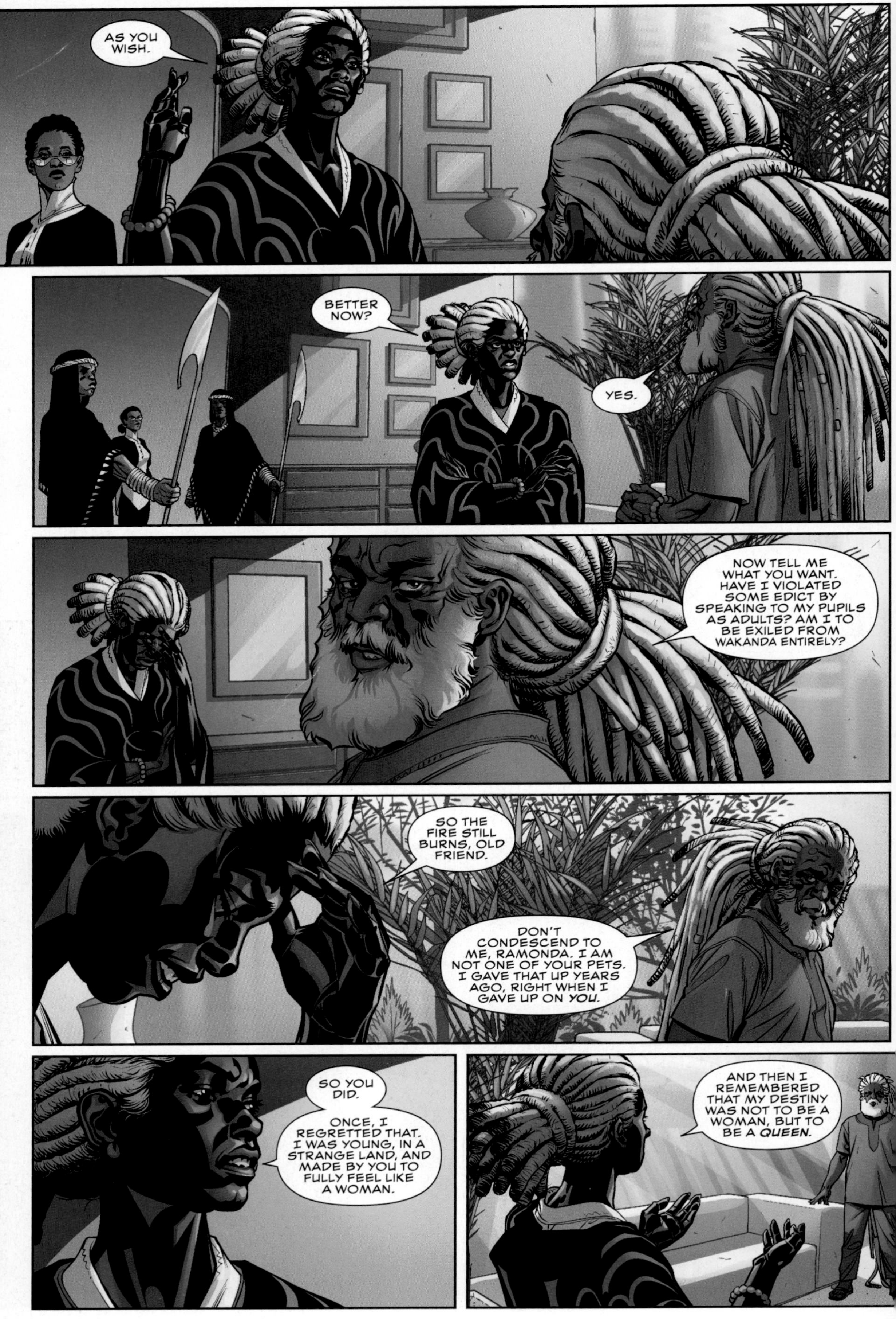
AS YOU WISH.
BETTER NOW?
YES.
NOW TELL ME WHAT YOU WANT. HAVE I VIOLATED SOME EDICT BY SPEAKING TO MY PUPILS AS ADULTS? AM I TO BE EXILED FROM WAKANDA ENTIRELY?
SO THE FIRE STILL BURNS, OLD FRIEND.
DON'T CONDESCEND TO ME, RAMONDA. I AM NOT ONE OF YOUR PETS. I GAVE THAT UP YEARS AGO, RIGHT WHEN I GAVE UP ON *YOU*.
SO YOU DID.
ONCE, I REGRETTED THAT. I WAS YOUNG, IN A STRANGE LAND, AND MADE BY YOU TO FULLY FEEL LIKE A WOMAN.
AND THEN I REMEMBERED THAT MY DESTINY WAS NOT TO BE A WOMAN, BUT TO BE A *QUEEN*.

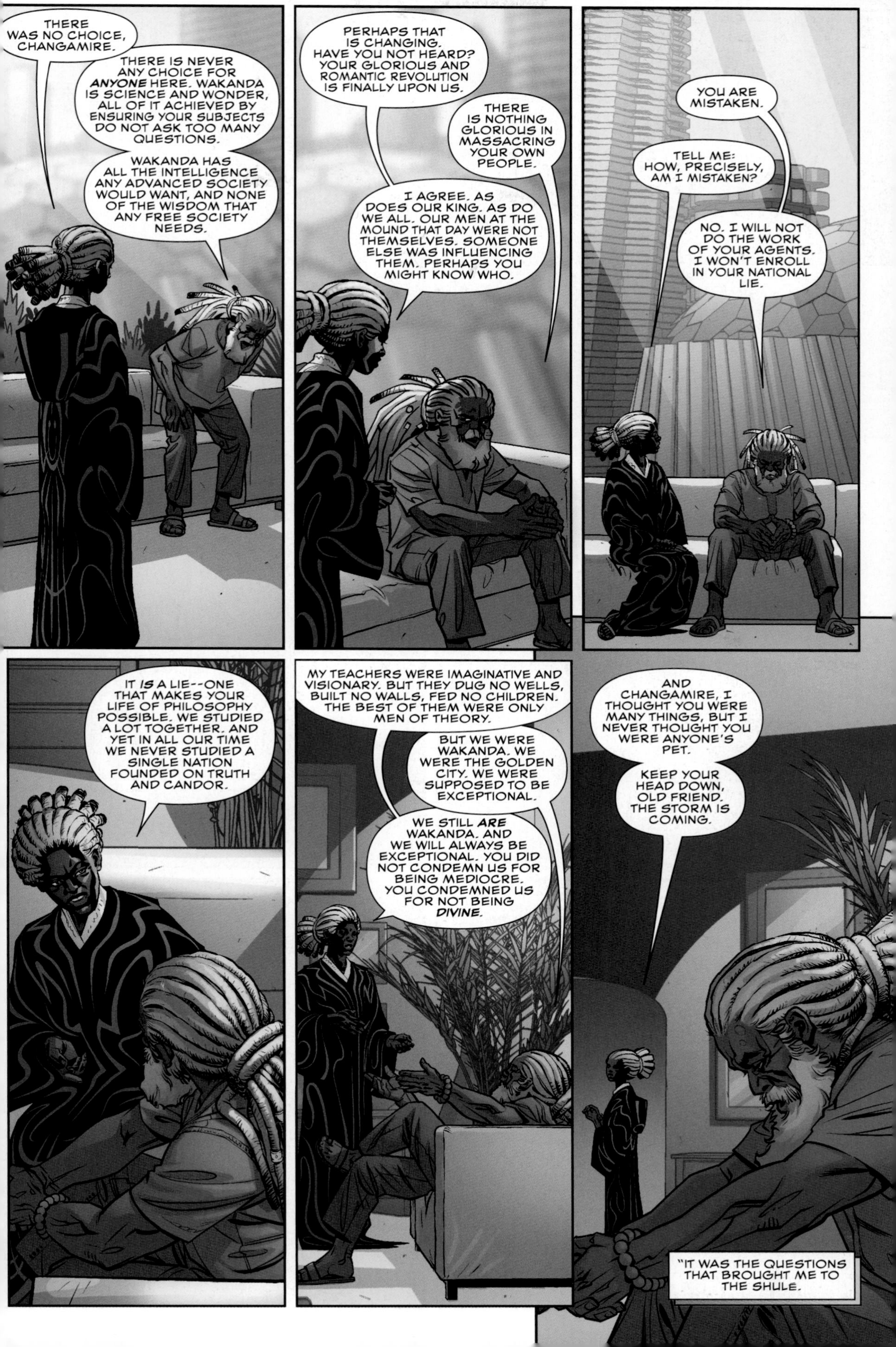
THERE WAS NO CHOICE, CHANGAMIRE.
THERE IS NEVER ANY CHOICE FOR ANYONE HERE. WAKANDA IS SCIENCE AND WONDER, ALL OF IT ACHIEVED BY ENSURING YOUR SUBJECTS DO NOT ASK TOO MANY QUESTIONS.
WAKANDA HAS ALL THE INTELLIGENCE ANY ADVANCED SOCIETY WOULD WANT, AND NONE OF THE WISDOM THAT ANY FREE SOCIETY NEEDS.
PERHAPS THAT IS CHANGING. HAVE YOU NOT HEARD? YOUR GLORIOUS AND ROMANTIC REVOLUTION IS FINALLY UPON US.
THERE IS NOTHING GLORIOUS IN MASSACRING YOUR OWN PEOPLE.
I AGREE. AS DOES OUR KING. AS DO WE ALL. OUR MEN AT THE MOUND THAT DAY WERE NOT THEMSELVES. SOMEONE ELSE WAS INFLUENCING THEM. PERHAPS YOU MIGHT KNOW WHO.
YOU ARE MISTAKEN.
TELL ME: HOW, PRECISELY, AM I MISTAKEN?
NO. I WILL NOT DO THE WORK OF YOUR AGENTS. I WON'T ENROLL IN YOUR NATIONAL LIE.
IT IS A LIE--ONE THAT MAKES YOUR LIFE OF PHILOSOPHY POSSIBLE. WE STUDIED A LOT TOGETHER. AND YET IN ALL OUR TIME WE NEVER STUDIED A SINGLE NATION FOUNDED ON TRUTH AND CANDOR.
MY TEACHERS WERE IMAGINATIVE AND VISIONARY. BUT THEY DUG NO WELLS, BUILT NO WALLS, FED NO CHILDREN. THE BEST OF THEM WERE ONLY MEN OF THEORY.
BUT WE WERE WAKANDA. WE WERE THE GOLDEN CITY. WE WERE SUPPOSED TO BE EXCEPTIONAL.
WE STILL ARE WAKANDA. AND WE WILL ALWAYS BE EXCEPTIONAL. YOU DID NOT CONDEMN US FOR BEING MEDIOCRE. YOU CONDEMNED US FOR NOT BEING DIVINE.
AND CHANGAMIRE, I THOUGHT YOU WERE MANY THINGS, BUT I NEVER THOUGHT YOU WERE ANYONE'S PET.
KEEP YOUR HEAD DOWN, OLD FRIEND. THE STORM IS COMING.
"IT WAS THE QUESTIONS THAT BROUGHT ME TO THE SHULE.

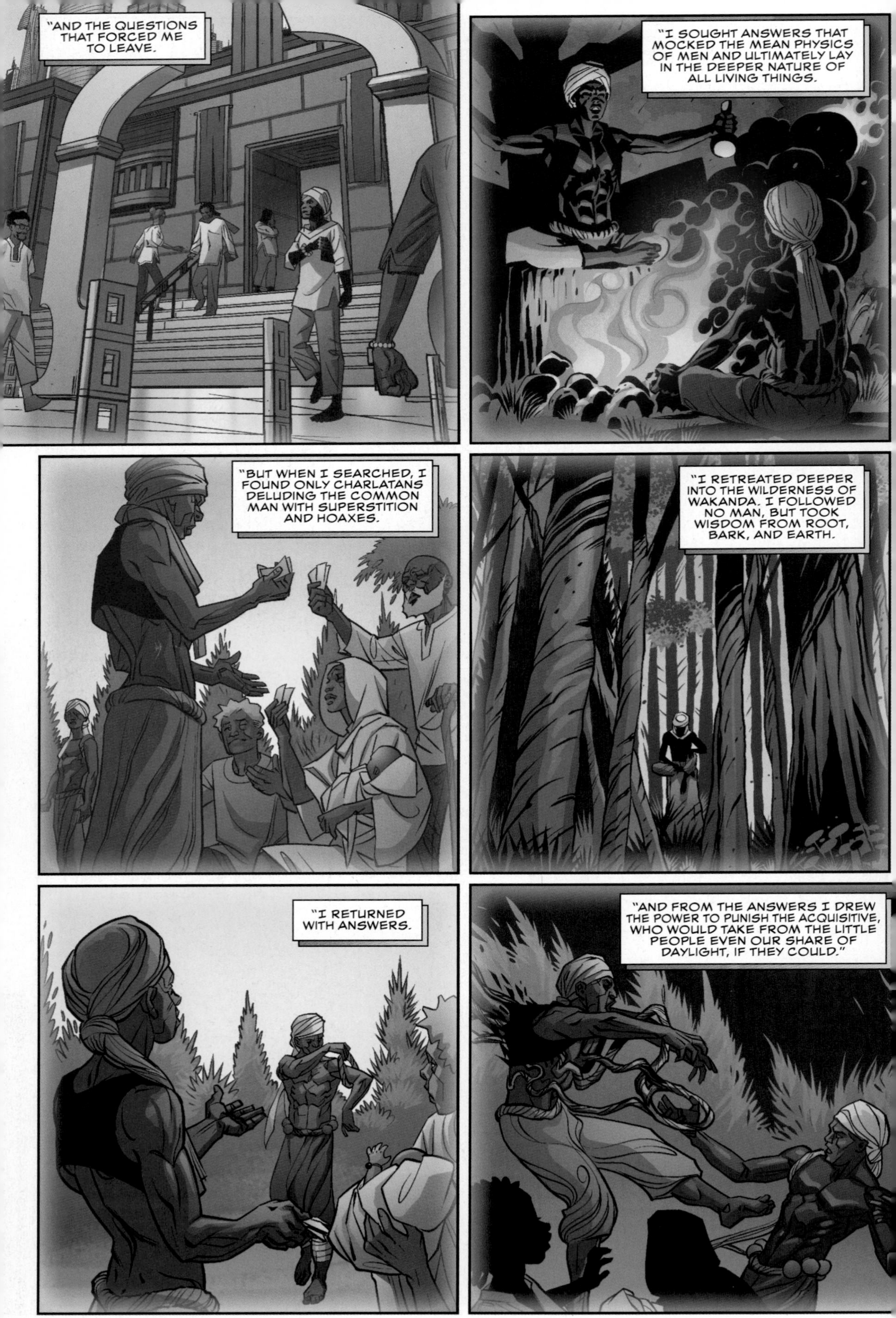
"AND THE QUESTIONS THAT FORCED ME TO LEAVE.
"I SOUGHT ANSWERS THAT MOCKED THE MEAN PHYSICS OF MEN AND ULTIMATELY LAY IN THE DEEPER NATURE OF ALL LIVING THINGS.
"BUT WHEN I SEARCHED, I FOUND ONLY CHARLATANS DELUDING THE COMMON MAN WITH SUPERSTITION AND HOAXES.
"I RETREATED DEEPER INTO THE WILDERNESS OF WAKANDA. I FOLLOWED NO MAN, BUT TOOK WISDOM FROM ROOT, BARK, AND EARTH.
"I RETURNED WITH ANSWERS.
"AND FROM THE ANSWERS I DREW THE POWER TO PUNISH THE ACQUISITIVE, WHO WOULD TAKE FROM THE LITTLE PEOPLE EVEN OUR SHARE OF DAYLIGHT, IF THEY COULD."

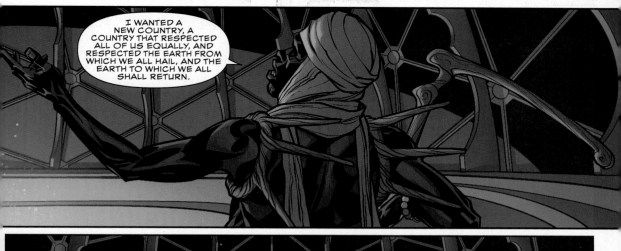

I WANTED A NEW COUNTRY, A COUNTRY THAT RESPECTED ALL OF US EQUALLY, AND RESPECTED THE EARTH FROM WHICH WE ALL HAIL, AND THE EARTH TO WHICH WE ALL SHALL RETURN.

I BELIEVE I HAVE FOUND THAT COUNTRY.

I COME TO OFFER YOU MY ADMIRATION. TOPPLING THE JABARI TYRANT WAS A GREAT SERVICE TO THE NATION. BUT MORE, I OFFER YOU MY ARMS. IT WILL NOT END WITH THE JABARI. *WAR* IS COMING.

TETU, EACH DAY ANOTHER OF OUR SISTERS JOINS THE CAUSE. EACH DAY WE GROW STRONGER.

THE MIDNIGHT ANGELS WERE ENOUGH FOR MANDLA. THEY WILL BE ENOUGH FOR *DAMISA-SARKI* TOO.

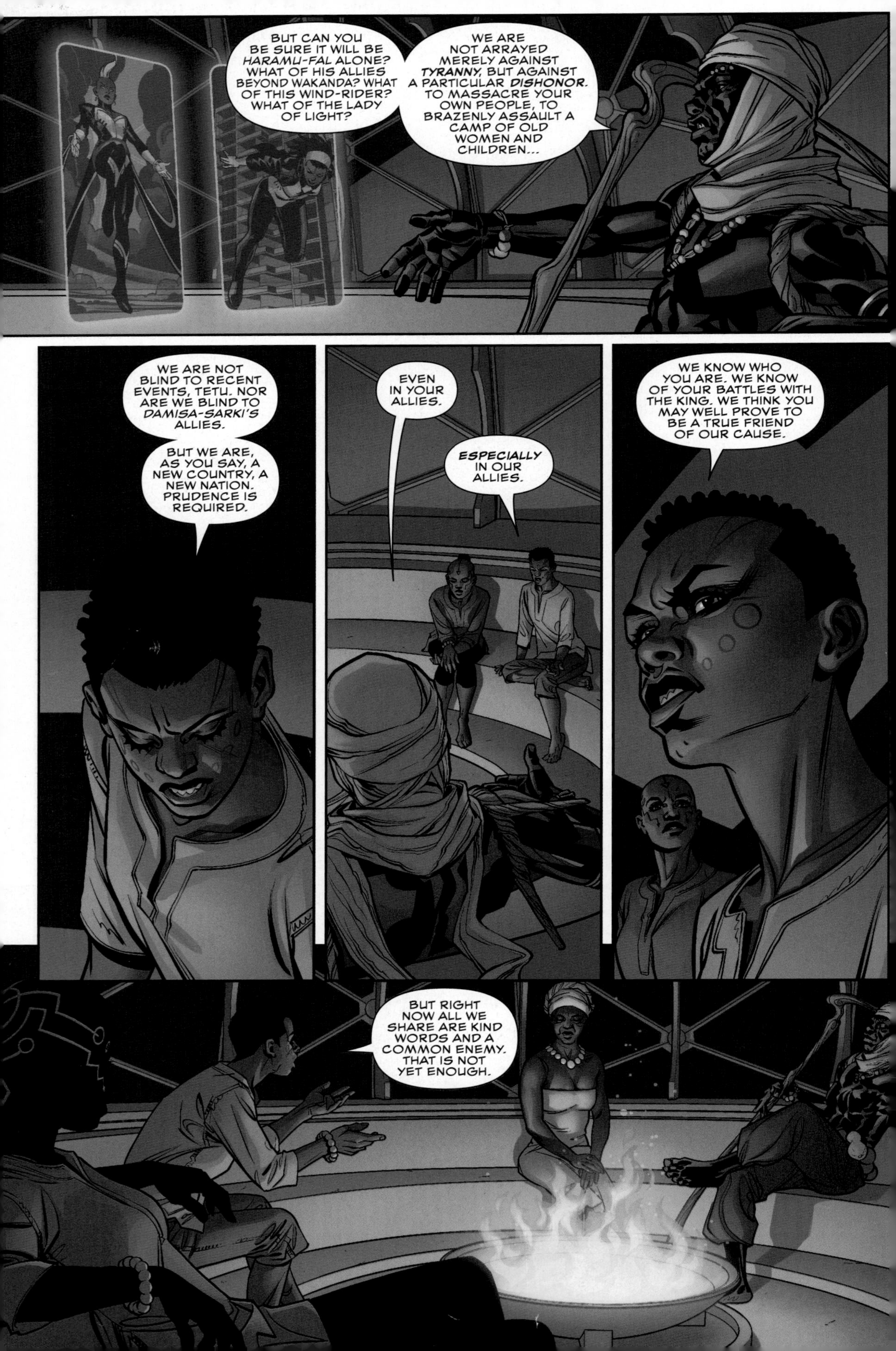
BUT CAN YOU BE SURE IT WILL BE HARAMU-FAL ALONE? WHAT OF HIS ALLIES BEYOND WAKANDA? WHAT OF THIS WIND-RIDER? WHAT OF THE LADY OF LIGHT?
WE ARE NOT ARRAYED MERELY AGAINST TYRANNY, BUT AGAINST A PARTICULAR DISHONOR. TO MASSACRE YOUR OWN PEOPLE, TO BRAZENLY ASSAULT A CAMP OF OLD WOMEN AND CHILDREN...
WE ARE NOT BLIND TO RECENT EVENTS, TETU. NOR ARE WE BLIND TO DAMISA-SARKI'S ALLIES.
BUT WE ARE, AS YOU SAY, A NEW COUNTRY, A NEW NATION. PRUDENCE IS REQUIRED.
EVEN IN YOUR ALLIES.
ESPECIALLY IN OUR ALLIES.
WE KNOW WHO YOU ARE. WE KNOW OF YOUR BATTLES WITH THE KING. WE THINK YOU MAY WELL PROVE TO BE A TRUE FRIEND OF OUR CAUSE.
BUT RIGHT NOW ALL WE SHARE ARE KIND WORDS AND A COMMON ENEMY. THAT IS NOT YET ENOUGH.

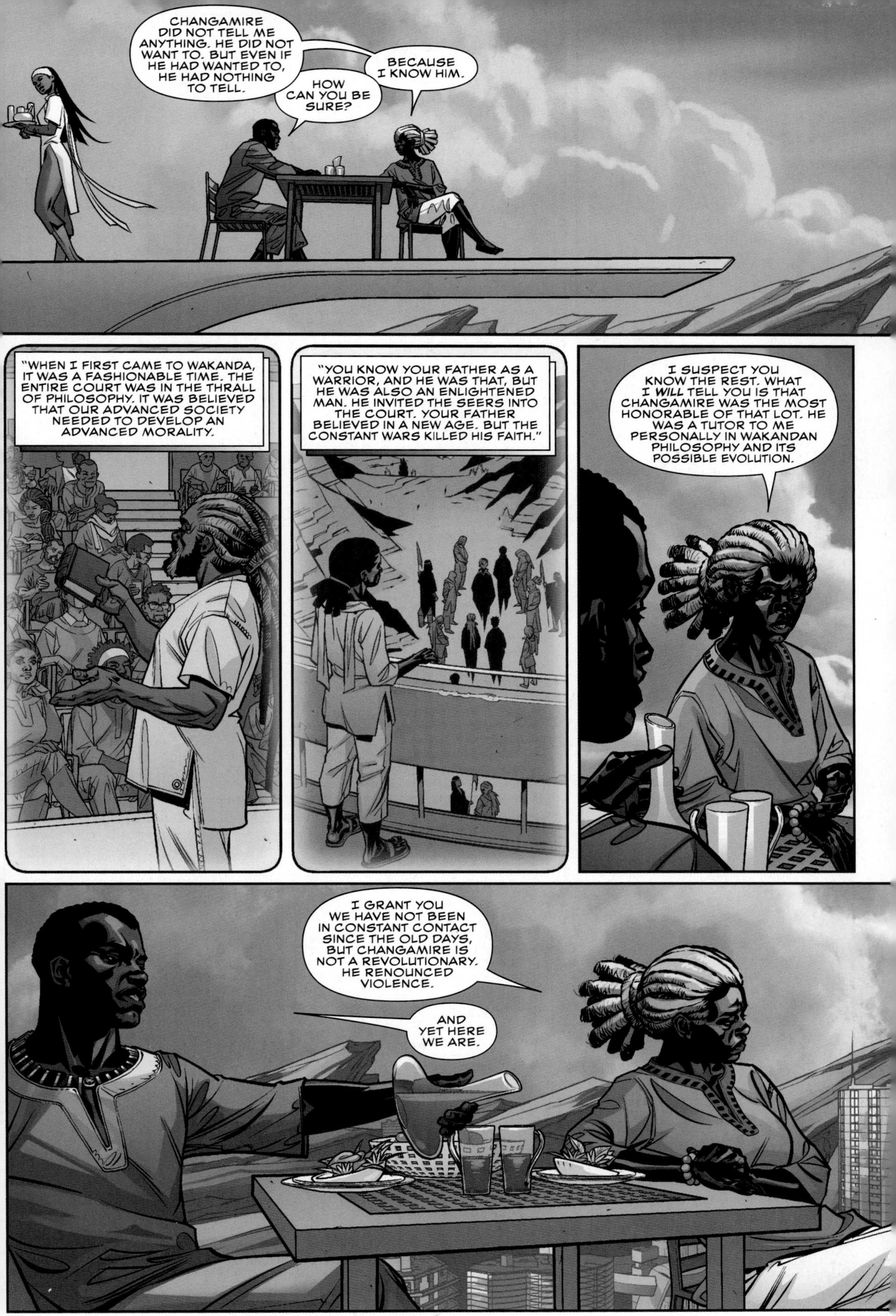
CHANGAMIRE DID NOT TELL ME ANYTHING. HE DID NOT WANT TO. BUT EVEN IF HE HAD WANTED TO, HE HAD NOTHING TO TELL.
HOW CAN YOU BE SURE?
BECAUSE I KNOW HIM.
"WHEN I FIRST CAME TO WAKANDA, IT WAS A FASHIONABLE TIME. THE ENTIRE COURT WAS IN THE THRALL OF PHILOSOPHY. IT WAS BELIEVED THAT OUR ADVANCED SOCIETY NEEDED TO DEVELOP AN ADVANCED MORALITY.
"YOU KNOW YOUR FATHER AS A WARRIOR, AND HE WAS THAT, BUT HE WAS ALSO AN ENLIGHTENED MAN. HE INVITED THE SEERS INTO THE COURT. YOUR FATHER BELIEVED IN A NEW AGE. BUT THE CONSTANT WARS KILLED HIS FAITH."
I SUSPECT YOU KNOW THE REST. WHAT I *WILL* TELL YOU IS THAT CHANGAMIRE WAS THE MOST HONORABLE OF THAT LOT. HE WAS A TUTOR TO ME PERSONALLY IN WAKANDAN PHILOSOPHY AND ITS POSSIBLE EVOLUTION.
I GRANT YOU WE HAVE NOT BEEN IN CONSTANT CONTACT SINCE THE OLD DAYS, BUT CHANGAMIRE IS NOT A REVOLUTIONARY. HE RENOUNCED VIOLENCE.
AND YET HERE WE ARE.

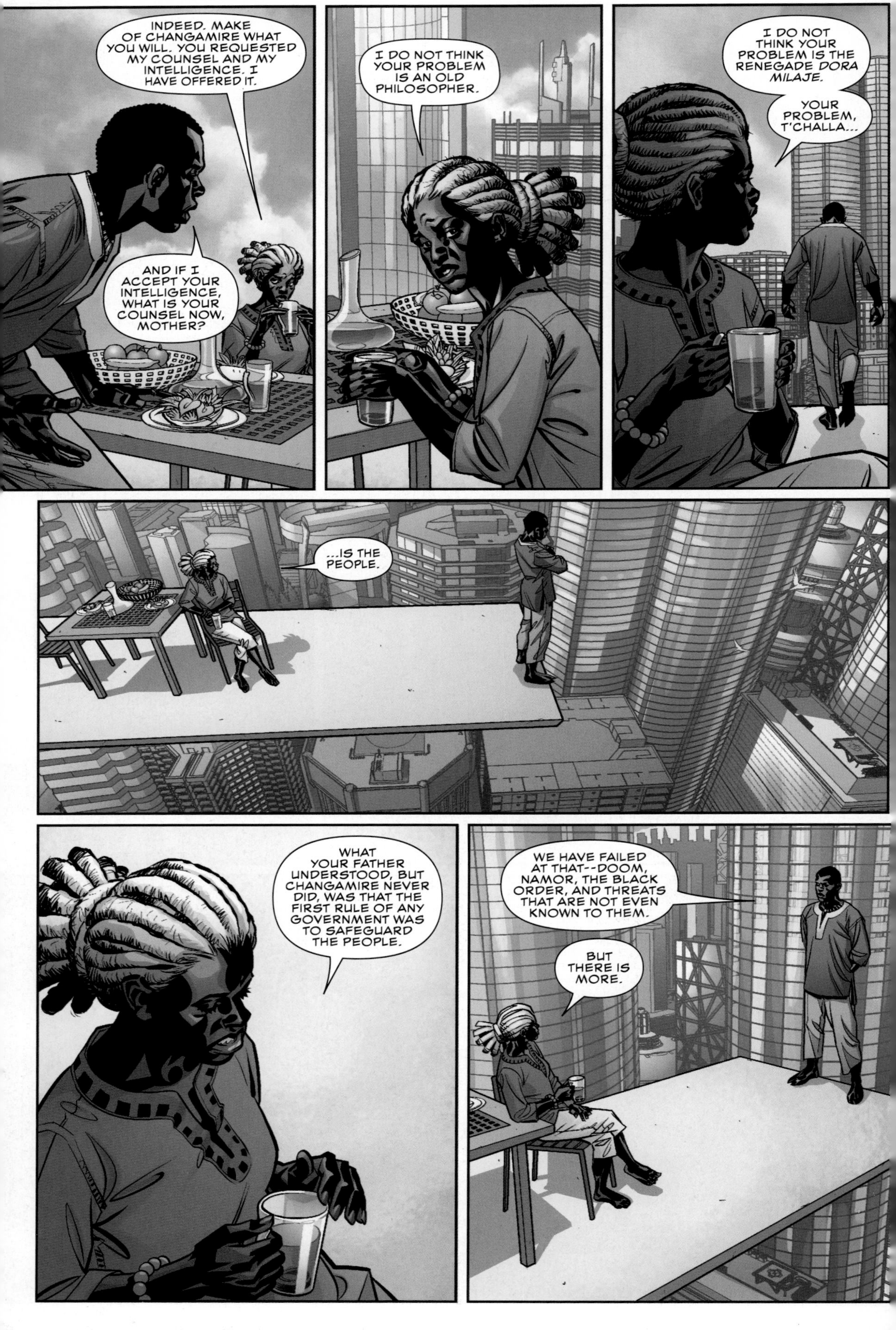
INDEED. MAKE OF CHANGAMIRE WHAT YOU WILL. YOU REQUESTED MY COUNSEL AND MY INTELLIGENCE. I HAVE OFFERED IT.
AND IF I ACCEPT YOUR INTELLIGENCE, WHAT IS YOUR COUNSEL NOW, MOTHER?
I DO NOT THINK YOUR PROBLEM IS AN OLD PHILOSOPHER.
I DO NOT THINK YOUR PROBLEM IS THE RENEGADE *DORA MILAJE*.
YOUR PROBLEM, T'CHALLA...
...IS THE PEOPLE.
WHAT YOUR FATHER UNDERSTOOD, BUT CHANGAMIRE NEVER DID, WAS THAT THE FIRST RULE OF ANY GOVERNMENT WAS TO SAFEGUARD THE PEOPLE.
WE HAVE FAILED AT THAT--DOOM, NAMOR, THE BLACK ORDER, AND THREATS THAT ARE NOT EVEN KNOWN TO THEM.
BUT THERE IS MORE.

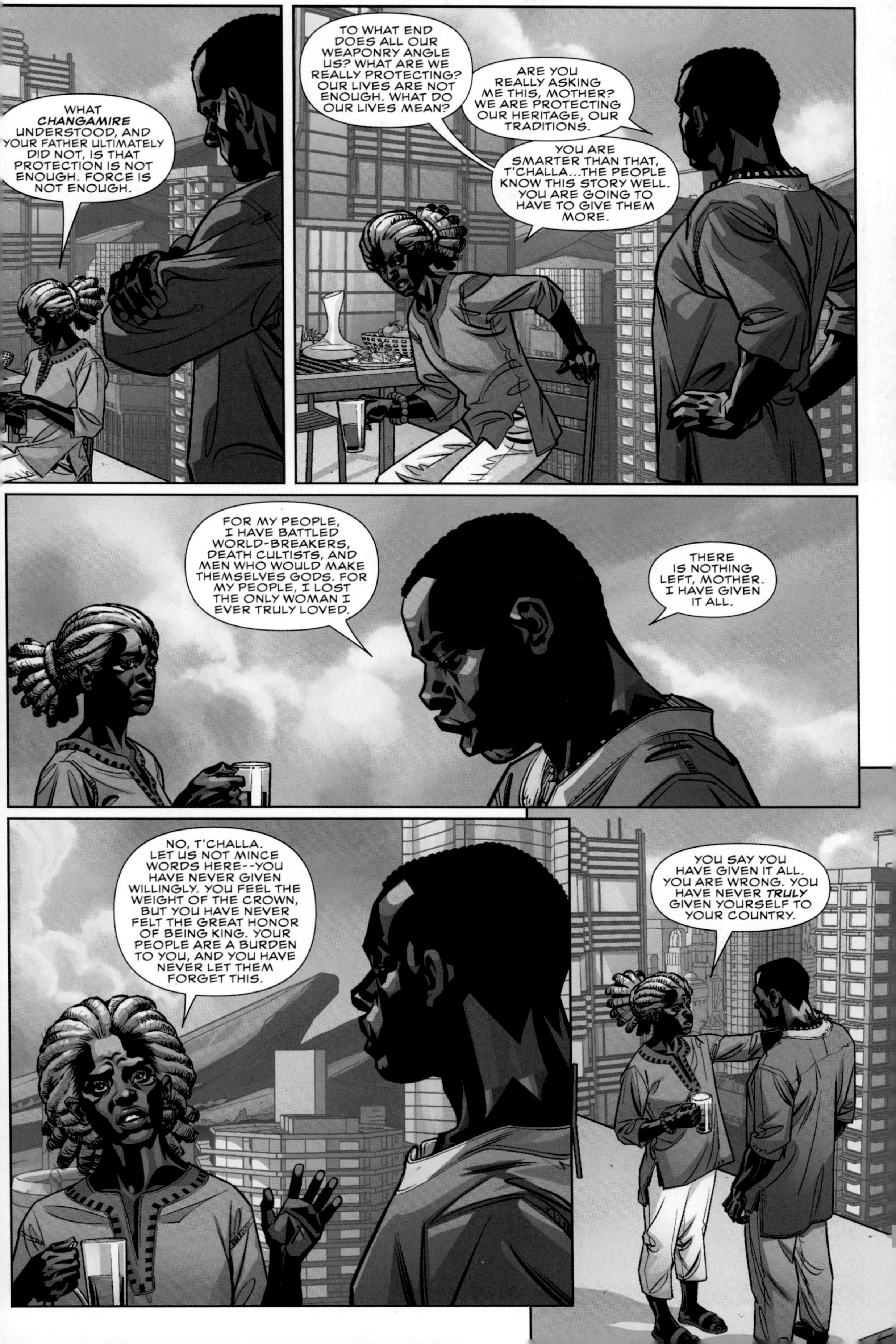
WHAT *CHANGAMIRE* UNDERSTOOD, AND YOUR FATHER ULTIMATELY DID NOT, IS THAT PROTECTION IS NOT ENOUGH. FORCE IS NOT ENOUGH.
TO WHAT END DOES ALL OUR WEAPONRY ANGLE US? WHAT ARE WE REALLY PROTECTING? OUR LIVES ARE NOT ENOUGH. WHAT DO OUR LIVES MEAN?
ARE YOU REALLY ASKING ME THIS, MOTHER? WE ARE PROTECTING OUR HERITAGE, OUR TRADITIONS.
YOU ARE SMARTER THAN THAT, T'CHALLA... THE PEOPLE KNOW THIS STORY WELL. YOU ARE GOING TO HAVE TO GIVE THEM MORE.
FOR MY PEOPLE, I HAVE BATTLED WORLD-BREAKERS, DEATH CULTISTS, AND MEN WHO WOULD MAKE THEMSELVES GODS. FOR MY PEOPLE, I LOST THE ONLY WOMAN I EVER TRULY LOVED.
THERE IS NOTHING LEFT, MOTHER. I HAVE GIVEN IT ALL.
NO, T'CHALLA. LET US NOT MINCE WORDS HERE--YOU HAVE NEVER GIVEN WILLINGLY. YOU FEEL THE WEIGHT OF THE CROWN, BUT YOU HAVE NEVER FELT THE GREAT HONOR OF BEING KING. YOUR PEOPLE ARE A BURDEN TO YOU, AND YOU HAVE NEVER LET THEM FORGET THIS.
YOU SAY YOU HAVE GIVEN IT ALL. YOU ARE WRONG. YOU HAVE NEVER *TRULY* GIVEN YOURSELF TO YOUR COUNTRY.

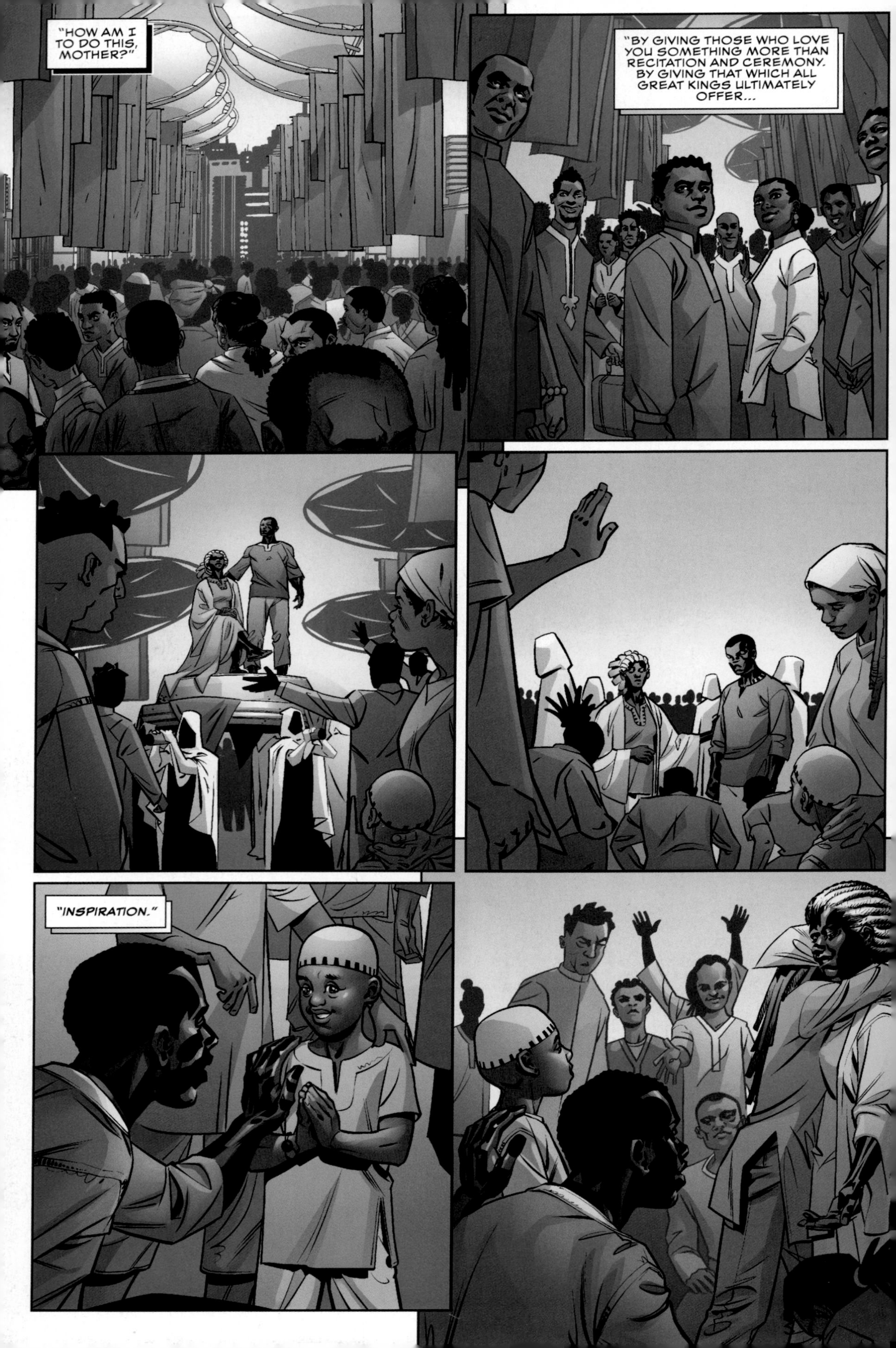
"HOW AM I TO DO THIS, MOTHER?"
"BY GIVING THOSE WHO LOVE YOU SOMETHING MORE THAN RECITATION AND CEREMONY. BY GIVING THAT WHICH ALL GREAT KINGS ULTIMATELY OFFER...
"INSPIRATION."

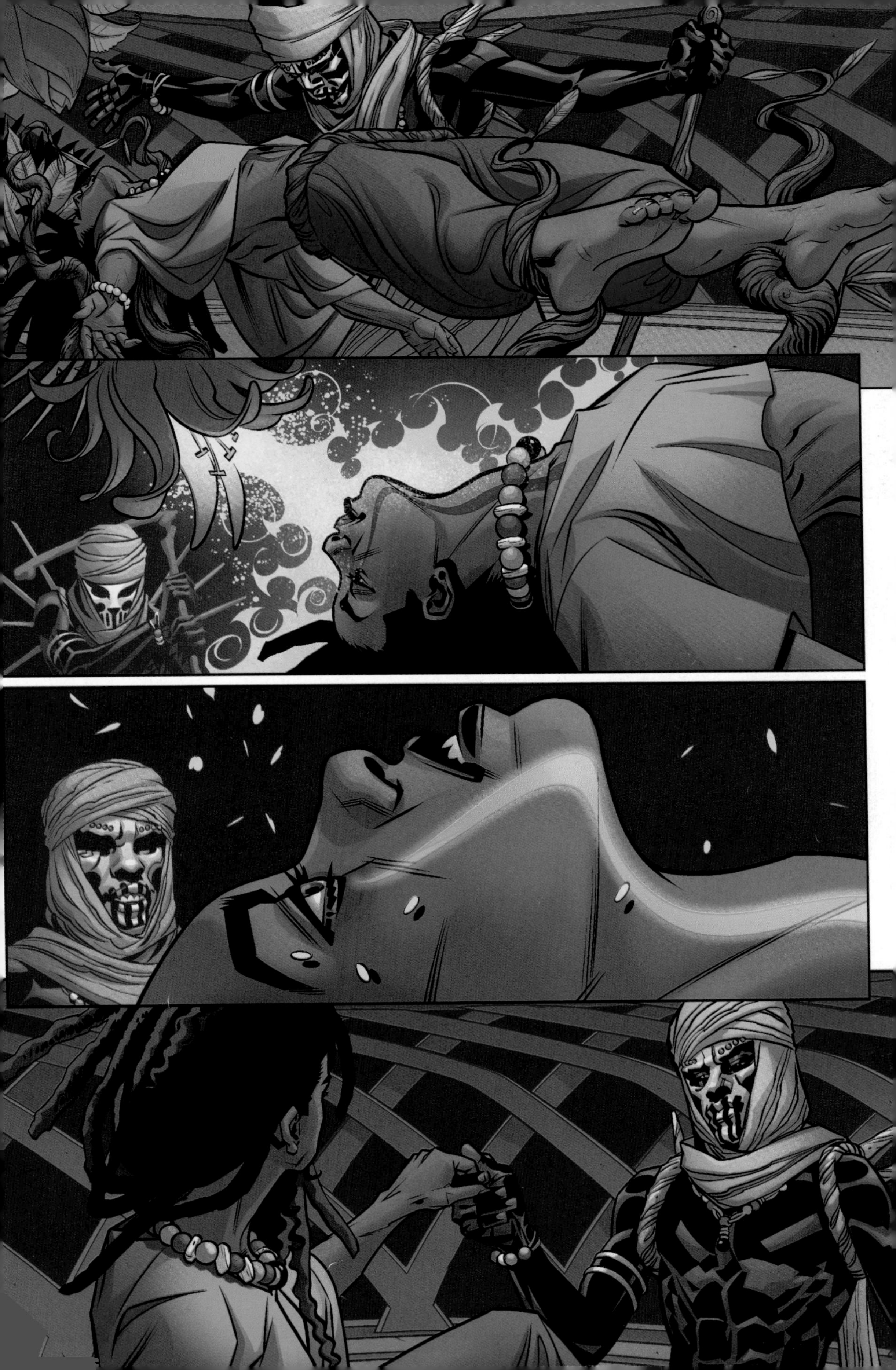

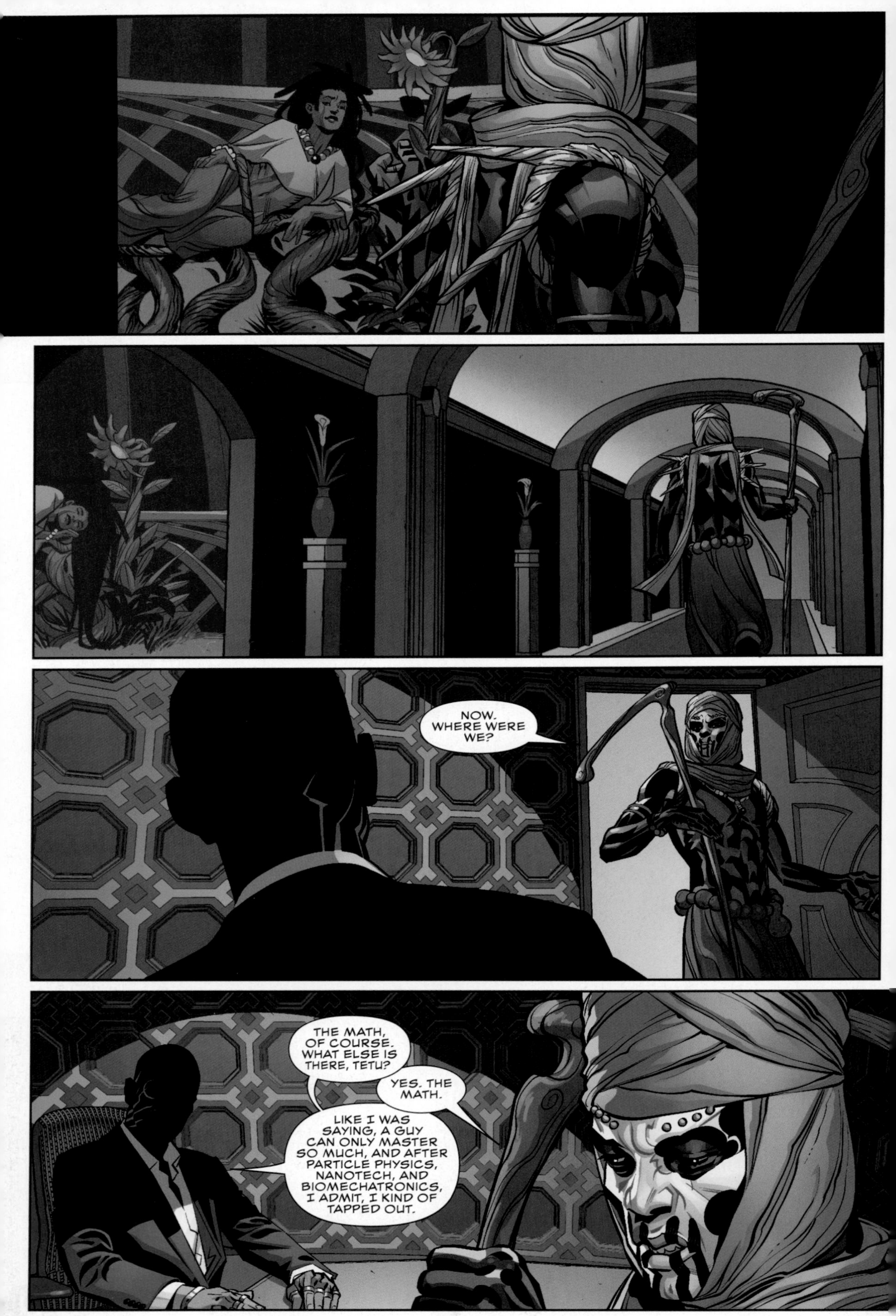
NOW. WHERE WERE WE?
THE MATH, OF COURSE. WHAT ELSE IS THERE, TETU?
YES. THE MATH.
LIKE I WAS SAYING, A GUY CAN ONLY MASTER SO MUCH, AND AFTER PARTICLE PHYSICS, NANOTECH, AND BIOMECHATRONICS, I ADMIT, I KIND OF TAPPED OUT.

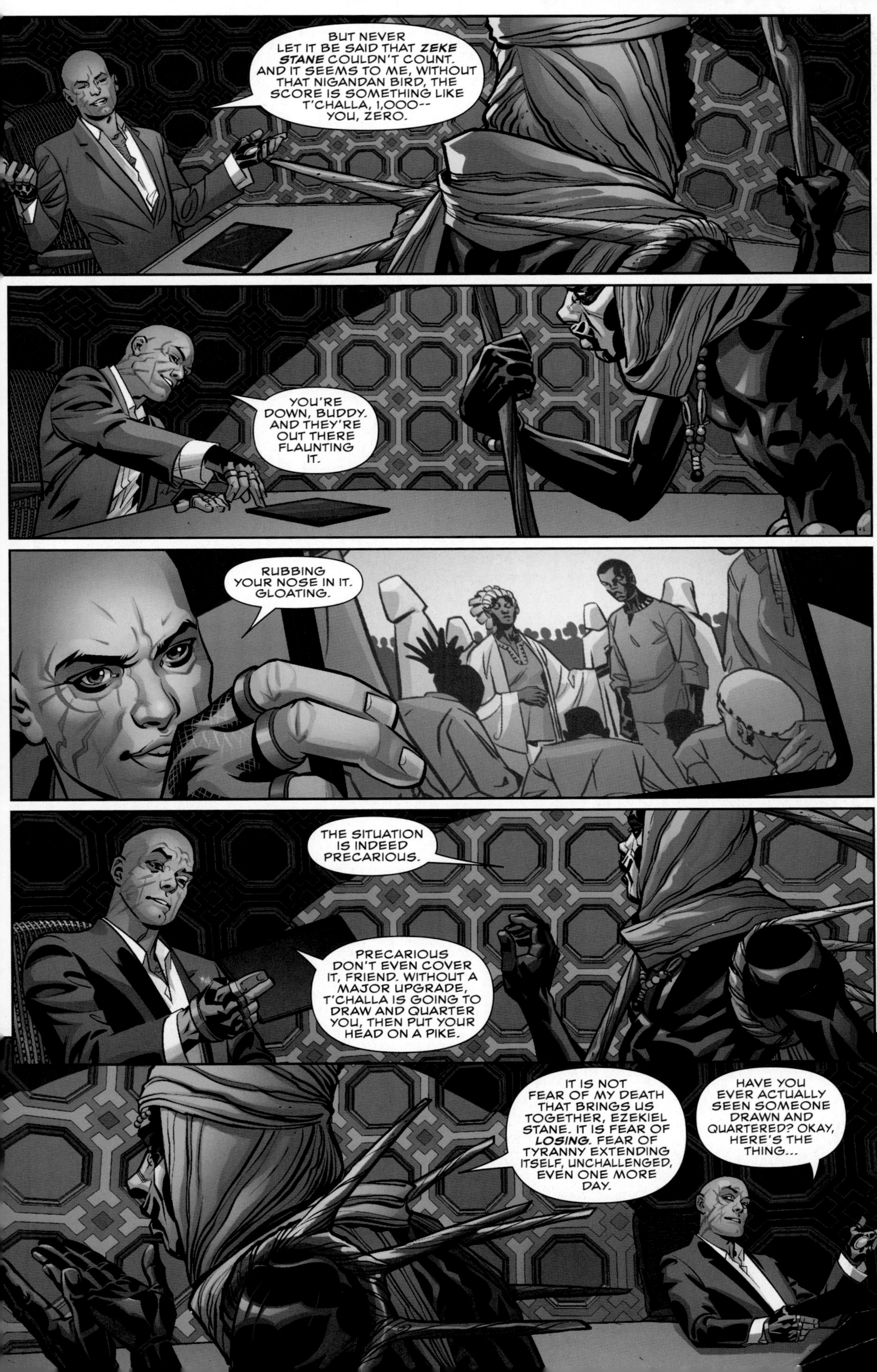
BUT NEVER LET IT BE SAID THAT ZEKE STANE COULDN'T COUNT. AND IT SEEMS TO ME, WITHOUT THAT NIGANDAN BIRD, THE SCORE IS SOMETHING LIKE T'CHALLA, 1,000-- YOU, ZERO.
YOU'RE DOWN, BUDDY. AND THEY'RE OUT THERE FLAUNTING IT.
RUBBING YOUR NOSE IN IT. GLOATING.
THE SITUATION IS INDEED PRECARIOUS.
PRECARIOUS DON'T EVEN COVER IT, FRIEND. WITHOUT A MAJOR UPGRADE, T'CHALLA IS GOING TO DRAW AND QUARTER YOU, THEN PUT YOUR HEAD ON A PIKE.
IT IS NOT FEAR OF MY DEATH THAT BRINGS US TOGETHER, EZEKIEL STANE. IT IS FEAR OF LOSING. FEAR OF TYRANNY EXTENDING ITSELF, UNCHALLENGED, EVEN ONE MORE DAY.
HAVE YOU EVER ACTUALLY SEEN SOMEONE DRAWN AND QUARTERED? OKAY, HERE'S THE THING...

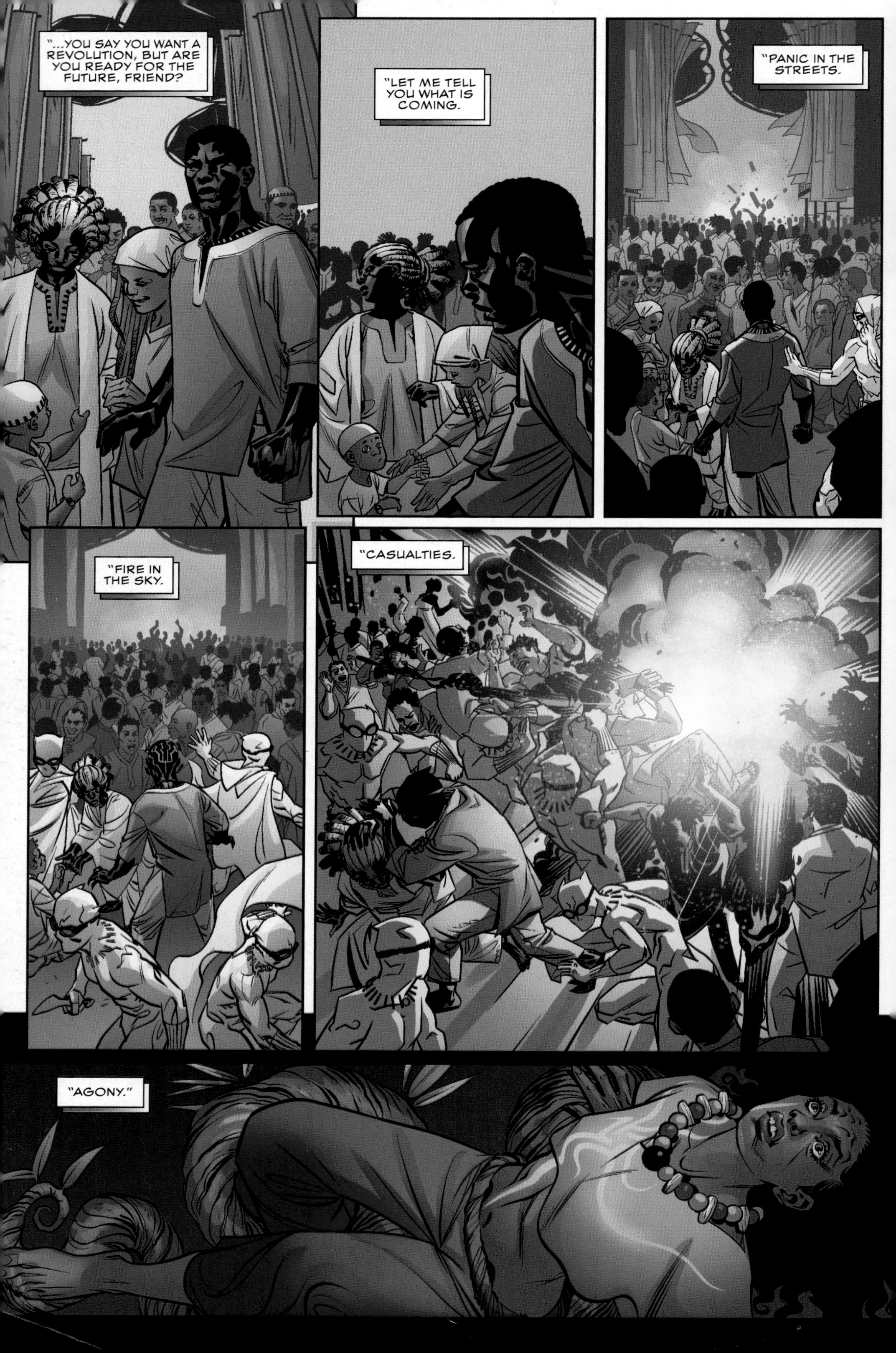
"...YOU SAY YOU WANT A REVOLUTION, BUT ARE YOU READY FOR THE FUTURE, FRIEND?
"LET ME TELL YOU WHAT IS COMING.
"PANIC IN THE STREETS.
"FIRE IN THE SKY.
"CASUALTIES.
"AGONY."

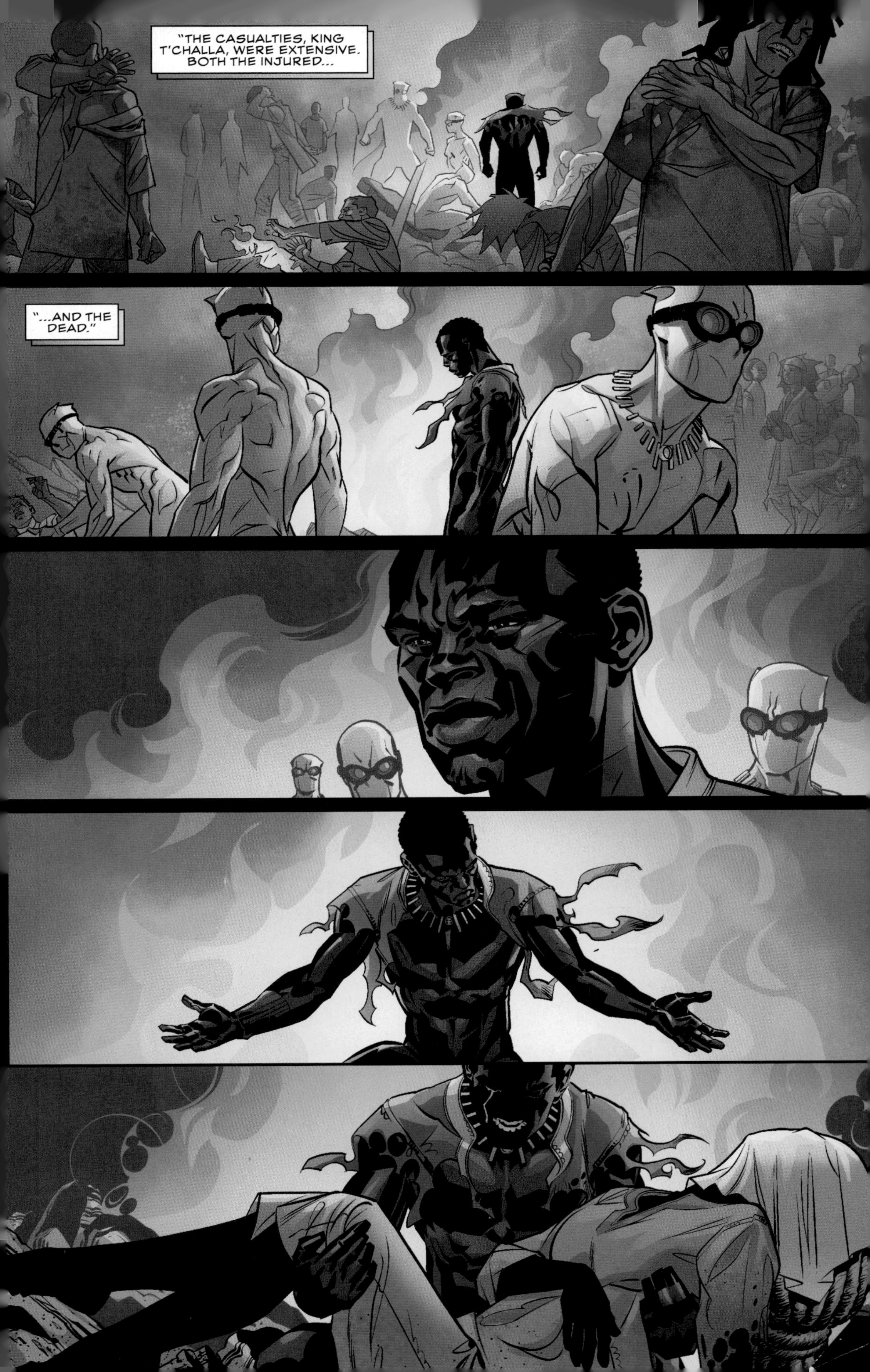
"THE CASUALTIES, KING T'CHALLA, WERE EXTENSIVE. BOTH THE INJURED...
"...AND THE DEAD."

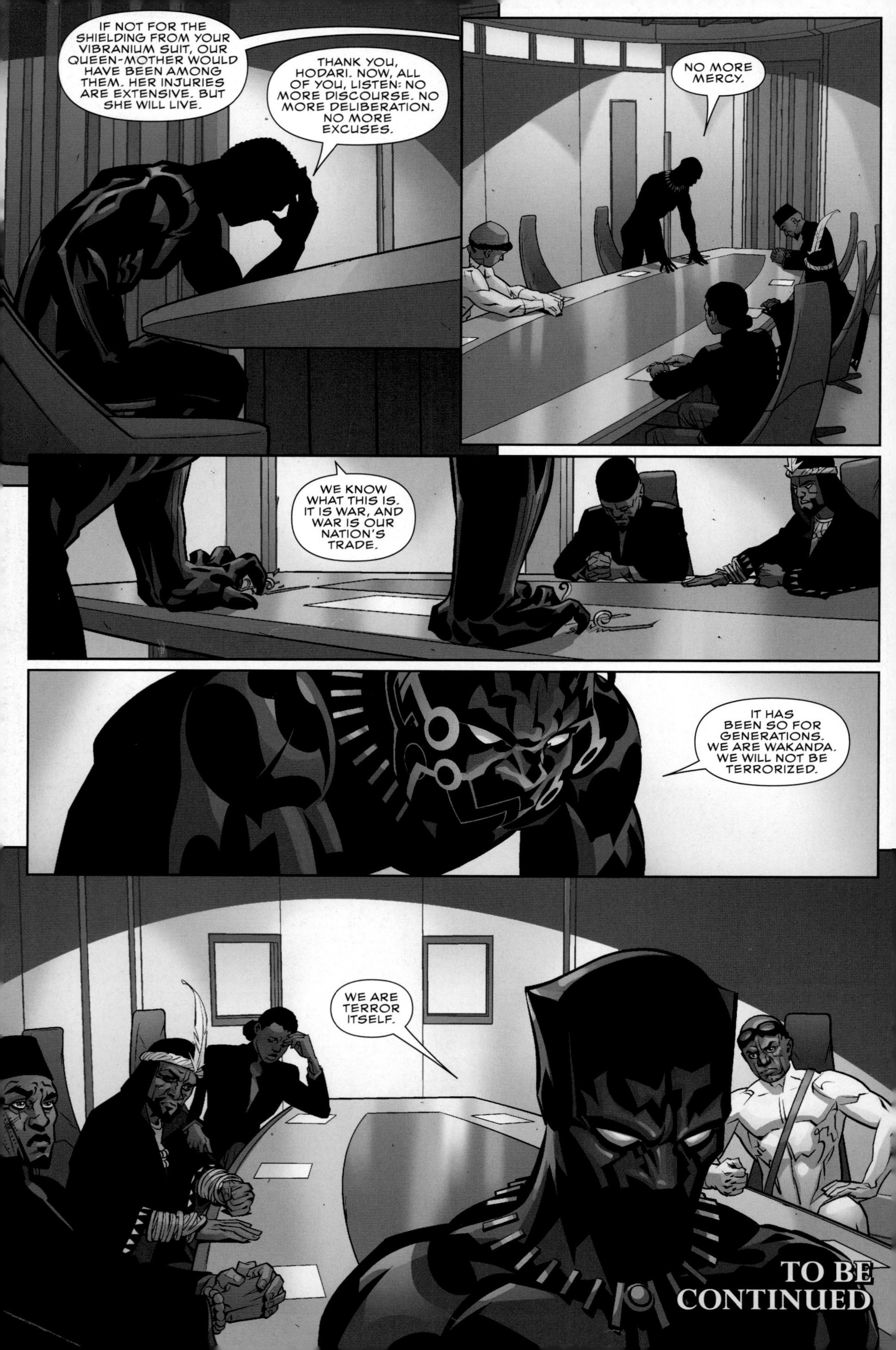
IF NOT FOR THE SHIELDING FROM YOUR VIBRANIUM SUIT, OUR QUEEN-MOTHER WOULD HAVE BEEN AMONG THEM. HER INJURIES ARE EXTENSIVE. BUT SHE WILL LIVE.
THANK YOU, HODARI. NOW, ALL OF YOU, LISTEN: NO MORE DISCOURSE. NO MORE DELIBERATION. NO MORE EXCUSES.
NO MORE MERCY.
WE KNOW WHAT THIS IS. IT IS WAR, AND WAR IS OUR NATION'S TRADE.
IT HAS BEEN SO FOR GENERATIONS. WE ARE WAKANDA. WE WILL NOT BE TERRORIZED.
WE ARE TERROR ITSELF.
TO BE CONTINUED

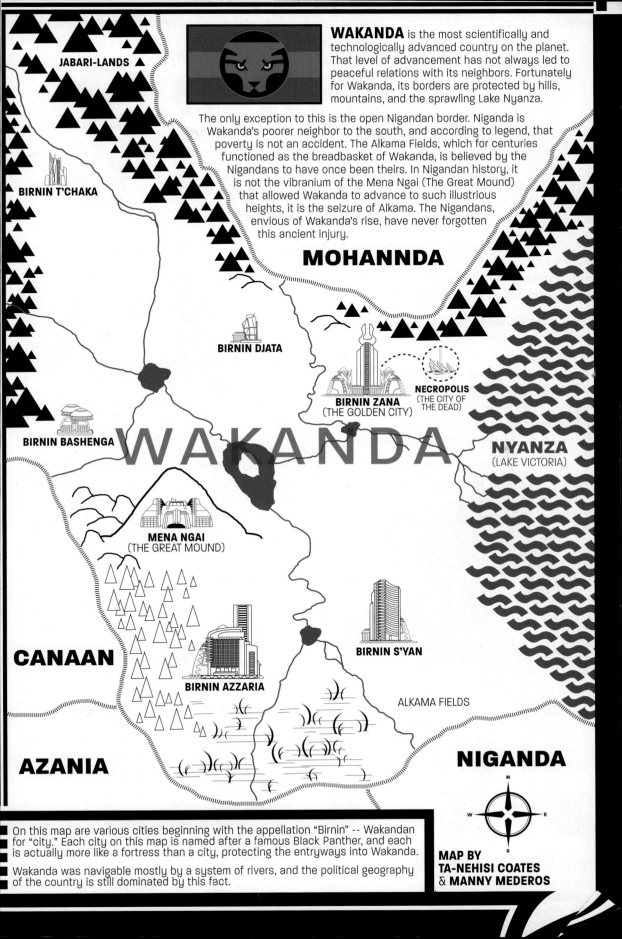

WAKANDA is the most scientifically and technologically advanced country on the planet. That level of advancement has not always led to peaceful relations with its neighbors. Fortunately for Wakanda, its borders are protected by hills, mountains, and the sprawling Lake Nyanza.

The only exception to this is the open Nigandan border. Niganda is Wakanda's poorer neighbor to the south, and according to legend, that poverty is not an accident. The Alkama Fields, which for centuries functioned as the breadbasket of Wakanda, is believed by the Nigandans to have once been theirs. In Nigandan history, it is not the vibranium of the Mena Ngai (The Great Mound) that allowed Wakanda to advance to such illustrious heights, it is the seizure of Alkama. The Nigandans, envious of Wakanda's rise, have never forgotten this ancient injury.

JABARI-LANDS

BIRNIN T'CHAKA

MOHANNDA

BIRNIN DJATA

NECROPOLIS
(THE CITY OF THE DEAD)

BIRNIN ZANA
(THE GOLDEN CITY)

BIRNIN BASHENGA

WAKANDA

NYANZA
(LAKE VICTORIA)

MENA NGAI
(THE GREAT MOUND)

CANAAN

BIRNIN S'YAN

BIRNIN AZZARIA

ALKAMA FIELDS

AZANIA

NIGANDA

On this map are various cities beginning with the appellation "Birnin" -- Wakandan for "city." Each city on this map is named after a famous Black Panther, and each is actually more like a fortress than a city, protecting the entryways into Wakanda.

Wakanda was navigable mostly by a system of rivers, and the political geography of the country is still dominated by this fact.

**MAP BY
TA-NEHISI COATES
& MANNY MEDEROS**

BEHIND THE SCENES
WITH BRIAN STELFREEZE

By TJ Dietsch for Marvel.com

Marvel: Ta-Nehisi is an accomplished writer, but hasn't worked in comics before. How has collaborating with him been different than other writers you've worked with?

Brian Stelfreeze: It's quite fascinating in a number of ways. Most established comic writers have a fixed style or methodology, so what you get on page one of the first issue is about the same for the last page of the series. Ta-Nehisi is still evolving as a comic book writer. It's really cool to see him not only learn the language of visual storytelling but also create new ways of doing it. I think Marvel brought me on to help him learn the ropes, but I find he's teaching me quite a bit as well.

BLACK PANTHER

Marvel: T'Challa's one of those classic characters whose costume has remained similar over the years but changed in small ways. What elements were you looking to update or change with your take?

Brian Stelfreeze: I've always liked the simplicity of the Black Panther costume. I've never liked when people give him flashy capes and other adornments. Perhaps if he was called the "Black Lion" those accoutrements would make sense, but "Black Panther" suggests a sleek efficiency so I'm staying simple. I'm adding small touches to make him feel more aggressive and catlike, but just keeping it simple.

Marvel: Black Panther also comes along with an amazing locale in Wakanda. What challenges does setting the book in that place offer you as an artist? Will it look different than we remember from previous incarnations?

Brian Stelfreeze: Wakanda is one of the biggest characters in this new series so we've given that quite a bit of thought. I want the country

to have a duality of old world and city of the future. Sometimes this juxtaposition should speak of a strong culture and heritage, but it should also hint at a growing schism. I've set the Golden City as a ring surrounding a giant crater lake to suggest that it's possibly the [result] of an ancient vibranium meteor strike.

Marvel: As you alluded to, Wakanda finds itself invaded and pushed to the edge by a terrorist organization called the People. What went into the design of those members? Did you draw from any existing groups in the process?

Brian Stelfreeze: Ta-Nehisi's script feels very African, so I wanted the art to reflect this. I'm pulling from cultures all over the continent to establish the look: Masai tribesmen, ancient Zulu warriors, and even modern Kalashnikov-wielding rebels will all influence the look of Wakanda.

Marvel: Even though Wakanda prefers to keep to itself, will readers see any familiar faces from the rest of the Marvel Universe as the story progresses?

Brian Stelfreeze: Not that it's a spoiler, but Namor shows up on page one. Wakanda is the Marvel world's most technologically advanced nation, and offensives there can have ramifications everywhere, so that leaves open great possibilities for cameos.

T'CHALLA

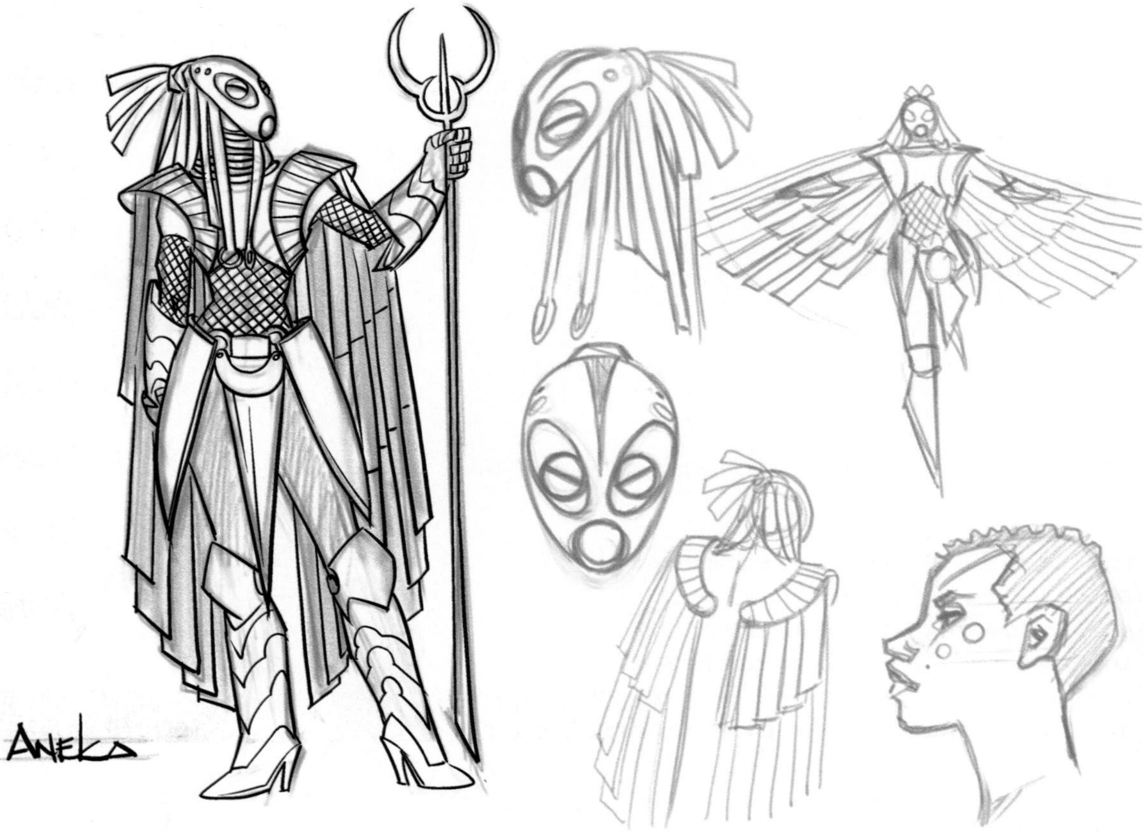
ANEKA

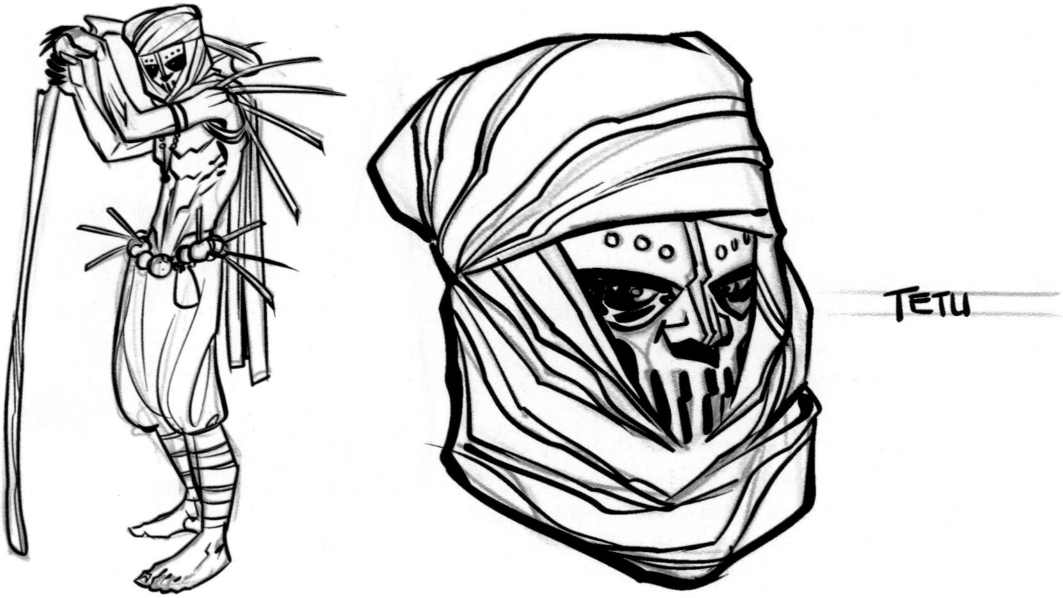
TETU

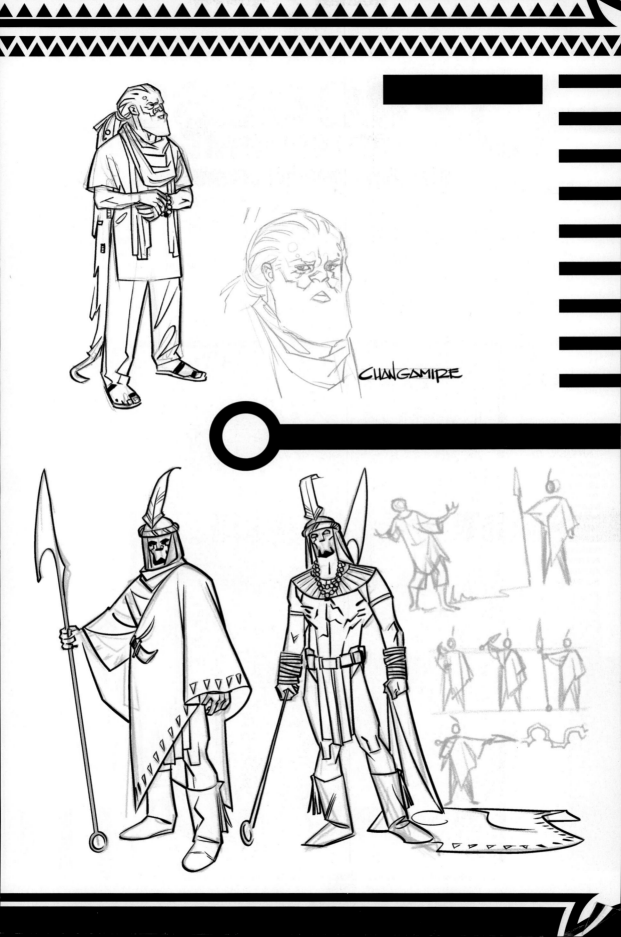

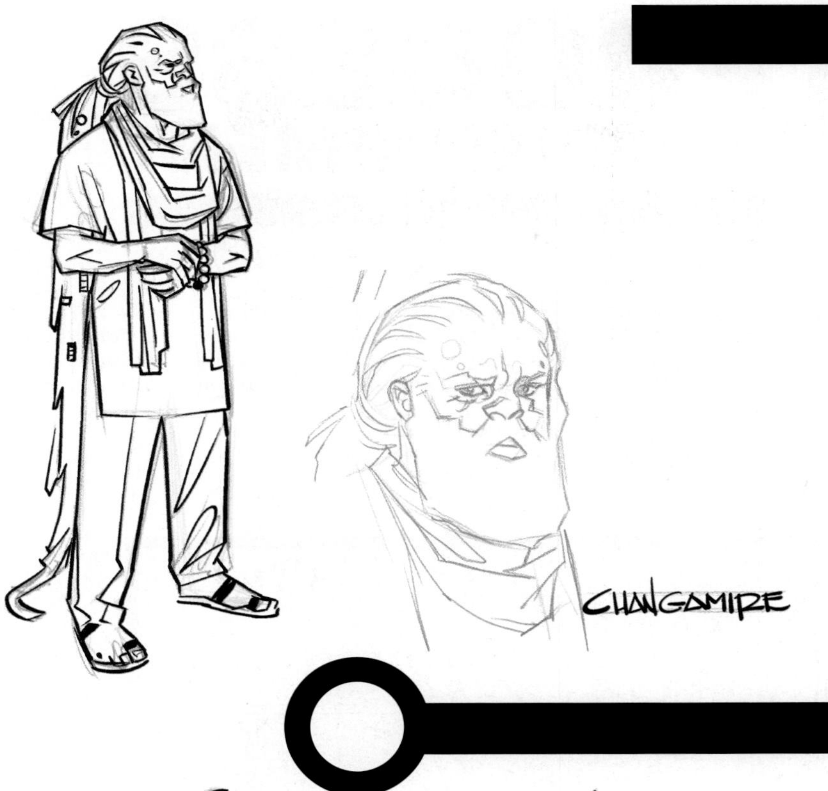
CHANGAMIRE

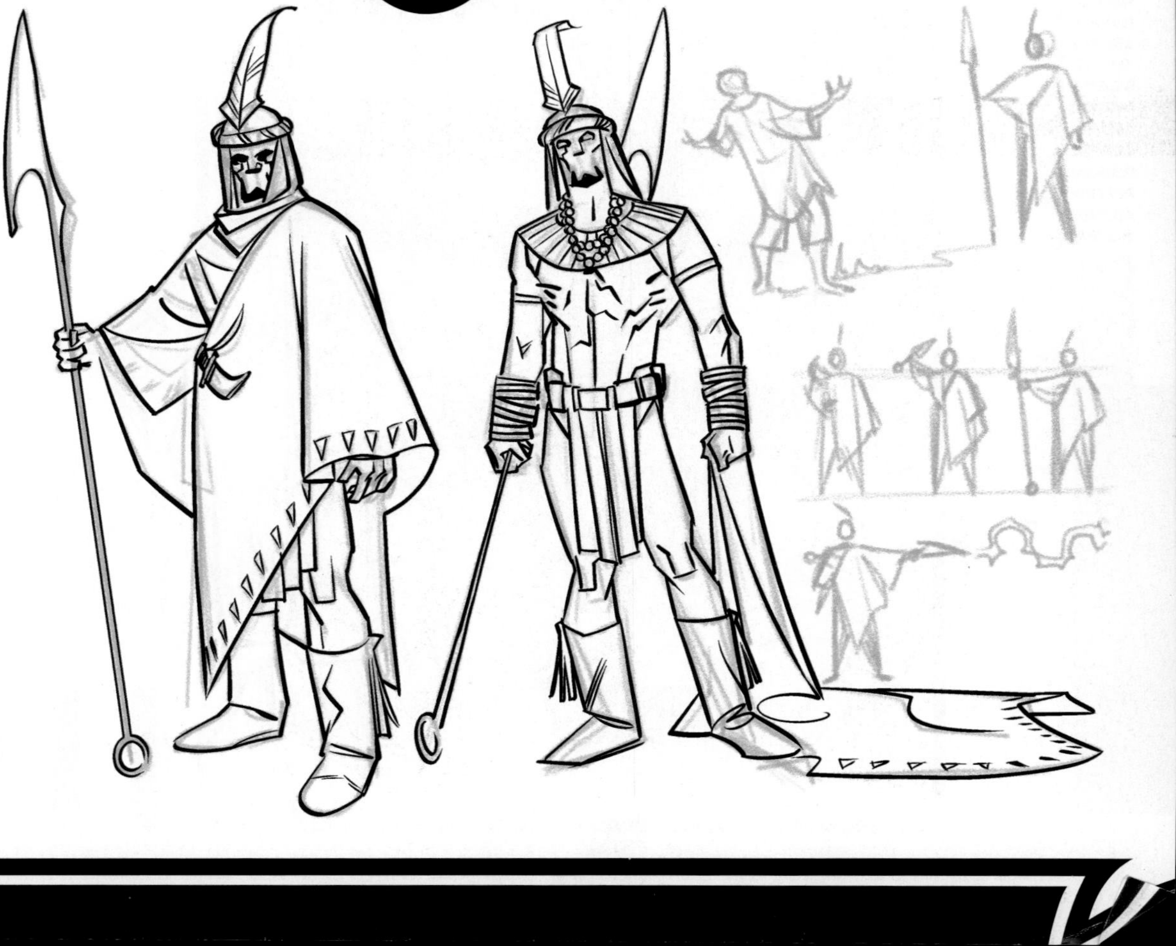

PROCESS AND DEVELOPMENT

PAGE 2

PANEL 1
Big splash page. Zoom out and see several members of the Wakandan army firing wildly into a crowd of charging miners. T'CHALLA kneels, wounded, amidst the chaos. The sense should be that the soldiers have lost control of themselves. We want to allude to the Boston Massacre. This is the onset of a revolution--soldiers firing into a peaceful crowd.

V/O CAPTION
"You have lost your soul."

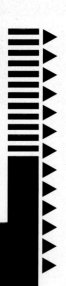

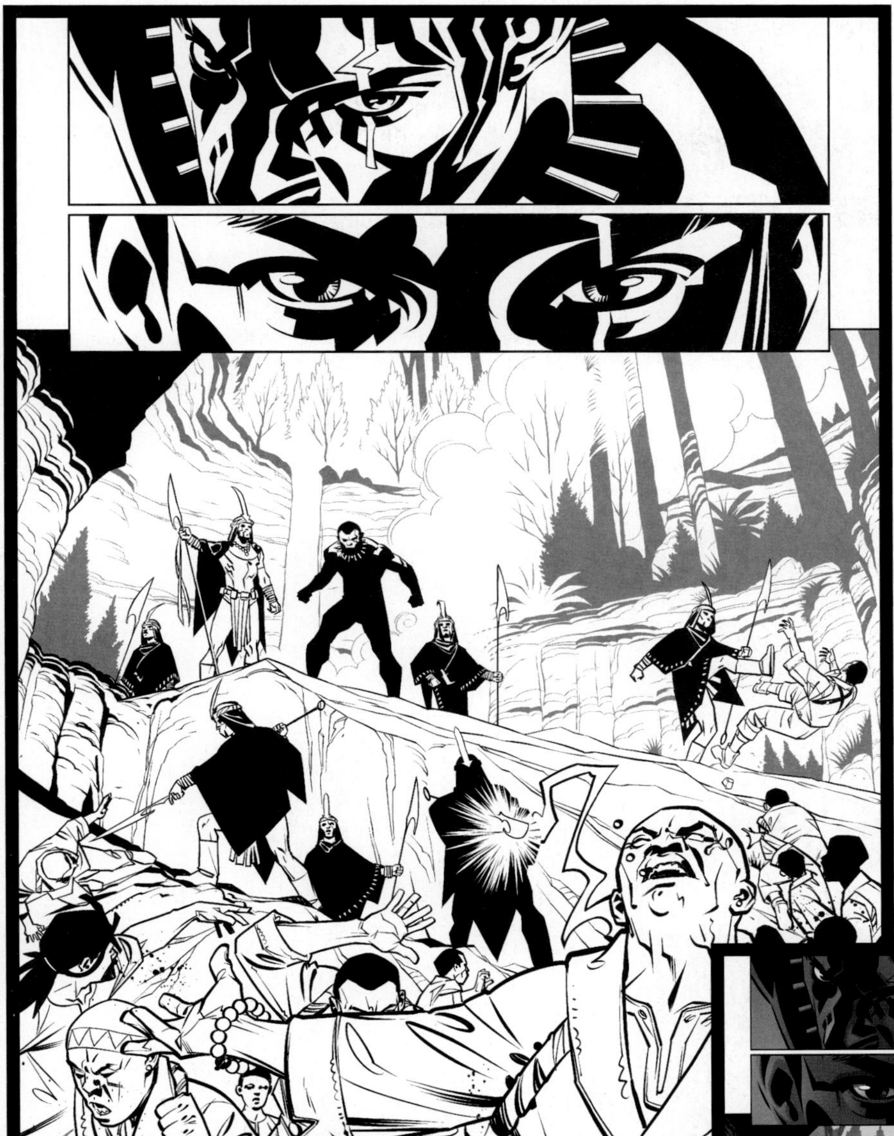

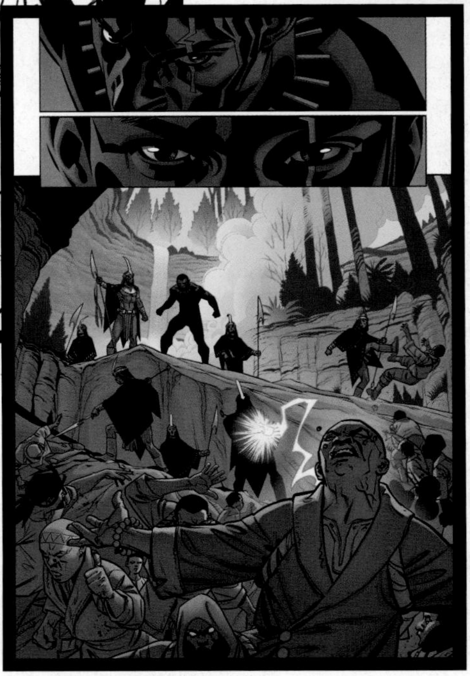

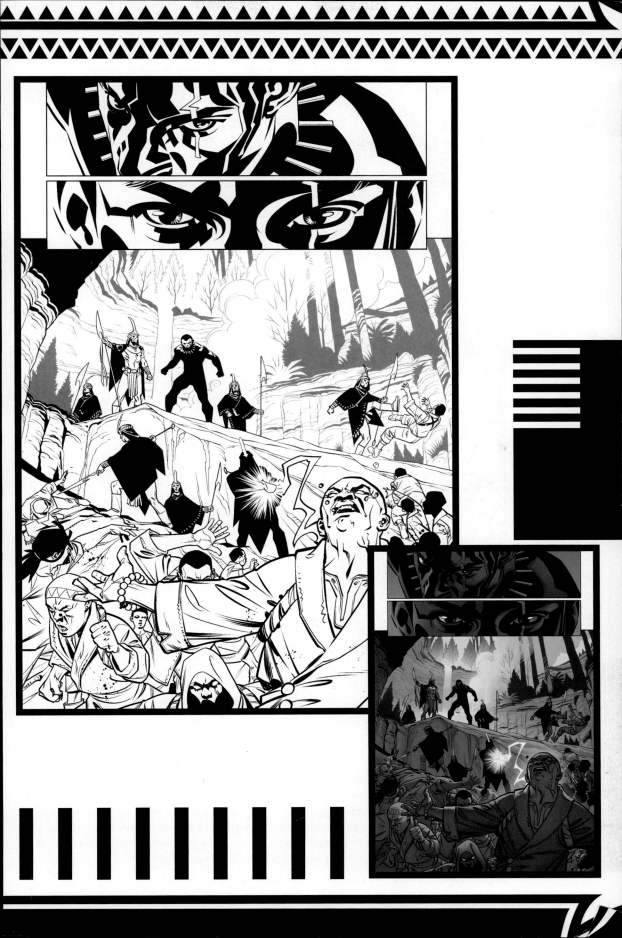

PRIME
BEAD

PRIME BEAD GIVEN AT BIRTH FOR
HEALTH CARE AND SUBSEQUENT
PAIRING FOR ADDITIONAL BEADS

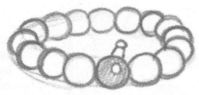

— WAKANDA BEAD BRACELET—
WAKANDIANS ADD TECH BEADS
AS NEEDED IN OCCUPATION
OR LIFESTYLE

BEADS CAN BE ADDED
FOR ANY SITUATION INCLUDING:
CELL PHONE
HOME AND PERSONAL SECURITY
GEO TRACKING
WHAT EVER PERSONAL TECH WE NEED

KIMOYO BAND

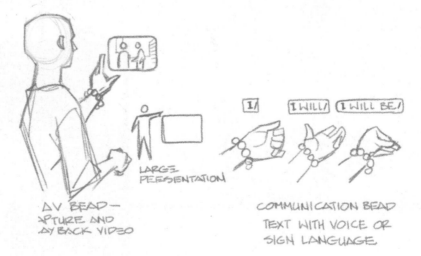

LARGE
PRESENTATION

I/   I WILL/   I WILL BE/

AV BEAD—
APTURE AND
AY BACK VIDEO

COMMUNICATION BEAD
TEXT WITH VOICE OR
SIGN LANGUAGE

"It's long been known that vibranium absorbs sound and kinetic energy, but that energy stays locked within the vibranium itself. Wakandan scientists can tap into this stored energy and use vibranium as a limitless power source, and this powers all Wakandan technology. All the military spears, and even the personal bracelets, network into this power source. This is why the extraordinary technology of Wakanda cannot be exported. It would be the equivalent of having the world's greatest laptop but with no battery. Perhaps this is a metaphor of the Wakandan people. They believe a part of their very soul exists within the country itself."

- Brian Stelfreeze

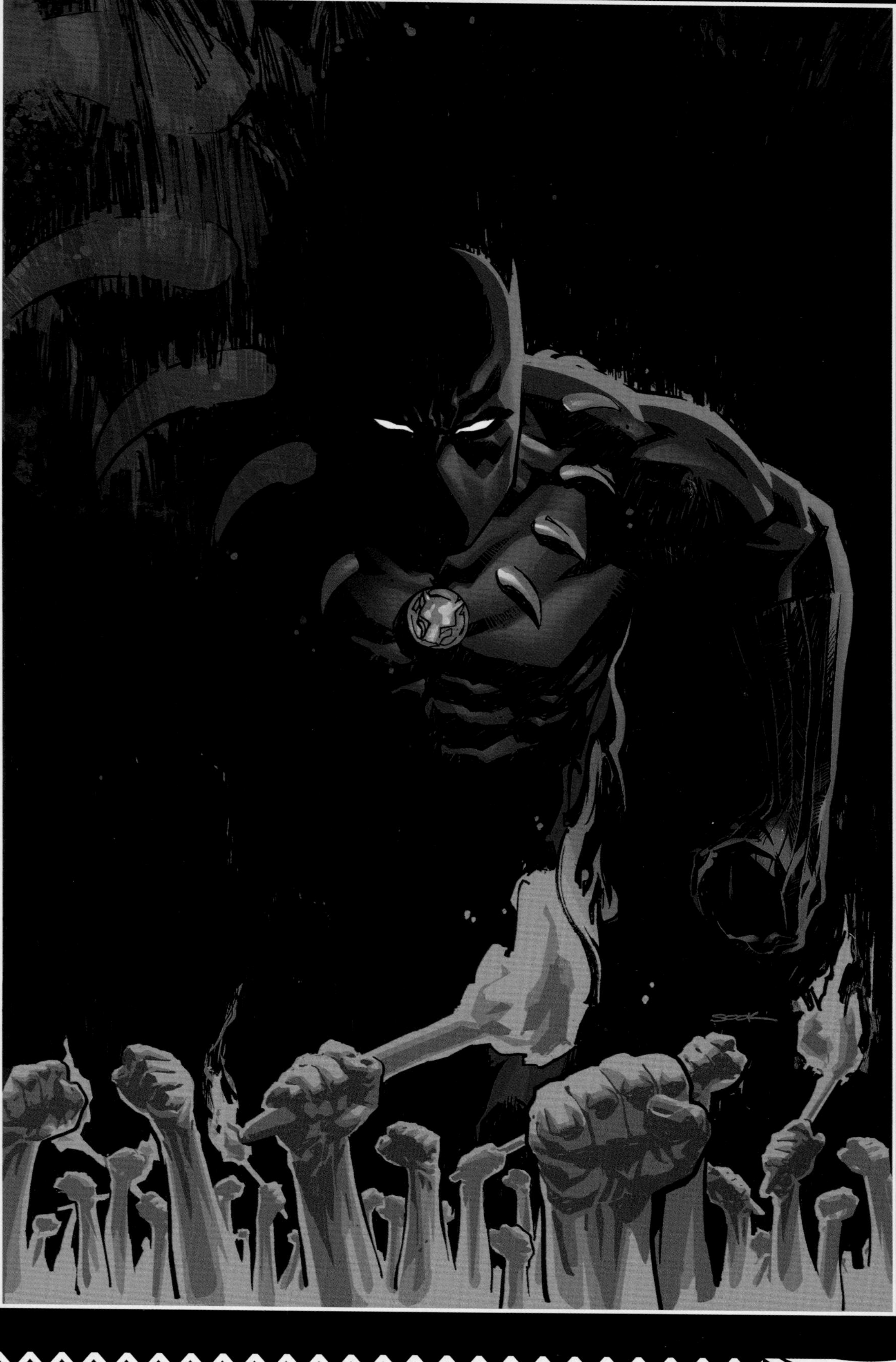
SOOK

#1 VARIANT BY **RYAN SOOK**

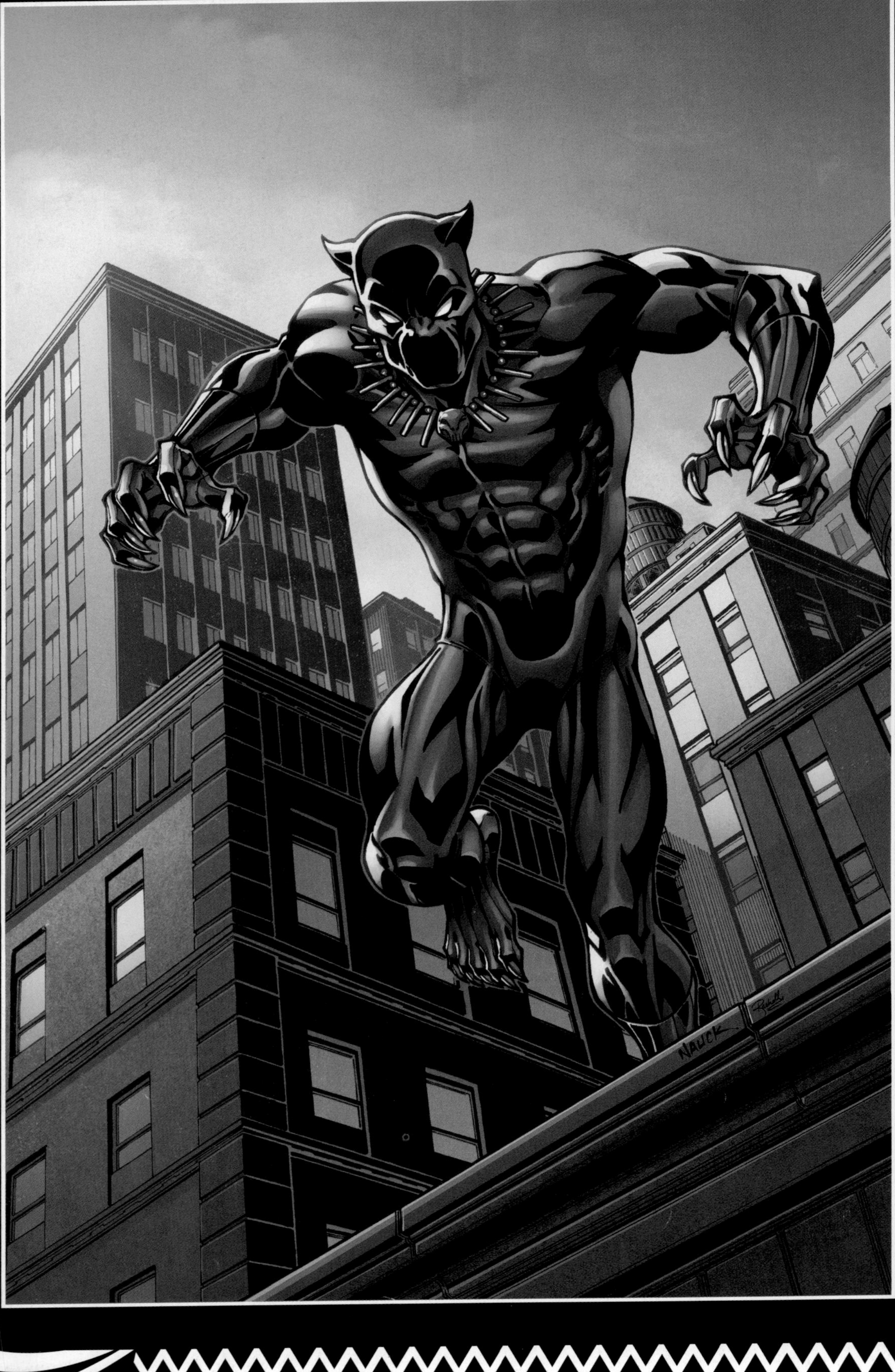
NAUCK

#1 VARIANT BY **TODD NAUCK** & **RACHELLE ROSENBERG**

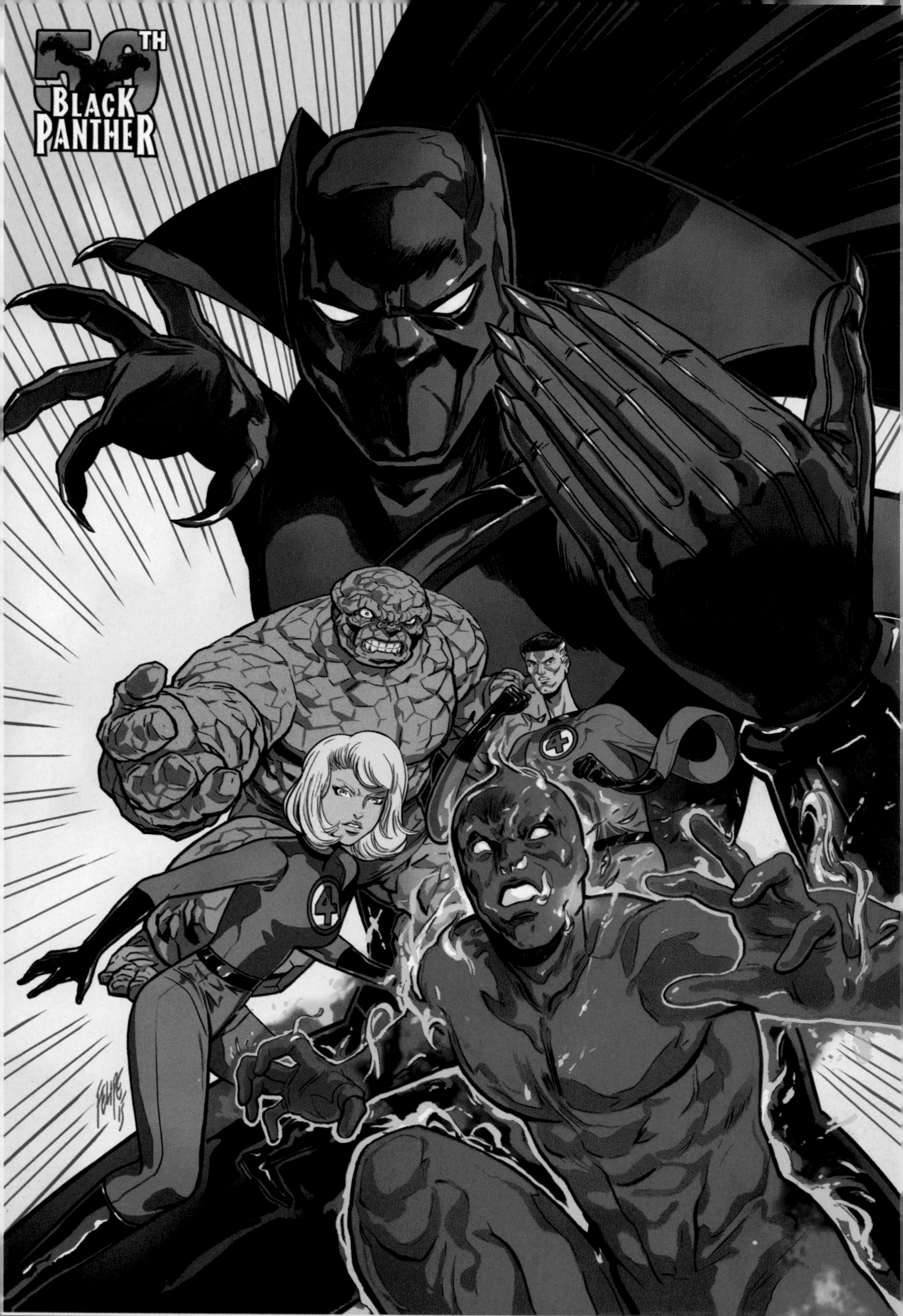
50TH
BLACK PANTHER

#1 50TH ANNIVERSARY VARIANT BY **FELIPE SMITH**

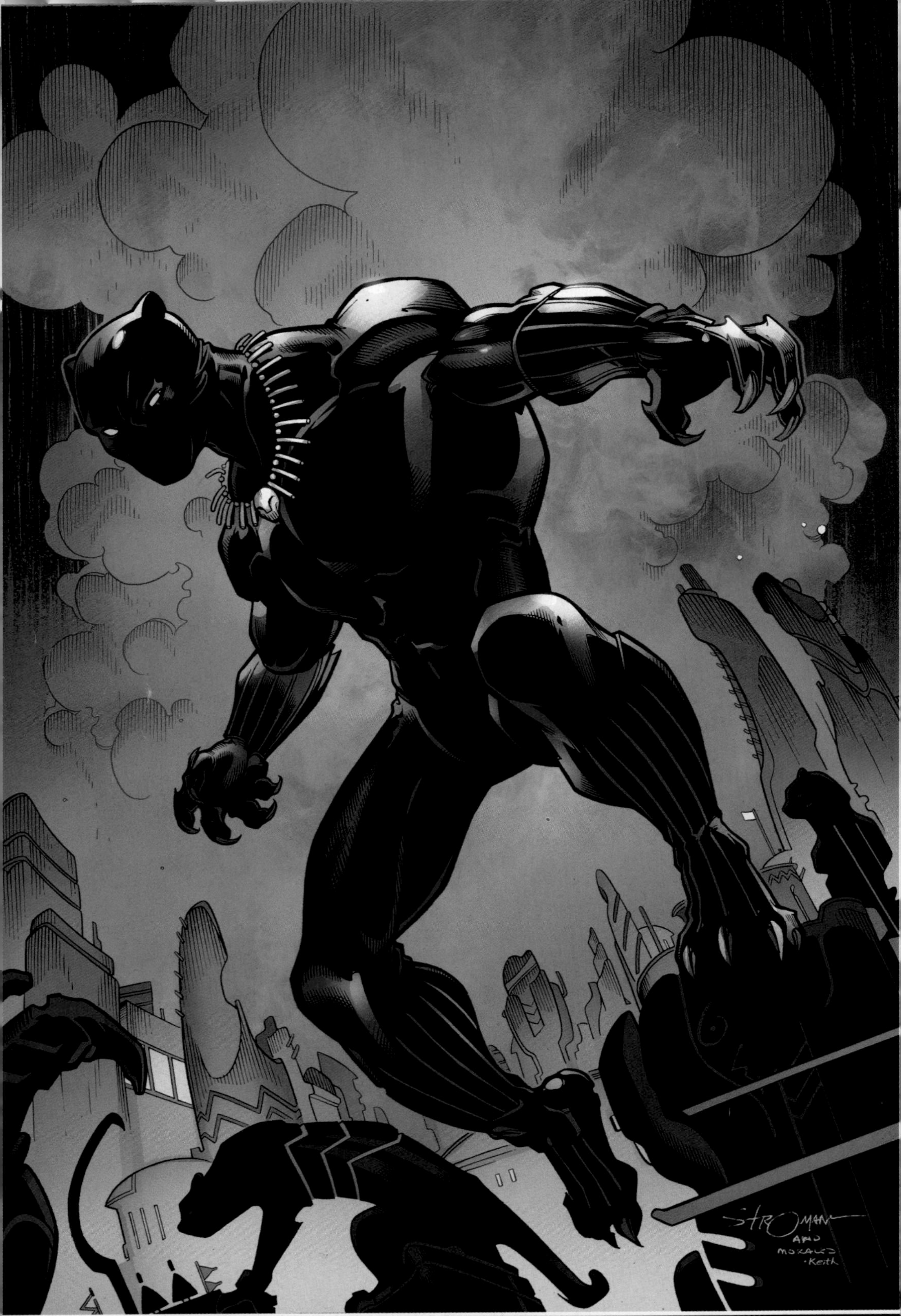

#1 VARIANT BY **LARRY STROMAN, MARK MORALES** & **JASON KEITH**

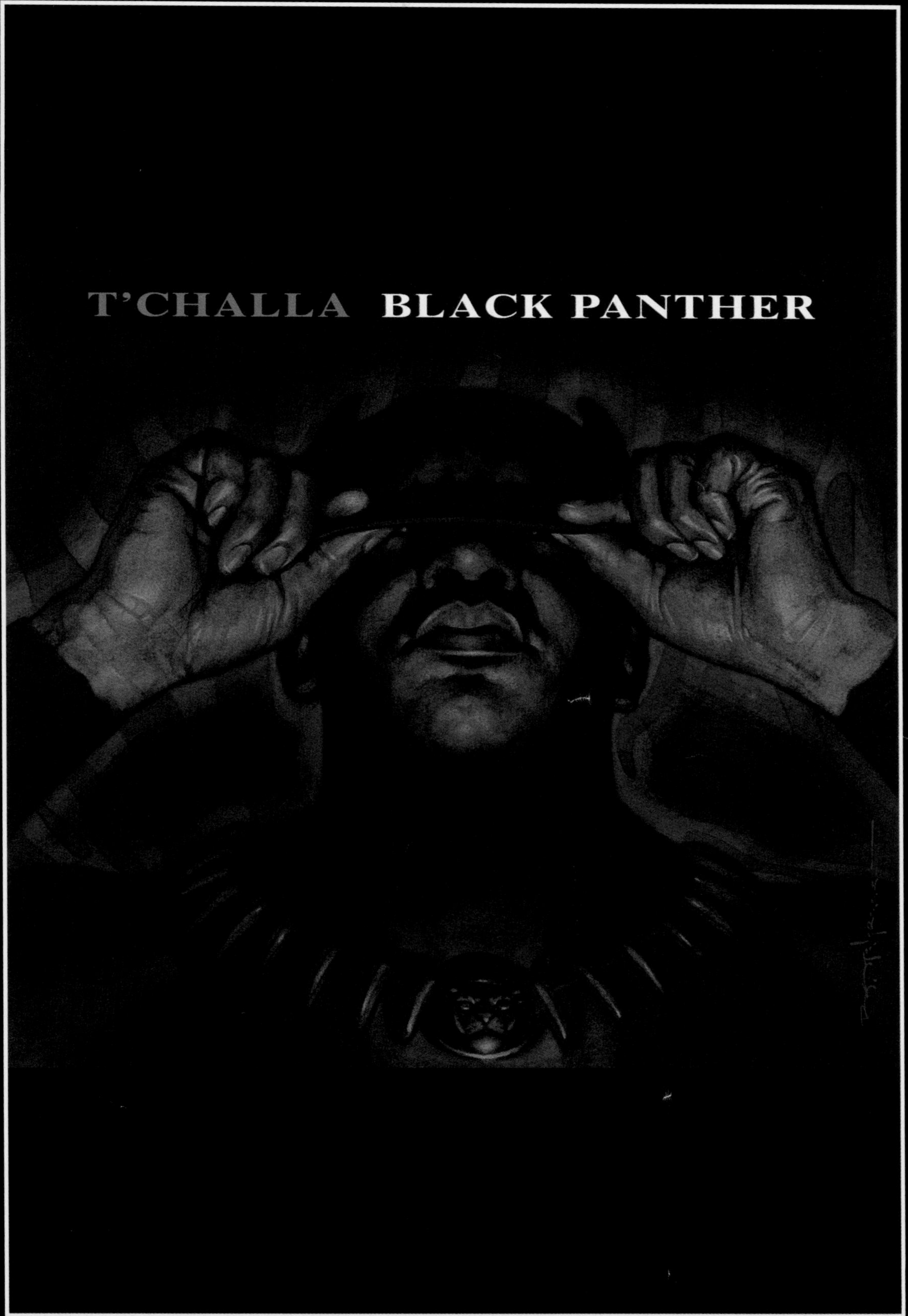
T'CHALLA BLACK PANTHER

#1 HIP-HOP VARIANT BY **BRIAN STELFREEZE**

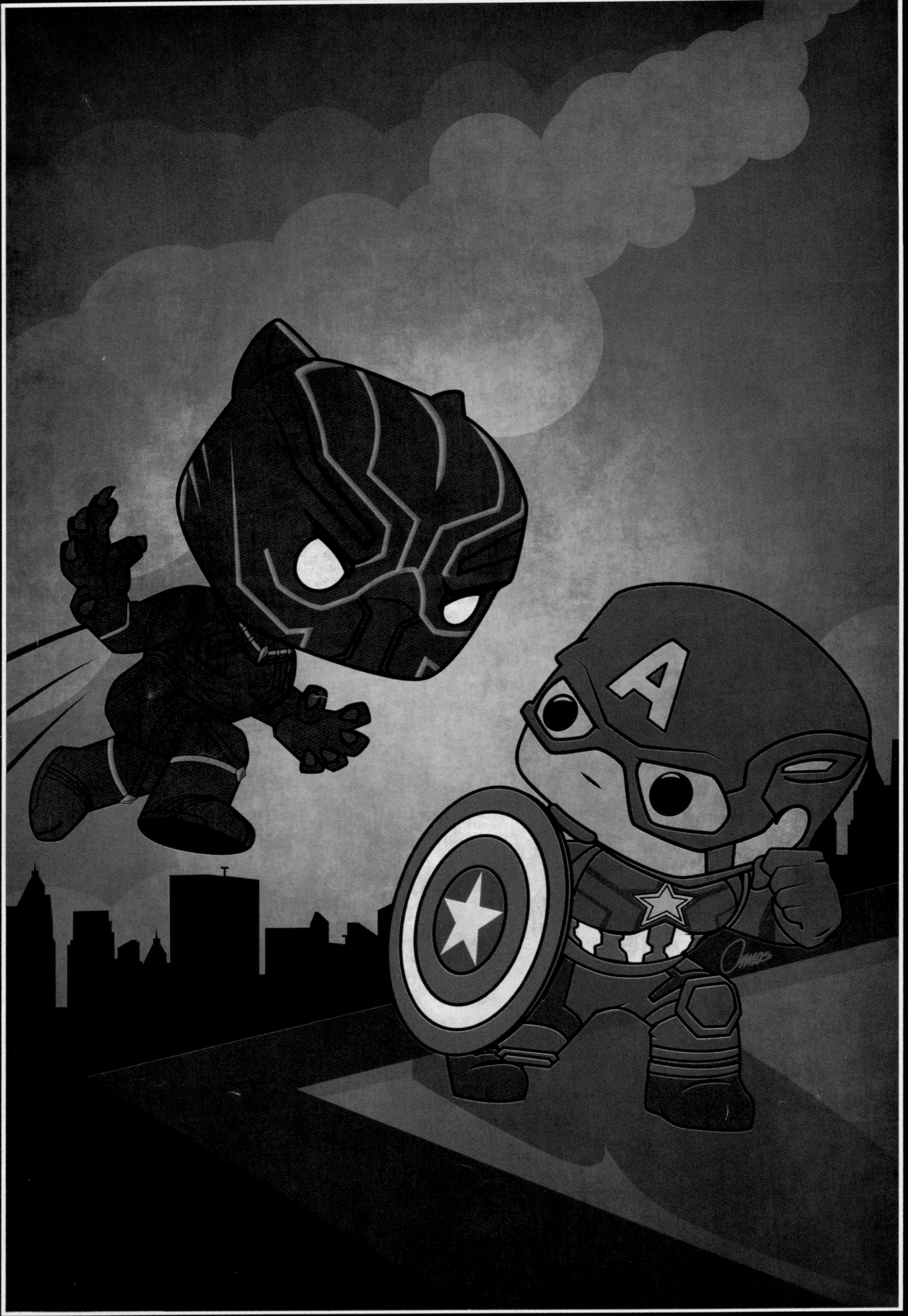

#1 FUNKO VARIANT

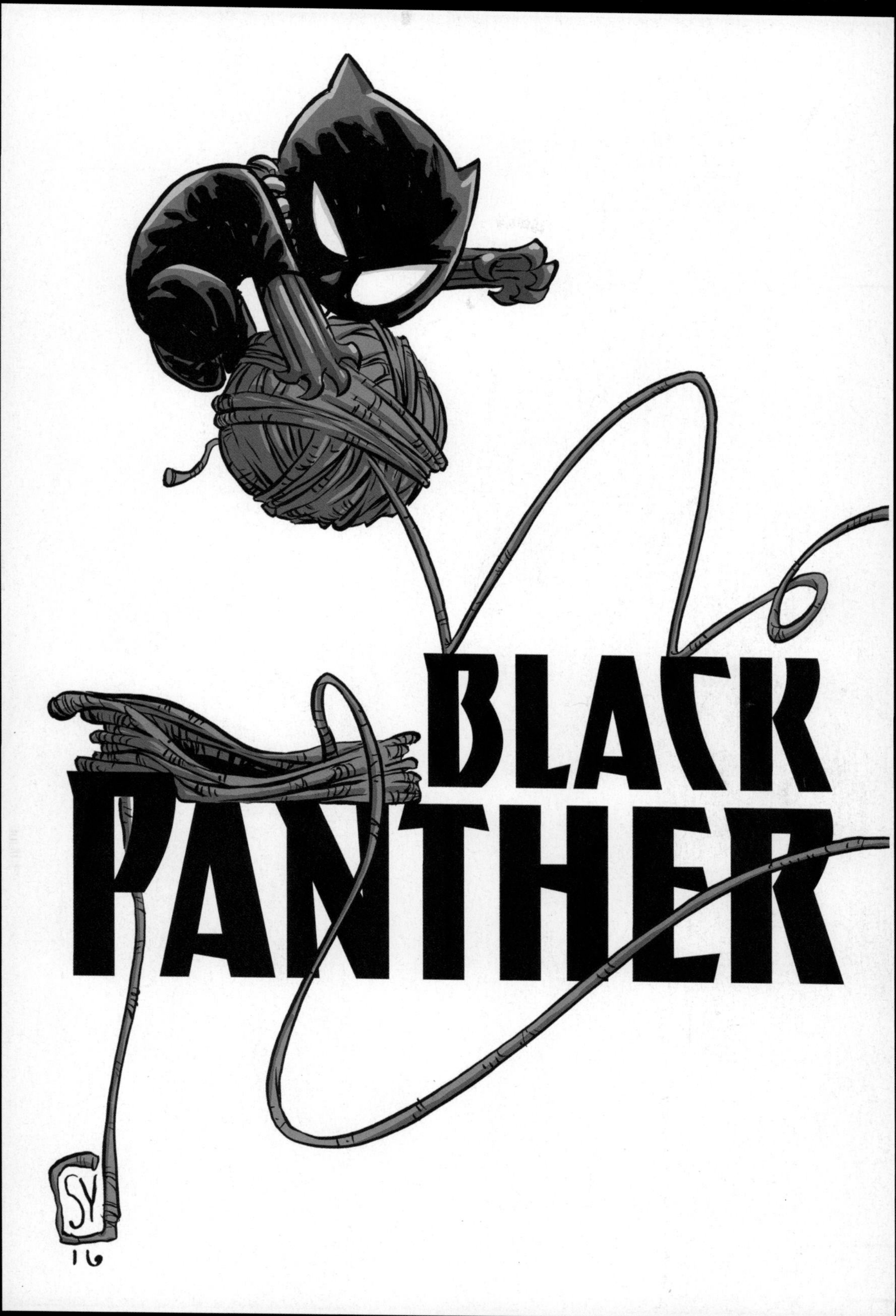
BLACK
PANTHER
SY
16

#1 VARIANT BY **SKOTTIE YOUNG**

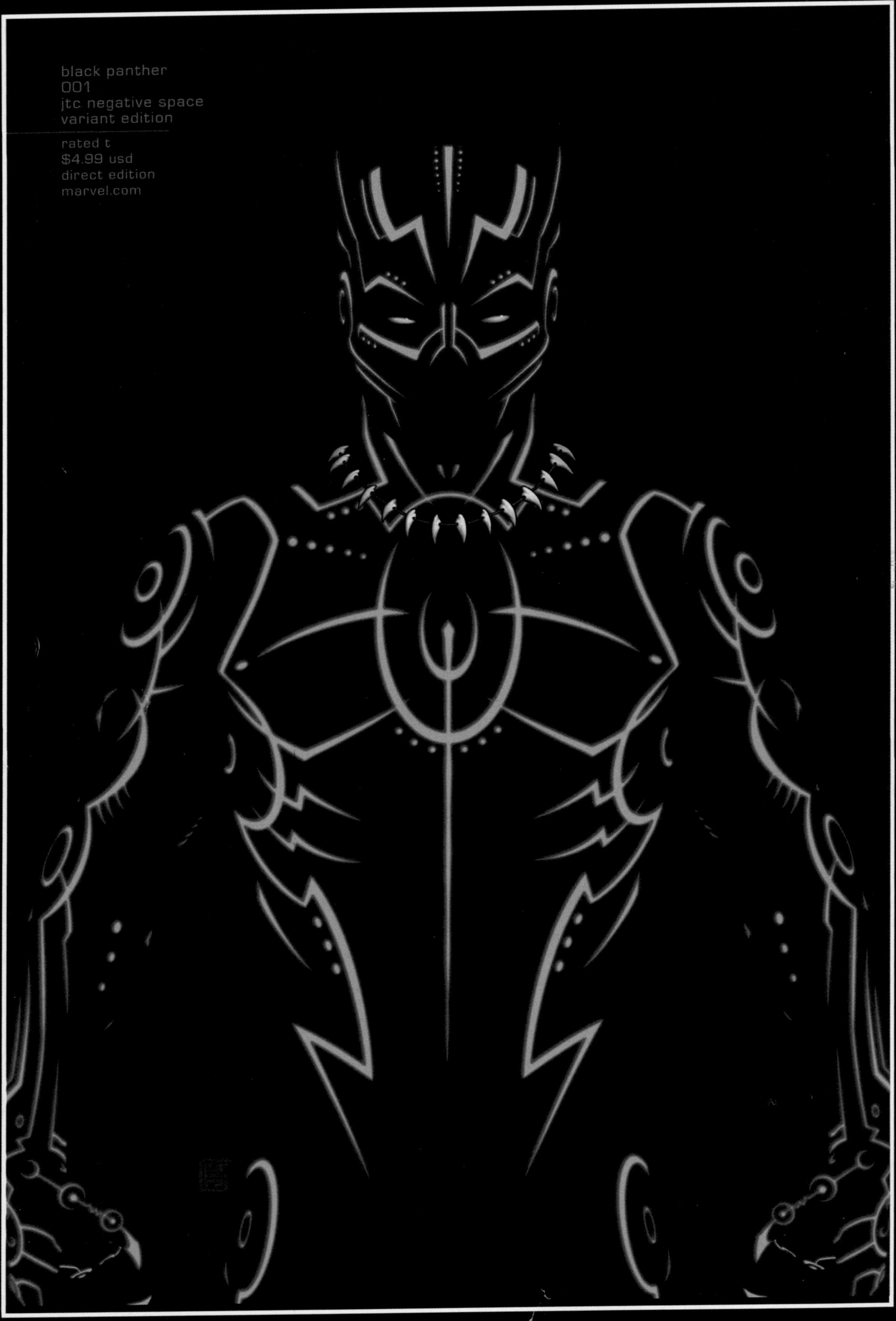
black panther
001
jtc negative space
variant edition
rated t
$4.99 usd
direct edition
marvel.com

#1 VARIANT BY **JOHN TYLER CHRISTOPHER**

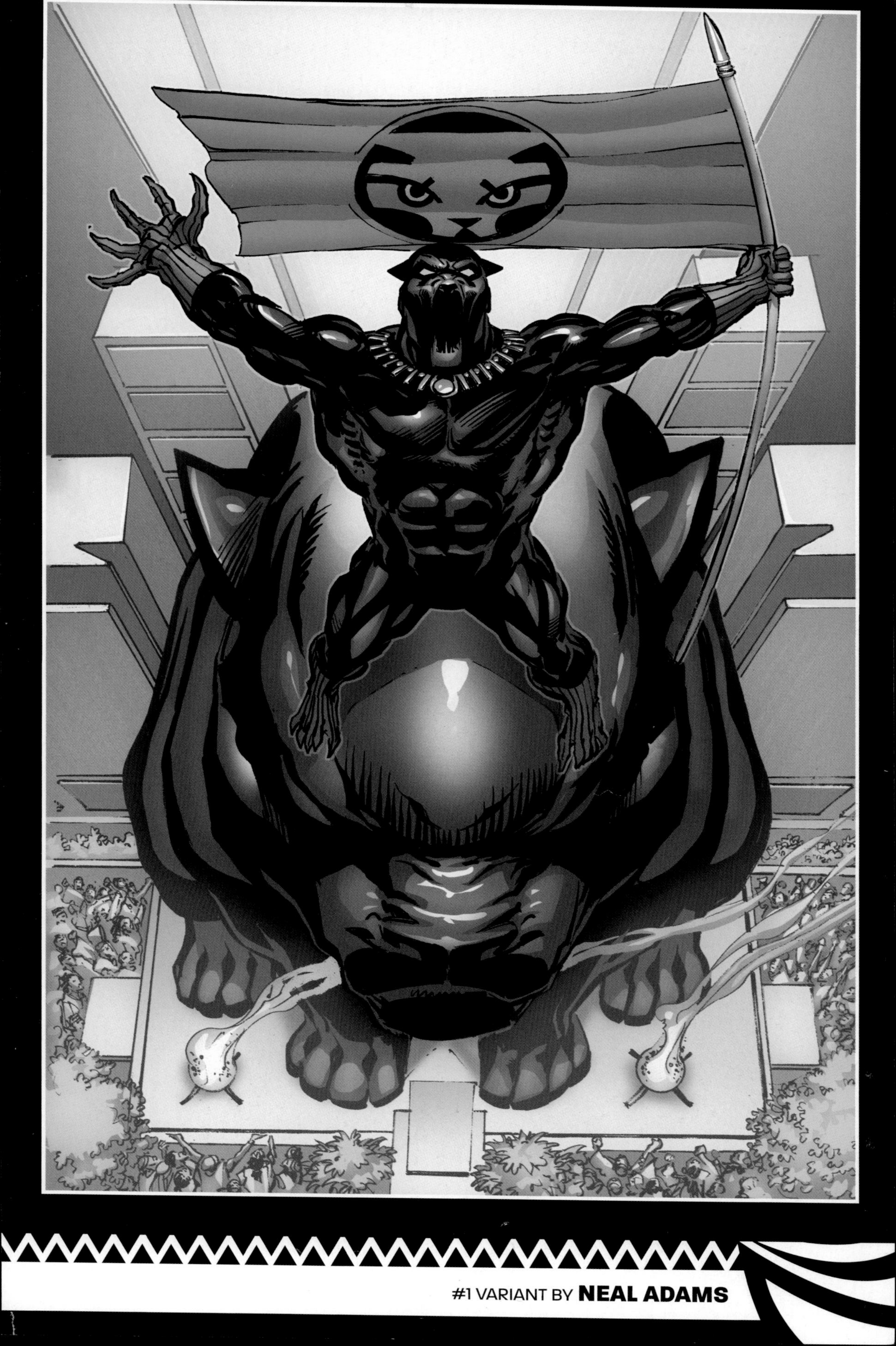

#1 VARIANT BY **NEAL ADAMS**

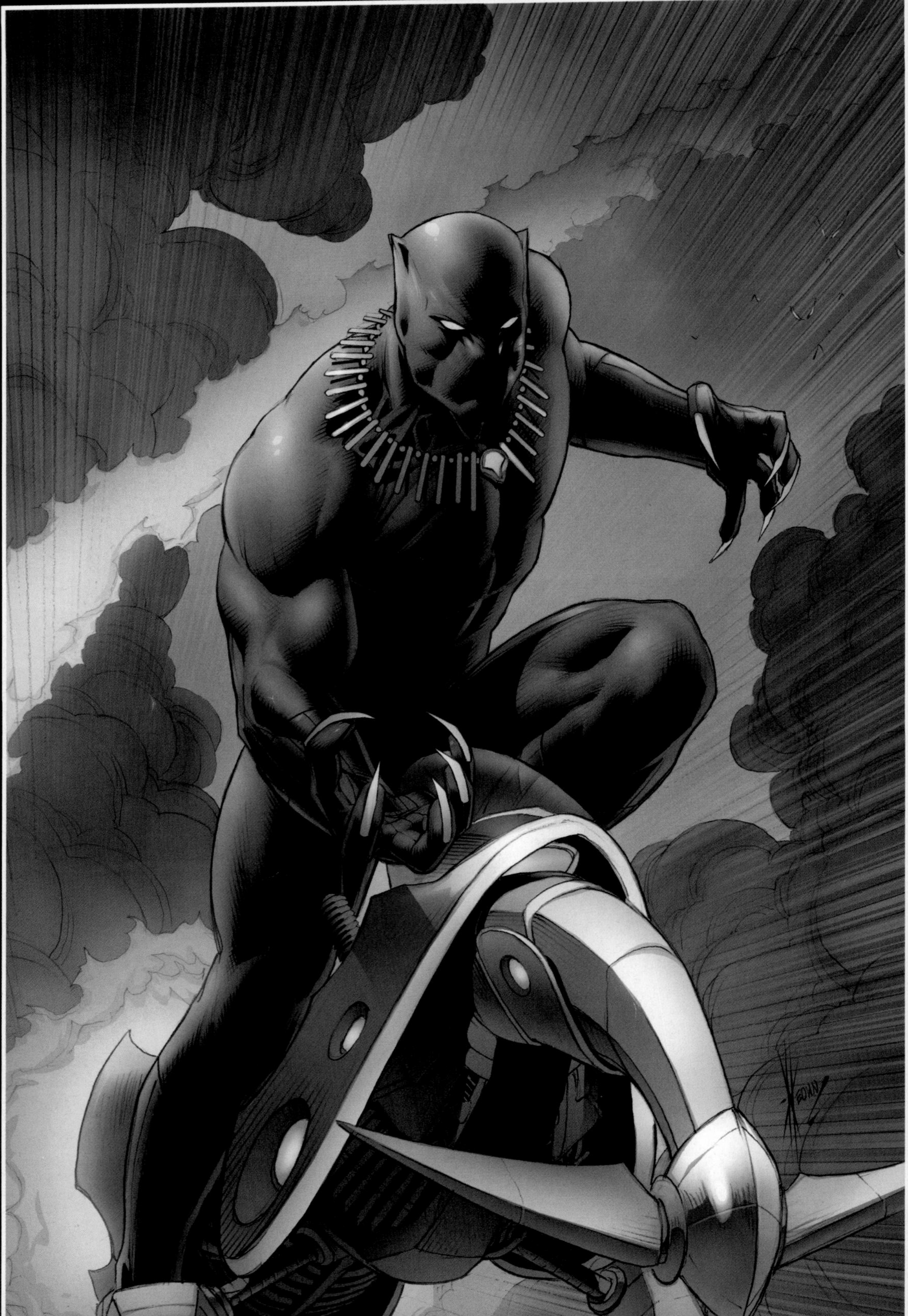

#1 VARIANT BY **DALE KEOWN**

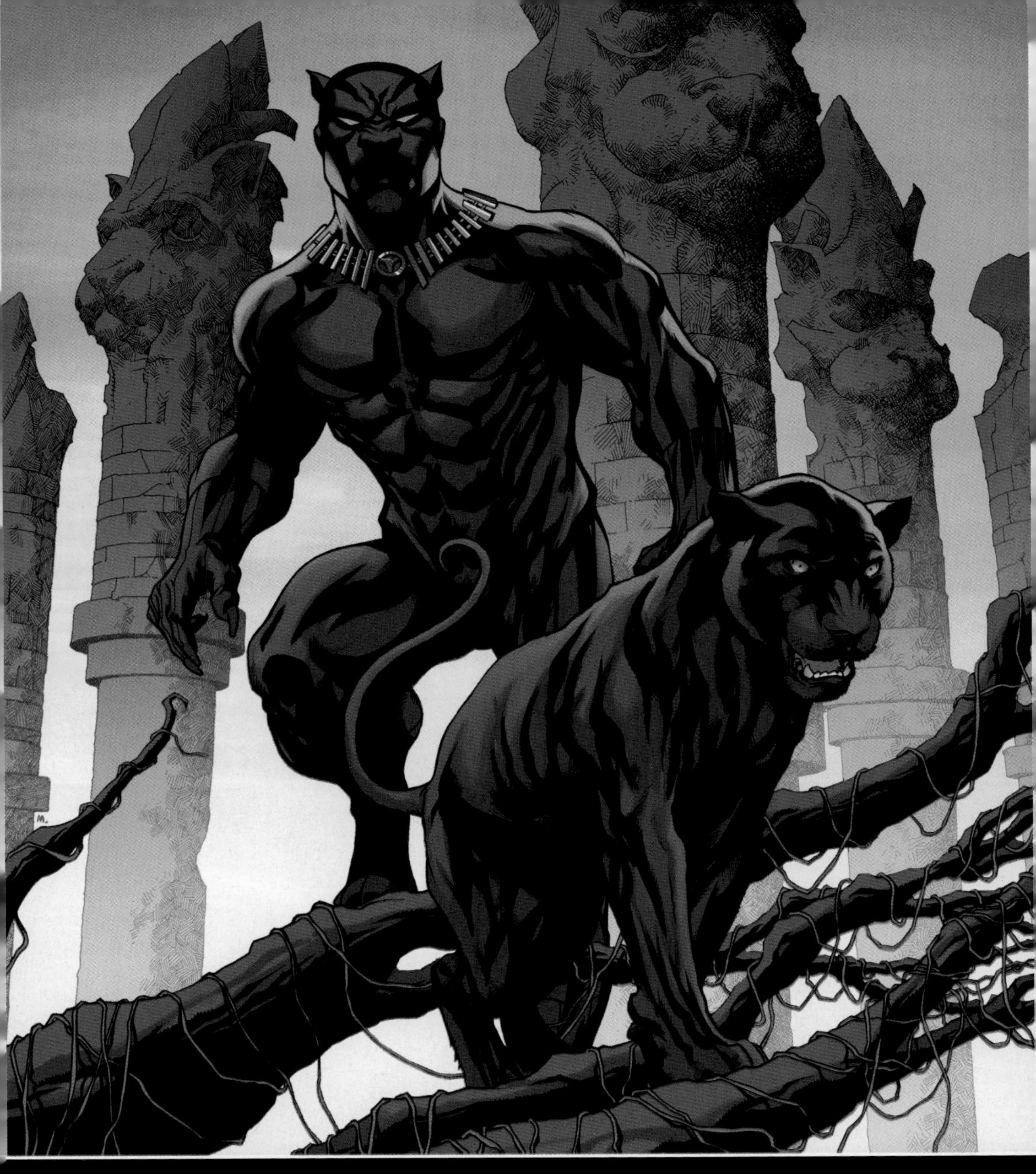

#1 VARIANT BY **MIKE McKONE** & **FRANK MARTIN**

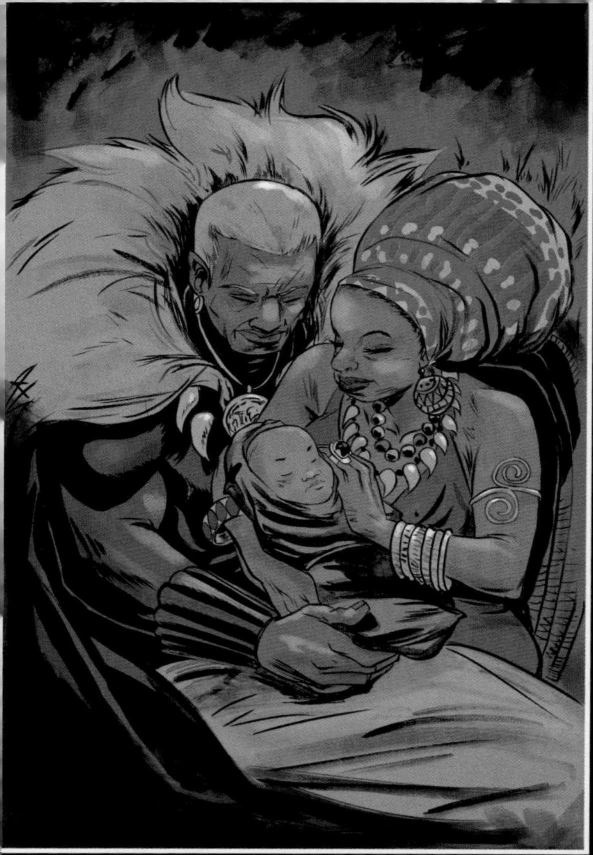
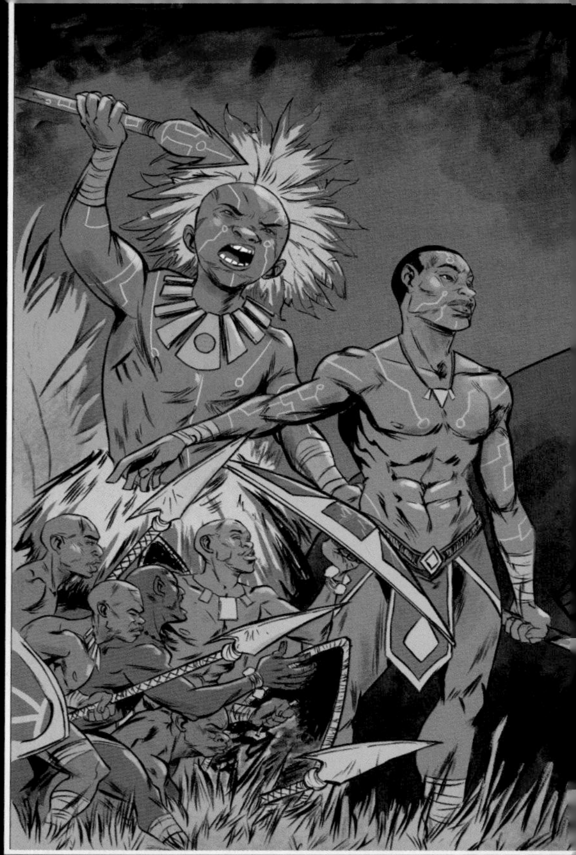

#1-4 VARIANTS BY **SANFORD GREENE**

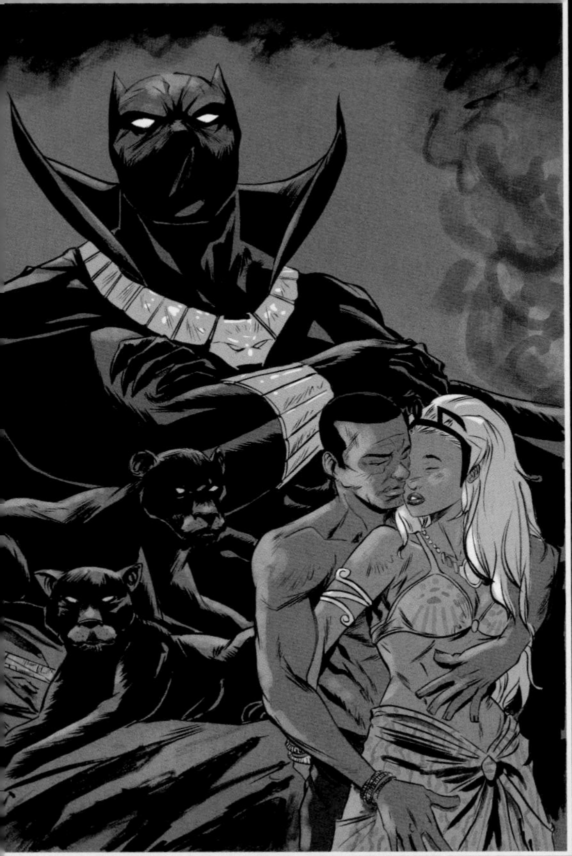

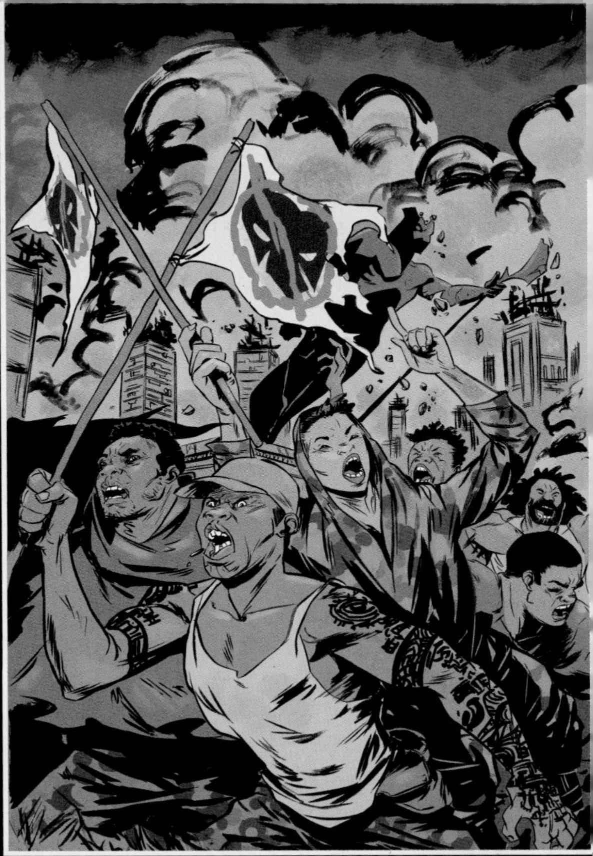

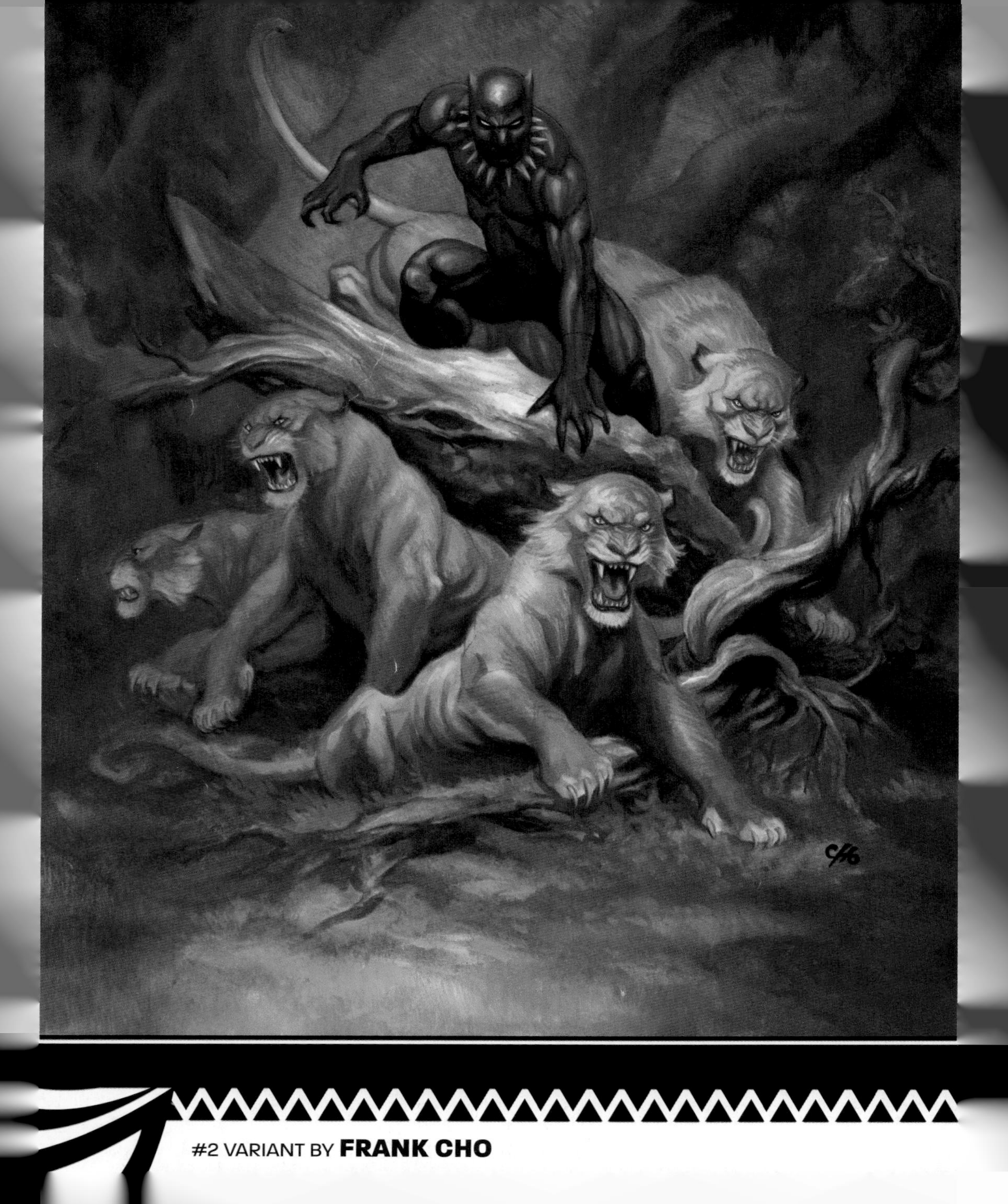
CHO

#2 VARIANT BY **FRANK CHO**

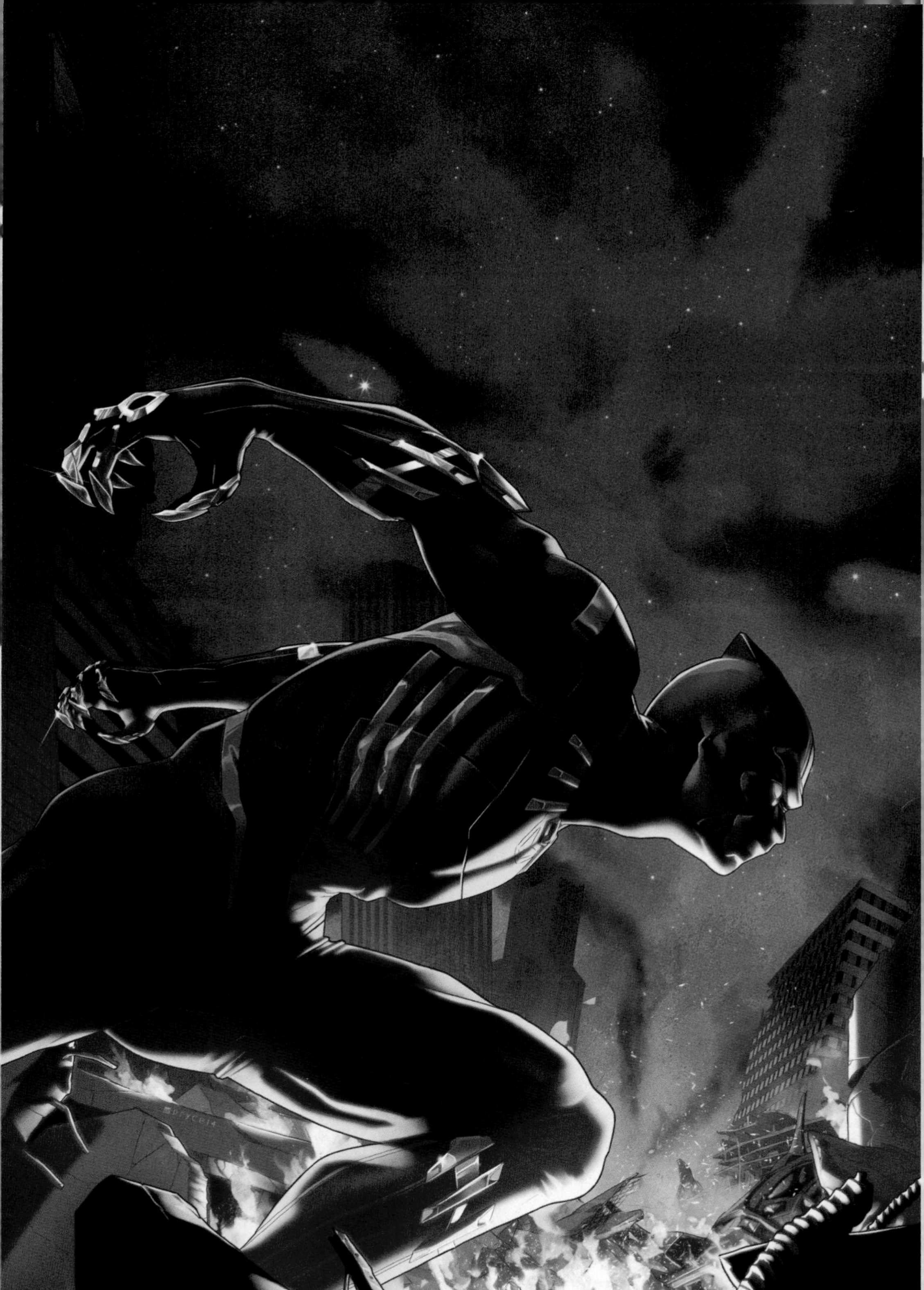

#2 AGE OF APOCALYPSE VARIANT BY **JAMAL CAMPBELL**

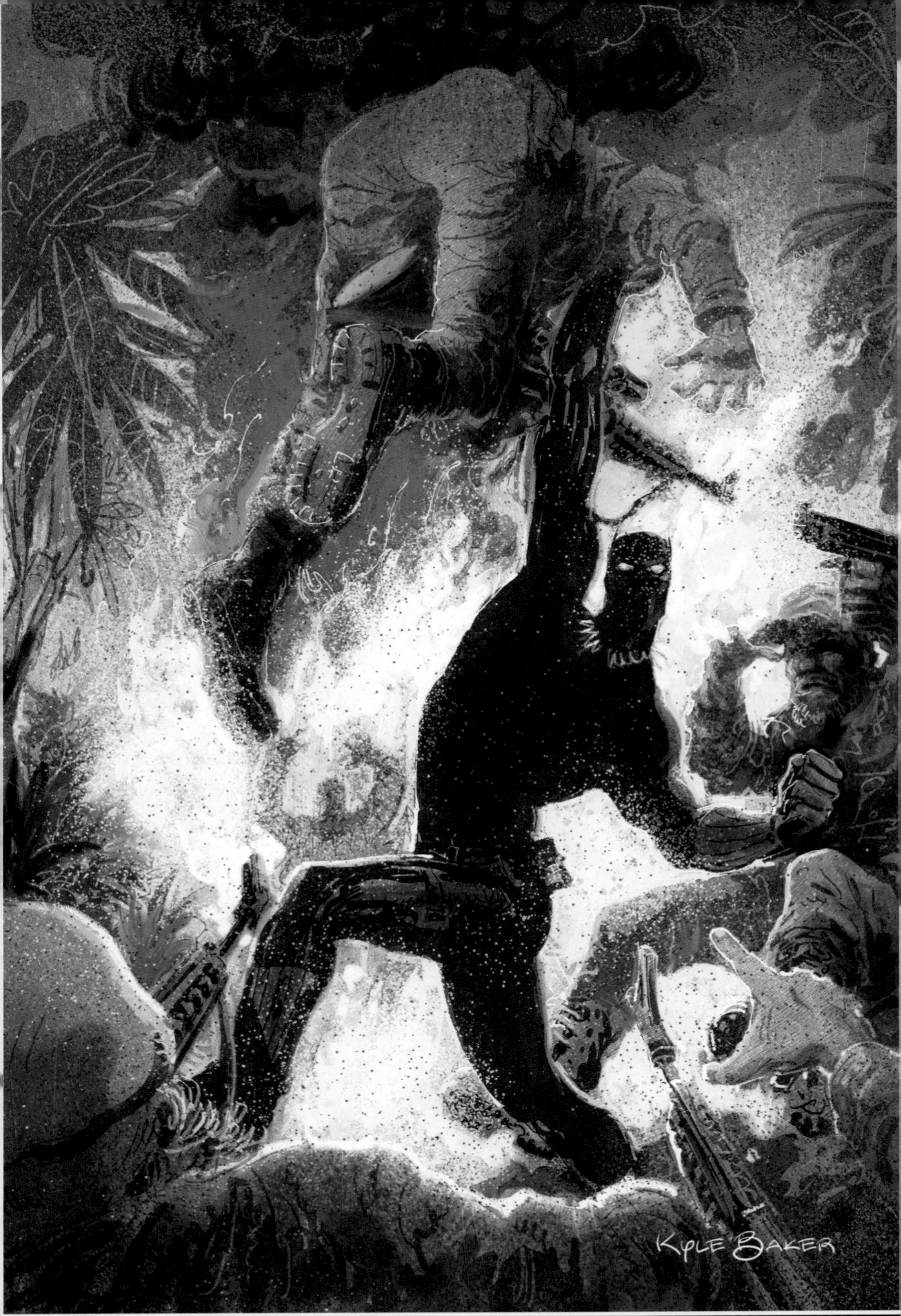
KYLE BAKER

#3 VARIANT BY **KYLE BAKER**

BLACK PANTHER CHRONOLOGY

As the king of the technologically advanced African nation Wakanda, T'Challa carries the hereditary mantle of the Black Panther, the protector of his people. As the world becomes aware of Wakanda's existence and its valuable natural resources, however, the Black Panther must journey out to the larger Marvel Universe where he encounters some of the world's greatest heroes.

Now you can see how it all began with these essential adventures from the Panther's storied history, from his first appearance in *Fantastic Four (1961) #52*, to his time as an Avenger, all the way to the present day.

"THE BLACK PANTHER!"

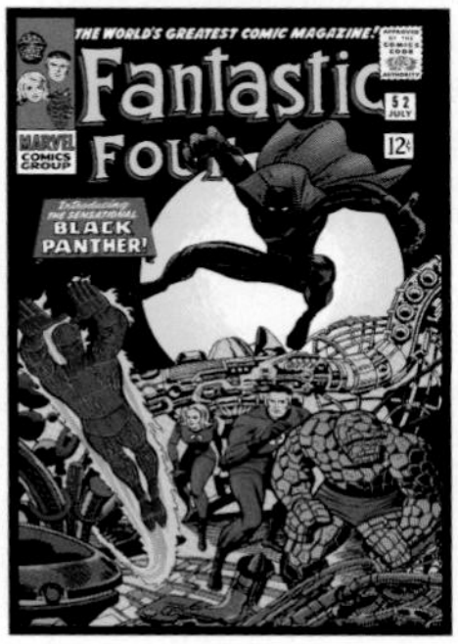

THE WORLD'S GREATEST COMIC MAGAZINE!
Fantastic Four
52 JULY
12¢
MARVEL COMICS GROUP
Introducing the sensational BLACK PANTHER!

In the Black Panther's first appearance, the King of Wakanda welcomes the Fabulous Foursome to his home country...only to attack the team upon their arrival! The FF must maneuver their way through the technologically advanced halls of Wakanda to discover the Panther's true agenda and learn his secret origin.

FANTASTIC FOUR (1961) #52

"DEATH CALLS FOR THE ARCH-HEROES"

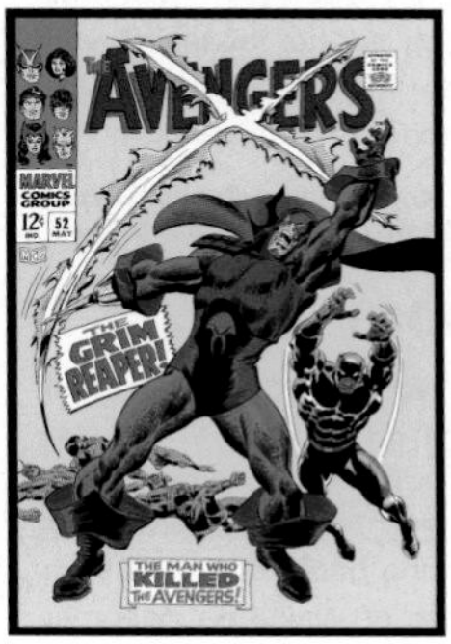

AVENGERS
MARVEL COMICS GROUP
12¢ 52 MAY
THE GRIM REAPER!
THE MAN WHO KILLED THE AVENGERS!

Stumbling upon an eerily quiet Avengers Mansion, Panther winds up trying out for Earth's Mightiest Heroes in a rather unconventional manner... by breaking into their headquarters! T'Challa's suspicions prove warranted, however, as he finds the team seemingly dead on the floor once he makes it in. Solving that mystery is just the beginning of the Black Panther's first mission as an Avenger!

AVENGERS (1963) #52

"PANTHER'S RAGE!"

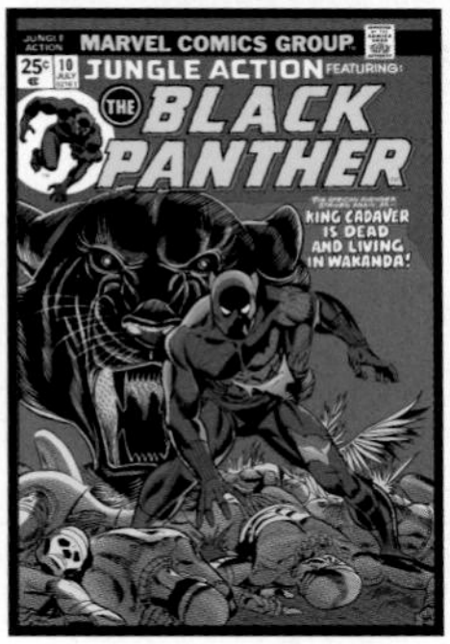

MARVEL COMICS GROUP
25¢ 18
JUNGLE ACTION FEATURING:
THE BLACK PANTHER
KING CADAVER IS DEAD AND LIVING IN WAKANDA!

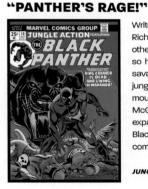

Writer Don McGregor and artists Rich Buckler, Billy Graham and others tell an epic adventure so huge it spanned across the savannah, into the deepest jungles and up snowcapped mountains. Over its course, McGregor would explore and expand the life and culture of Black Panther's Wakanda in compelling detail.

JUNGLE ACTION (1972) #6 - 17

"KING SOLOMON'S FROG!"

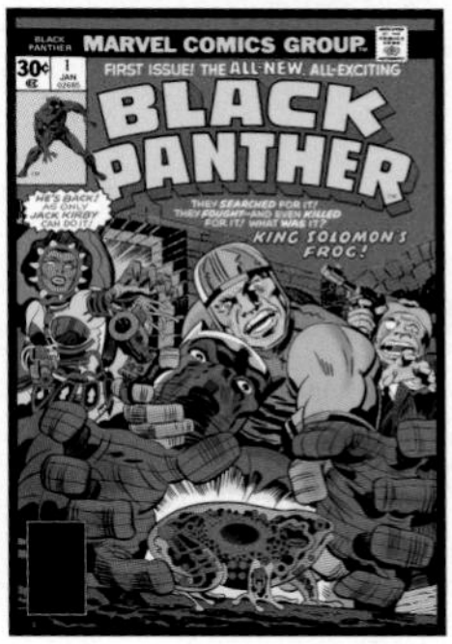

MARVEL COMICS GROUP
30¢ 1
FIRST ISSUE! THE ALL-NEW, ALL-EXCITING
BLACK PANTHER
KING SOLOMON'S FROG!

The Black Panther's co-creator, Jack Kirby, returned to write and draw new adventures for the hero in his first solo series! Kirby added a touch of the far-out to Panther's life beginning with this first adventure, in which the King of Wakanda chases after the mystically powered King Solomon's Frogs! Trust us—the Frog's true secret has to be seen to be believed.

BLACK PANTHER (1977) #1

"THE CLIENT"

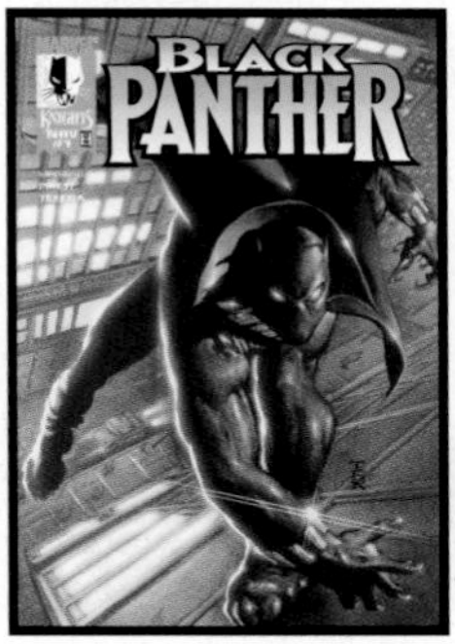

BLACK PANTHER

Writer Christopher Priest began his seminal Black Panther run with this story, introducing a new supporting cast for the Wakandan regent—including the pantsless Everett K. Ross—and infusing a healthy dose of humor and political intrigue to the Panther's adventures. This first arc alone features the devil, super hero action, geopolitics, and much more!

BLACK PANTHER (1998) #1

"WHO IS THE BLACK PANTHER"

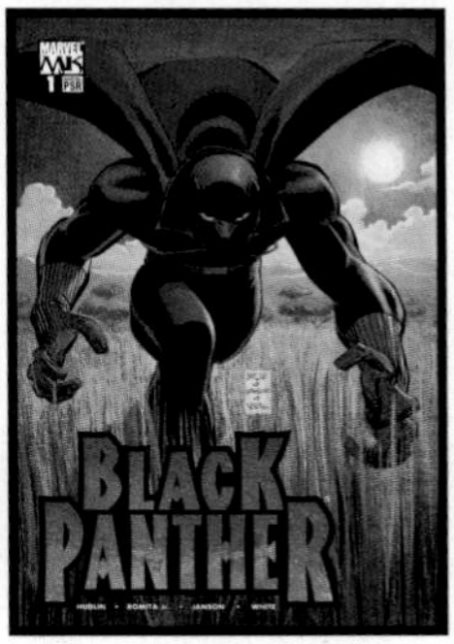

MARVEL
BLACK PANTHER

Writer Reginald Hudlin and artist John Romita Jr. return to the Panther's origins, updating T'Challa's early adventures to the modern day! Learn how our hero first donned the mantle of the Black Panther, and witness his early encounters with the larger Marvel Universe as he faces one of his greatest foes, the treacherous Klaw.

BLACK PANTHER (2005) #1

BLACK PANTHER CHRONOLOGY

"FLAGS OF OUR FATHERS"

CAPTAIN AMERICA
BLACK PANTHER
FLAGS OF OUR FATHERS

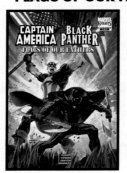

Journey back to World War II to witness Captain America's first encounter with the man who held the Black Panther mantle before T'Challa—his father, T'Chaka. Guest-starring Nick Fury and the Howling Commandos, this saga reveals the deeper roots of the Black Panther's heroic legacy as he faces off with some of the baddest Nazi villains in the Marvel U!

CAPTAIN AMERICA/BLACK PANTHER: FLAGS OF OUR FATHERS (2010) #1

"INERT"

MARVEL
FANTASTIC FOUR

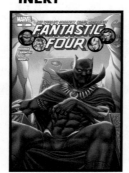

In recent years, writer Jonathan Hickman has taken Black Panther on his most trying journey yet, and it all began here as the Fantastic Four visit their old friend in Wakanda. When the dead rise to attack the FF and Wakandan dignitaries, the Black Panther sets out to learn the true nature of what's going on...and soon he must take on a shocking new role to bring balance to his country.

FANTASTIC FOUR (2012) #607

BLACK PANTHER (2008)

MARVEL
DARK REIGN
BLACK PANTHER

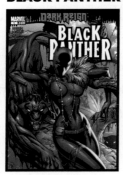

As Norman Osborn's "Dark Reign" affected the entire globe, T'Challa's jet crashes on his way to Wakanda, leaving the king badly burned. Storm, Queen of Wakanda, assumes the mantle of Black Panther to defend her people in their time of need against all who threaten their way of life!

DOOMWAR (2010)

DOOMWAR
MARVEL

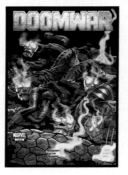

Seeking Wakanda's precious Vibranium, Doctor Doom captures Storm and conquers the nation! It will take the combined forces of two Black Panthers, the X-Men, and the Fantastic Four to stop the maniacal Doom from executing Storm, pitting the world's most powerful super heroes against the villainous ruler of Latveria.

KLAWS OF THE PANTHER (2010)

MARVEL
KLAWS OF THE PANTHER

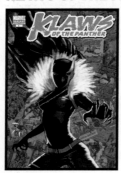

Klaw, the villain composed of living sound, has hatched a new scheme to spill blood all the way from the Savage Land to the streets of New York City! The only one who can stop him is Shuri, the new Black Panther, who must learn to control her inner rage if she hopes to destroy this monster once and for all.

NEW AVENGERS (2013)

NEW AVENGERS
#1
JONATHAN HICKMAN
RICK MAGYAR
MARVEL NOW!
STEVE EPTING
FRANK D'ARMATA
JOIN THE REVOLUTION
001

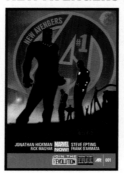

The entire world is at stake when Black Panther and the rest of the Illuminati learn their planet is on a collision course with a parallel Earth! It will take the smartest and most powerful heroes to prevent this cataclysmic event from coming to pass, paving the way for the events of the all-new *Black Panther* series.

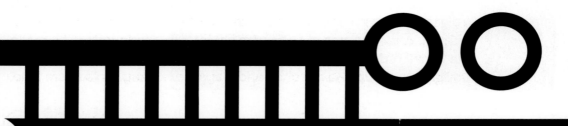

TA-NEHISI COATES

Ta-Nehisi Coates is a national correspondent for *The Atlantic* where he writes about politics and culture. In 2015, Coates published *Between the World and Me*, which won the National Book Award. Coates is also the recipient of a MacArthur Fellowship, a National Magazine Award, and the George Polk Award. He lives in New York with his wife and son.

BRIAN STELFREEZE

Brian Stelfreeze has worked in the comic book industry for over 25 years as a writer, penciler, inker, colorist, and painter. He has worked for almost every major American comics publisher, and has the distinction of producing over 50 consecutive covers for *Batman: Shadow of the Bat*, and being one of the founding members of Atlanta's Gaijin Studios. His most recent work includes BOOM!'s *Day Men* and Marvel's *Black Panther*.

LAURA MARTIN

A winner of multiple Eisner and Eagle awards, Laura Martin is one of the most acclaimed colorists in comics. Starting with Jim Lee's WildStorm Studios, some of her earliest professional work included coloring John Cassaday's *Planetary* and Bryan Hitch's *The Authority*. After a period as art director for CrossGen Comics, she began work with Marvel, serving again as Cassaday's colorist on *Astonishing X-Men*. Other credits include J. Michael Straczynski's *Thor* and Brian Michael Bendis' *Siege*.

JOE SABINO

Hailing from New Jersey, Joe Sabino majored in Computer Animation at Fairleigh Dickinson University. He first started at Marvel helping launch a digital comics initiative and soon transferred into the infamous Marvel Bullpen. After two-and-a-half years at Marvel's headquarters, he made the transition into being a freelance letterer with Chris Eliopoulos' Virtual Calligraphy group. He coaches and plays ice hockey in his spare time.

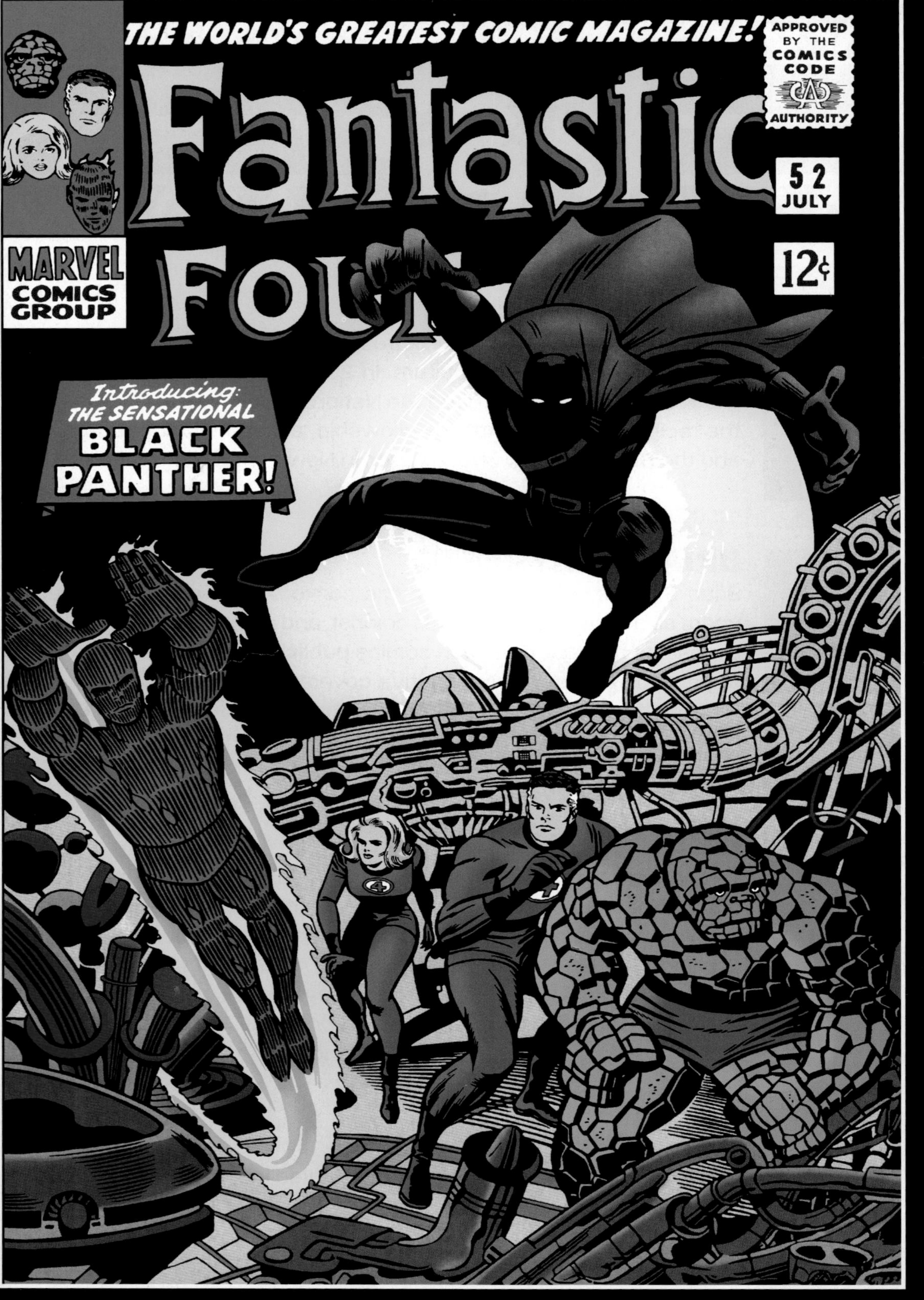
THE WORLD'S GREATEST COMIC MAGAZINE!
APPROVED BY THE COMICS CODE AUTHORITY
Fantastic Four
52 JULY
MARVEL COMICS GROUP
12¢
Introducing: THE SENSATIONAL BLACK PANTHER!

NOW PRESENTING THE CLASSIC FIRST APPEARANCE OF BLACK PANTHER!

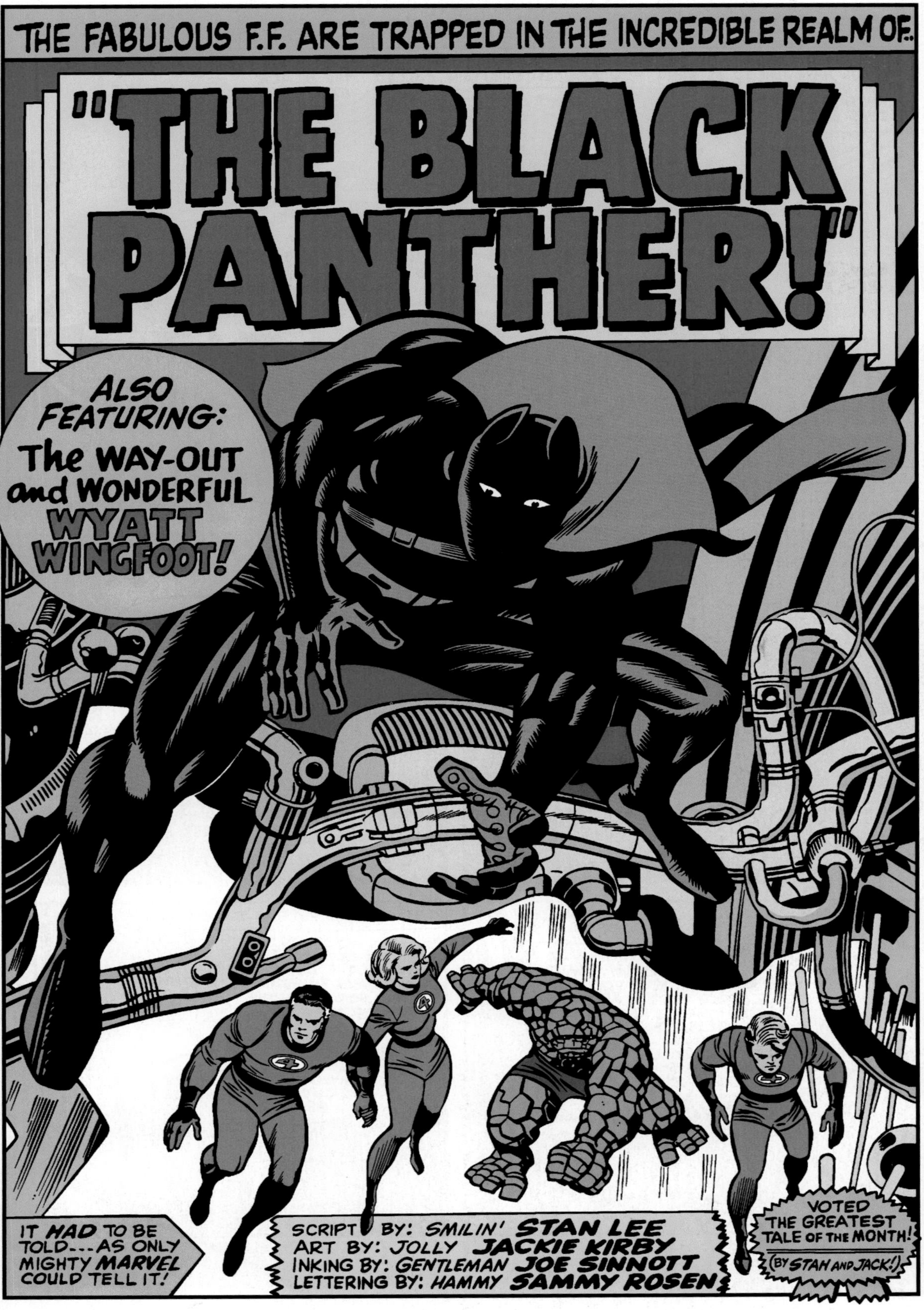
THE FABULOUS F.F. ARE TRAPPED IN THE INCREDIBLE REALM OF..
"THE BLACK PANTHER!"
ALSO FEATURING: The WAY-OUT and WONDERFUL WYATT WINGFOOT!
IT HAD TO BE TOLD--- AS ONLY MIGHTY MARVEL COULD TELL IT!
SCRIPT BY: SMILIN' STAN LEE
ART BY: JOLLY JACKIE KIRBY
INKING BY: GENTLEMAN JOE SINNOTT
LETTERING BY: HAMMY SAMMY ROSEN
VOTED THE GREATEST TALE OF THE MONTH!
(BY STAN AND JACK!)

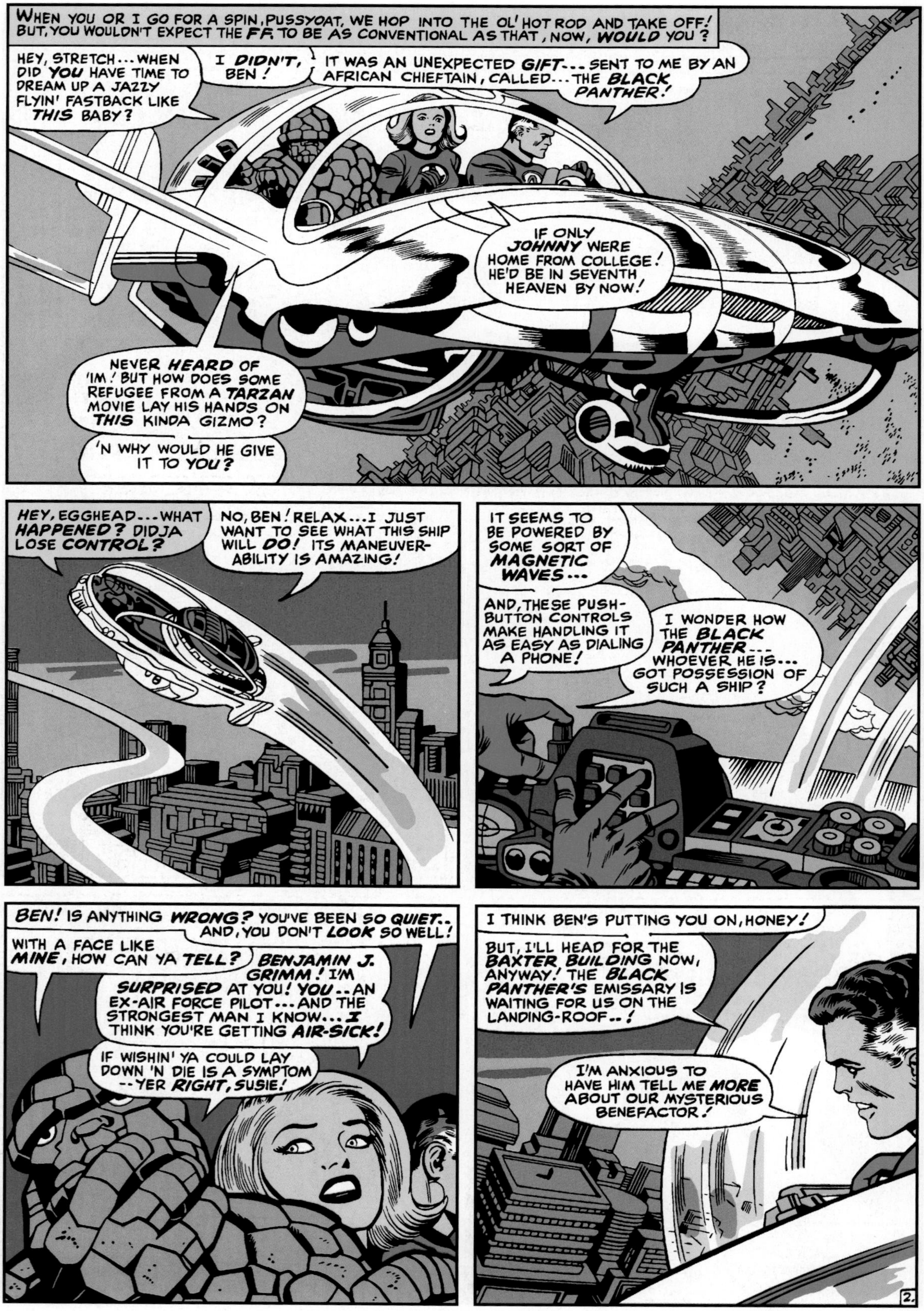
WHEN YOU OR I GO FOR A SPIN, PUSSYCAT, WE HOP INTO THE OL' HOT ROD AND TAKE OFF! BUT, YOU WOULDN'T EXPECT THE FF TO BE AS CONVENTIONAL AS THAT, NOW, WOULD YOU?
HEY, STRETCH... WHEN DID YOU HAVE TIME TO DREAM UP A JAZZY FLYIN' FASTBACK LIKE THIS BABY?
I DIDN'T, BEN!
IT WAS AN UNEXPECTED GIFT... SENT TO ME BY AN AFRICAN CHIEFTAIN, CALLED... THE BLACK PANTHER!
IF ONLY JOHNNY WERE HOME FROM COLLEGE! HE'D BE IN SEVENTH HEAVEN BY NOW!
NEVER HEARD OF 'IM! BUT HOW DOES SOME REFUGEE FROM A TARZAN MOVIE LAY HIS HANDS ON THIS KINDA GIZMO?
'N WHY WOULD HE GIVE IT TO YOU?
HEY, EGGHEAD... WHAT HAPPENED? DIDJA LOSE CONTROL?
NO, BEN! RELAX... I JUST WANT TO SEE WHAT THIS SHIP WILL DO! ITS MANEUVER-ABILITY IS AMAZING!
IT SEEMS TO BE POWERED BY SOME SORT OF MAGNETIC WAVES...
AND, THESE PUSH-BUTTON CONTROLS MAKE HANDLING IT AS EASY AS DIALING A PHONE!
I WONDER HOW THE BLACK PANTHER--- WHOEVER HE IS... GOT POSSESSION OF SUCH A SHIP?
BEN! IS ANYTHING WRONG? YOU'VE BEEN SO QUIET.. AND, YOU DON'T LOOK SO WELL!
WITH A FACE LIKE MINE, HOW CAN YA TELL?
BENJAMIN J. GRIMM! I'M SURPRISED AT YOU! YOU.. AN EX-AIR FORCE PILOT... AND THE STRONGEST MAN I KNOW... I THINK YOU'RE GETTING AIR-SICK!
IF WISHIN' YA COULD LAY DOWN 'N DIE IS A SYMPTOM --YER RIGHT, SUSIE!
I THINK BEN'S PUTTING YOU ON, HONEY!
BUT, I'LL HEAD FOR THE BAXTER BUILDING NOW, ANYWAY! THE BLACK PANTHER'S EMISSARY IS WAITING FOR US ON THE LANDING-ROOF..!
I'M ANXIOUS TO HAVE HIM TELL ME MORE ABOUT OUR MYSTERIOUS BENEFACTOR!
2.

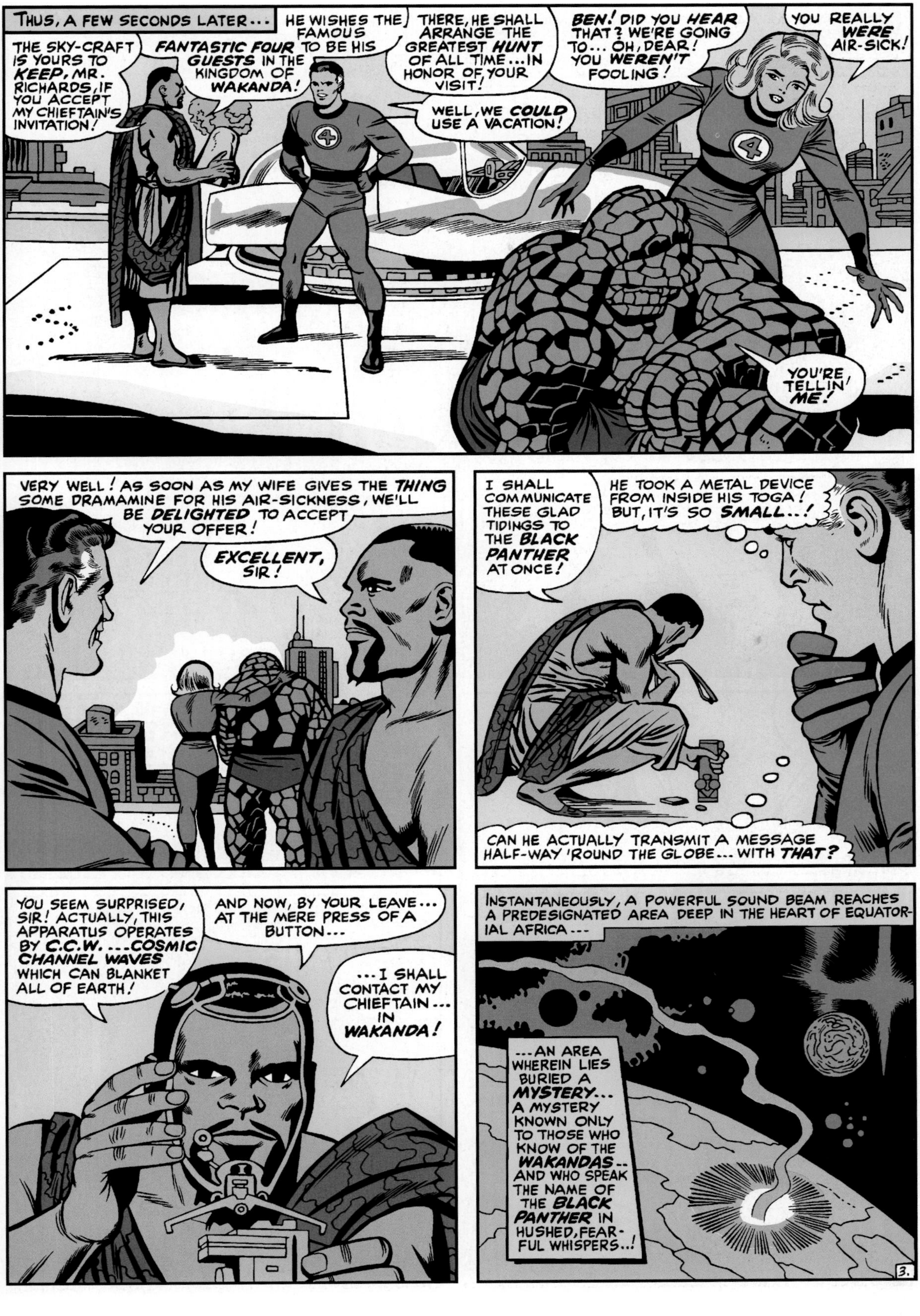
THUS, A FEW SECONDS LATER...
THE SKY-CRAFT IS YOURS TO KEEP, MR. RICHARDS, IF YOU ACCEPT MY CHIEFTAIN'S INVITATION!
HE WISHES THE FAMOUS FANTASTIC FOUR TO BE HIS GUESTS IN THE KINGDOM OF WAKANDA!
THERE, HE SHALL ARRANGE THE GREATEST HUNT OF ALL TIME... IN HONOR OF YOUR VISIT!
WELL, WE COULD USE A VACATION!
BEN! DID YOU HEAR THAT? WE'RE GOING TO... OH, DEAR! YOU WEREN'T FOOLING!
YOU REALLY WERE AIR-SICK!
YOU'RE TELLIN' ME!
VERY WELL! AS SOON AS MY WIFE GIVES THE THING SOME DRAMAMINE FOR HIS AIR-SICKNESS, WE'LL BE DELIGHTED TO ACCEPT YOUR OFFER!
EXCELLENT, SIR!
I SHALL COMMUNICATE THESE GLAD TIDINGS TO THE BLACK PANTHER AT ONCE!
HE TOOK A METAL DEVICE FROM INSIDE HIS TOGA! BUT, IT'S SO SMALL...!
CAN HE ACTUALLY TRANSMIT A MESSAGE HALF-WAY 'ROUND THE GLOBE... WITH THAT?
YOU SEEM SURPRISED, SIR! ACTUALLY, THIS APPARATUS OPERATES BY C.C.W. ...COSMIC CHANNEL WAVES WHICH CAN BLANKET ALL OF EARTH!
AND NOW, BY YOUR LEAVE... AT THE MERE PRESS OF A BUTTON...
...I SHALL CONTACT MY CHIEFTAIN... IN WAKANDA!
INSTANTANEOUSLY, A POWERFUL SOUND BEAM REACHES A PREDESIGNATED AREA DEEP IN THE HEART OF EQUATORIAL AFRICA---
...AN AREA WHEREIN LIES BURIED A MYSTERY... A MYSTERY KNOWN ONLY TO THOSE WHO KNOW OF THE WAKANDAS.. AND WHO SPEAK THE NAME OF THE BLACK PANTHER IN HUSHED, FEARFUL WHISPERS..!
3.

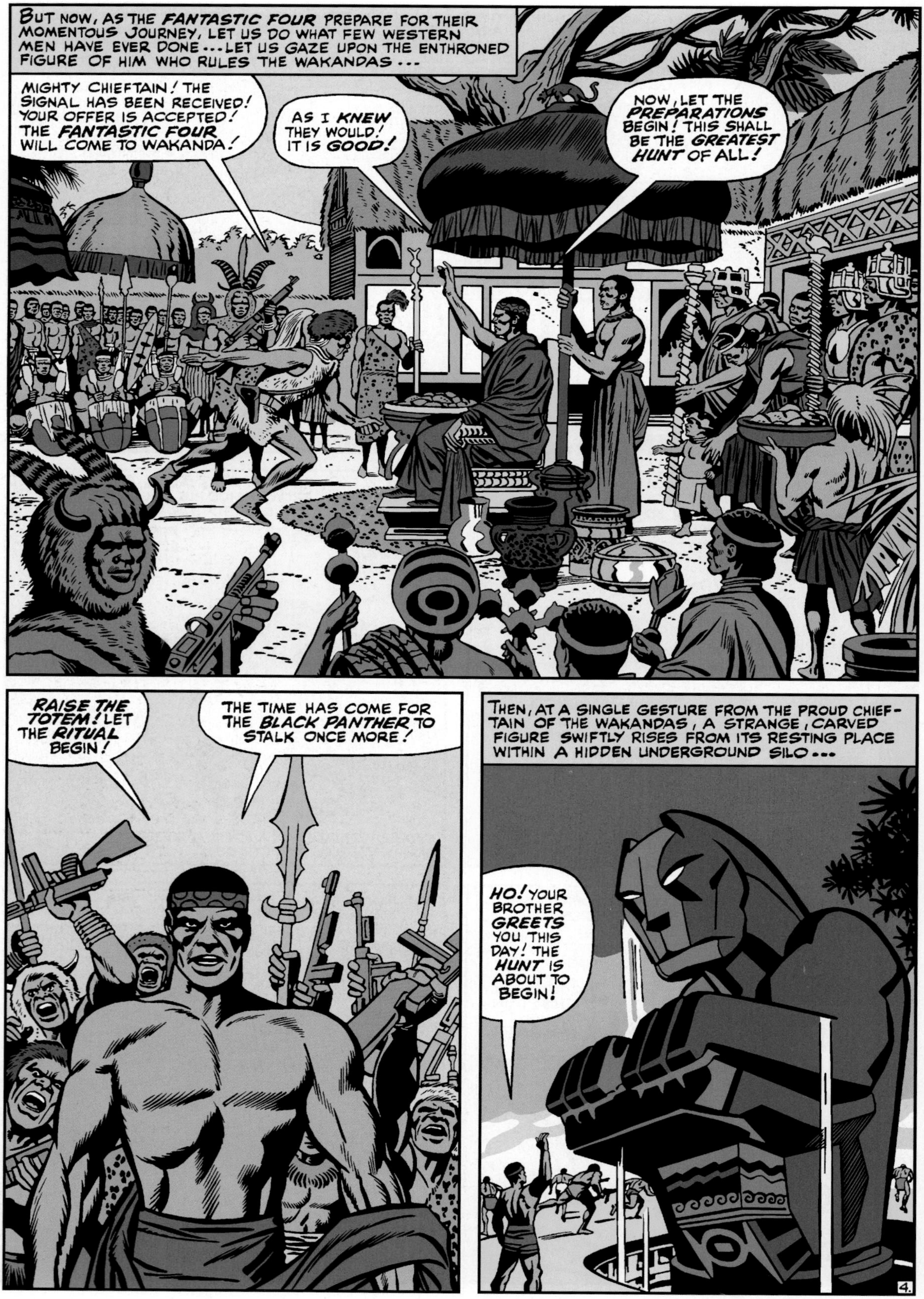

BUT NOW, AS THE FANTASTIC FOUR PREPARE FOR THEIR MOMENTOUS JOURNEY, LET US DO WHAT FEW WESTERN MEN HAVE EVER DONE... LET US GAZE UPON THE ENTHRONED FIGURE OF HIM WHO RULES THE WAKANDAS...
MIGHTY CHIEFTAIN! THE SIGNAL HAS BEEN RECEIVED! YOUR OFFER IS ACCEPTED! THE FANTASTIC FOUR WILL COME TO WAKANDA!
AS I KNEW THEY WOULD! IT IS GOOD!
NOW, LET THE PREPARATIONS BEGIN! THIS SHALL BE THE GREATEST HUNT OF ALL!
RAISE THE TOTEM! LET THE RITUAL BEGIN!
THE TIME HAS COME FOR THE BLACK PANTHER TO STALK ONCE MORE!
THEN, AT A SINGLE GESTURE FROM THE PROUD CHIEFTAIN OF THE WAKANDAS, A STRANGE, CARVED FIGURE SWIFTLY RISES FROM ITS RESTING PLACE WITHIN A HIDDEN UNDERGROUND SILO...
HO! YOUR BROTHER GREETS YOU THIS DAY! THE HUNT IS ABOUT TO BEGIN!
4.

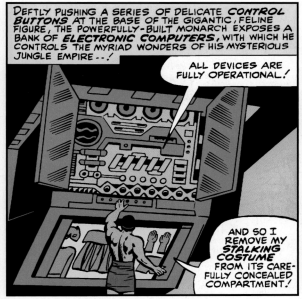

DEFTLY PUSHING A SERIES OF DELICATE *CONTROL BUTTONS* AT THE BASE OF THE GIGANTIC, FELINE FIGURE, THE POWERFULLY-BUILT MONARCH EXPOSES A BANK OF *ELECTRONIC COMPUTERS*, WITH WHICH HE CONTROLS THE MYRIAD WONDERS OF HIS MYSTERIOUS JUNGLE EMPIRE...!

ALL DEVICES ARE FULLY OPERATIONAL!

AND SO I REMOVE MY *STALKING COSTUME* FROM ITS CAREFULLY CONCEALED COMPARTMENT!

NOW, LET THE FANTASTIC FOUR *COME!*

THE *BLACK PANTHER* SHALL GREET THEM... AS THEY HAVE NEVER BEEN GREETED BEFORE!

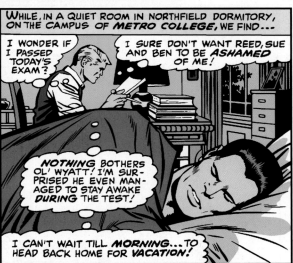

WHILE, IN A QUIET ROOM IN NORTHFIELD DORMITORY, ON THE CAMPUS OF *METRO COLLEGE*, WE FIND...

I WONDER IF I PASSED TODAY'S EXAM?

I SURE DON'T WANT REED, SUE AND BEN TO BE *ASHAMED* OF ME!

NOTHING BOTHERS OL' WYATT! I'M SURPRISED HE EVEN MANAGED TO STAY AWAKE *DURING* THE TEST!

I CAN'T WAIT TILL *MORNING*...TO HEAD BACK HOME FOR *VACATION!*

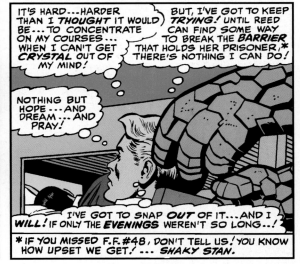

IT'S HARD...HARDER THAN I *THOUGHT* IT WOULD BE...TO CONCENTRATE ON MY COURSES... WHEN I CAN'T GET *CRYSTAL* OUT OF MY MIND!

BUT, I'VE GOT TO KEEP *TRYING!* UNTIL REED CAN FIND SOME WAY TO BREAK THE *BARRIER* THAT HOLDS HER PRISONER,* THERE'S NOTHING I CAN DO!

NOTHING BUT HOPE...AND DREAM...AND PRAY!

I'VE GOT TO SNAP *OUT* OF IT...AND I *WILL!* IF ONLY THE *EVENINGS* WEREN'T SO LONG...!

* IF YOU MISSED F.F. #48, DON'T TELL US! YOU KNOW HOW UPSET WE GET! --- SHAKY STAN.

HEY!! HOLY HANNAH!! WHAT THE...?!!

SURPRISE!

HIYA, JOE COLLEGE! WHAT'S THE GOOD WORD, LITTLE ITTY BITTY BUDDY?

I'LL ITTY BITTY BUDDY *YOU,* YOU BLUE-EYED BIRDBRAIN!!

I *KNOWED* YA'D BE AS GOOD-NATURED AS EVER, JUNIOR!

LEGGO, BEFORE I GIVE YOU A HOT-FOOT BETWEEN WHERE YOUR *EARS* OUGHTTA BE!

5.

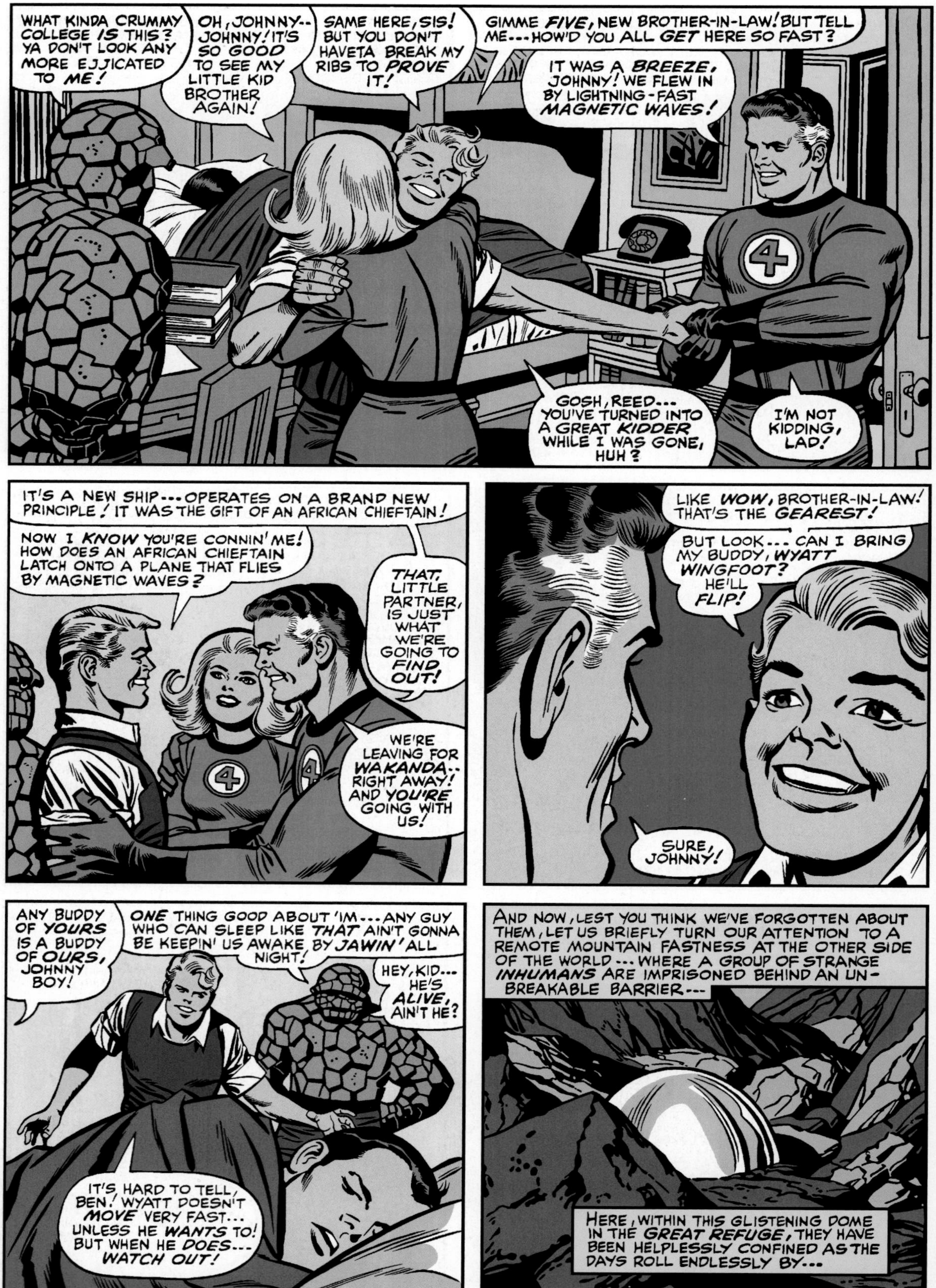
WHAT KINDA CRUMMY COLLEGE IS THIS? YA DON'T LOOK ANY MORE EJJICATED TO ME!
OH, JOHNNY-- JOHNNY! IT'S SO GOOD TO SEE MY LITTLE KID BROTHER AGAIN!
SAME HERE, SIS! BUT YOU DON'T HAVETA BREAK MY RIBS TO PROVE IT!
GIMME FIVE, NEW BROTHER-IN-LAW! BUT TELL ME--- HOW'D YOU ALL GET HERE SO FAST?
IT WAS A BREEZE, JOHNNY! WE FLEW IN BY LIGHTNING-FAST MAGNETIC WAVES!
GOSH, REED... YOU'VE TURNED INTO A GREAT KIDDER WHILE I WAS GONE, HUH?
I'M NOT KIDDING, LAD!
IT'S A NEW SHIP--- OPERATES ON A BRAND NEW PRINCIPLE! IT WAS THE GIFT OF AN AFRICAN CHIEFTAIN!
NOW I KNOW YOU'RE CONNIN' ME! HOW DOES AN AFRICAN CHIEFTAIN LATCH ONTO A PLANE THAT FLIES BY MAGNETIC WAVES?
THAT, LITTLE PARTNER, IS JUST WHAT WE'RE GOING TO FIND OUT!
WE'RE LEAVING FOR WAKANDA.. RIGHT AWAY! AND YOU'RE GOING WITH US!
LIKE WOW, BROTHER-IN-LAW! THAT'S THE GEAREST!
BUT LOOK... CAN I BRING MY BUDDY, WYATT WINGFOOT? HE'LL FLIP!
SURE, JOHNNY!
ANY BUDDY OF YOURS IS A BUDDY OF OURS, JOHNNY BOY!
ONE THING GOOD ABOUT 'IM--- ANY GUY WHO CAN SLEEP LIKE THAT AIN'T GONNA BE KEEPIN' US AWAKE BY JAWIN' ALL NIGHT!
HEY, KID... HE'S ALIVE, AIN'T HE?
IT'S HARD TO TELL, BEN! WYATT DOESN'T MOVE VERY FAST... UNLESS HE WANTS TO! BUT WHEN HE DOES--- WATCH OUT!
AND NOW, LEST YOU THINK WE'VE FORGOTTEN ABOUT THEM, LET US BRIEFLY TURN OUR ATTENTION TO A REMOTE MOUNTAIN FASTNESS AT THE OTHER SIDE OF THE WORLD--- WHERE A GROUP OF STRANGE INHUMANS ARE IMPRISONED BEHIND AN UN-BREAKABLE BARRIER---
HERE, WITHIN THIS GLISTENING DOME IN THE GREAT REFUGE, THEY HAVE BEEN HELPLESSLY CONFINED AS THE DAYS ROLL ENDLESSLY BY...
6.

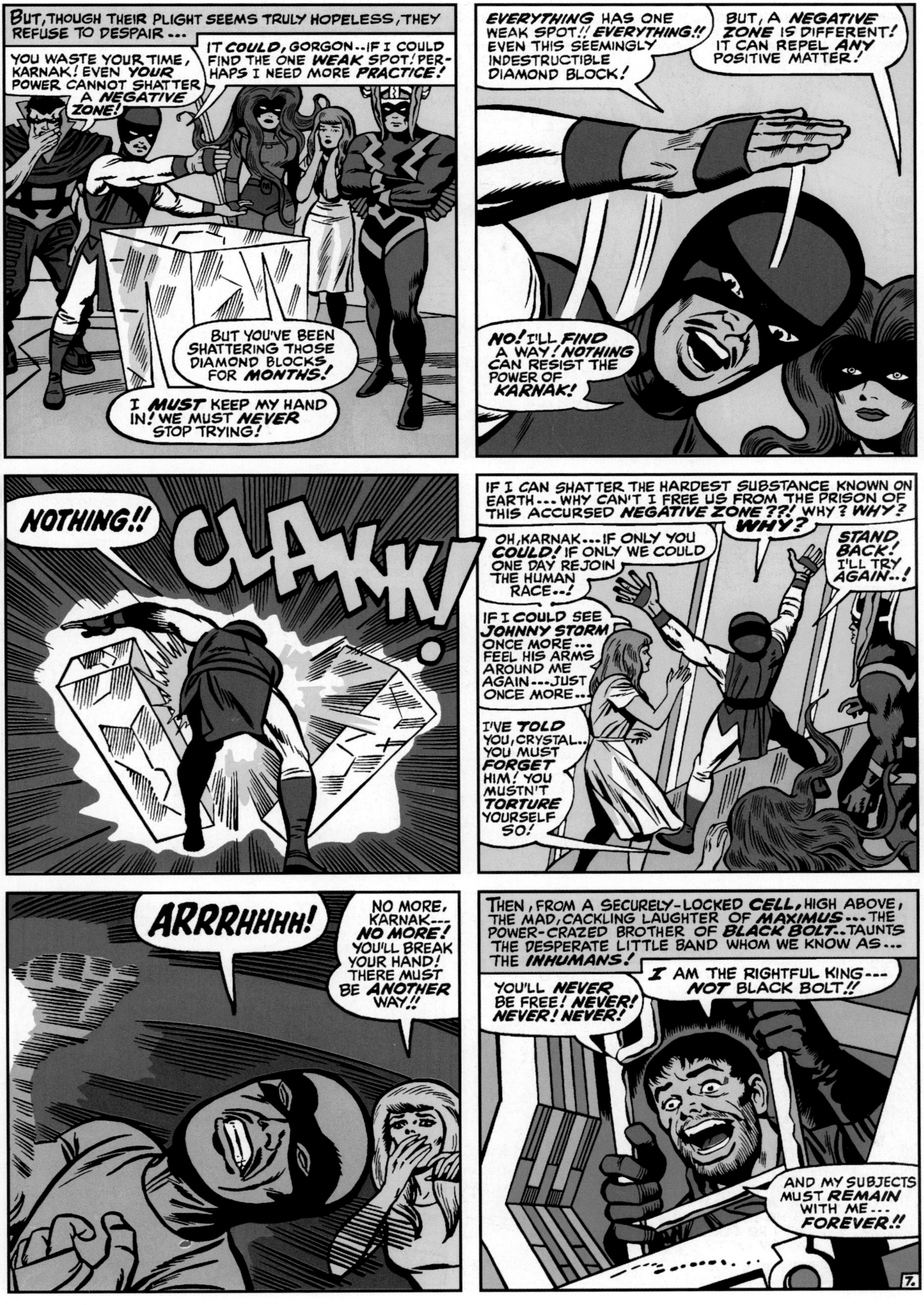

BUT, THOUGH THEIR PLIGHT SEEMS TRULY HOPELESS, THEY REFUSE TO DESPAIR...
YOU WASTE YOUR TIME, KARNAK! EVEN YOUR POWER CANNOT SHATTER A NEGATIVE ZONE!
IT COULD, GORGON--IF I COULD FIND THE ONE WEAK SPOT! PERHAPS I NEED MORE PRACTICE!
BUT YOU'VE BEEN SHATTERING THOSE DIAMOND BLOCKS FOR MONTHS!
I MUST KEEP MY HAND IN! WE MUST NEVER STOP TRYING!
EVERYTHING HAS ONE WEAK SPOT!! EVERYTHING!! EVEN THIS SEEMINGLY INDESTRUCTIBLE DIAMOND BLOCK!
BUT, A NEGATIVE ZONE IS DIFFERENT! IT CAN REPEL ANY POSITIVE MATTER!
NO! I'LL FIND A WAY! NOTHING CAN RESIST THE POWER OF KARNAK!
NOTHING!!
CLAKK!
IF I CAN SHATTER THE HARDEST SUBSTANCE KNOWN ON EARTH--- WHY CAN'T I FREE US FROM THE PRISON OF THIS ACCURSED NEGATIVE ZONE??! WHY? WHY? WHY?
OH, KARNAK--- IF ONLY YOU COULD! IF ONLY WE COULD ONE DAY REJOIN THE HUMAN RACE--!
IF I COULD SEE JOHNNY STORM ONCE MORE... FEEL HIS ARMS AROUND ME AGAIN---JUST ONCE MORE...
STAND BACK! I'LL TRY AGAIN--!
I'VE TOLD YOU, CRYSTAL... YOU MUST FORGET HIM! YOU MUSTN'T TORTURE YOURSELF SO!
ARRRHHHH!
NO MORE, KARNAK--- NO MORE! YOU'LL BREAK YOUR HAND! THERE MUST BE ANOTHER WAY!!
THEN, FROM A SECURELY-LOCKED CELL, HIGH ABOVE, THE MAD, CACKLING LAUGHTER OF MAXIMUS--- THE POWER-CRAZED BROTHER OF BLACK BOLT-- TAUNTS THE DESPERATE LITTLE BAND WHOM WE KNOW AS... THE INHUMANS!
YOU'LL NEVER BE FREE! NEVER! NEVER! NEVER!
I AM THE RIGHTFUL KING--- NOT BLACK BOLT!!
AND MY SUBJECTS MUST REMAIN WITH ME--- FOREVER!!
7.

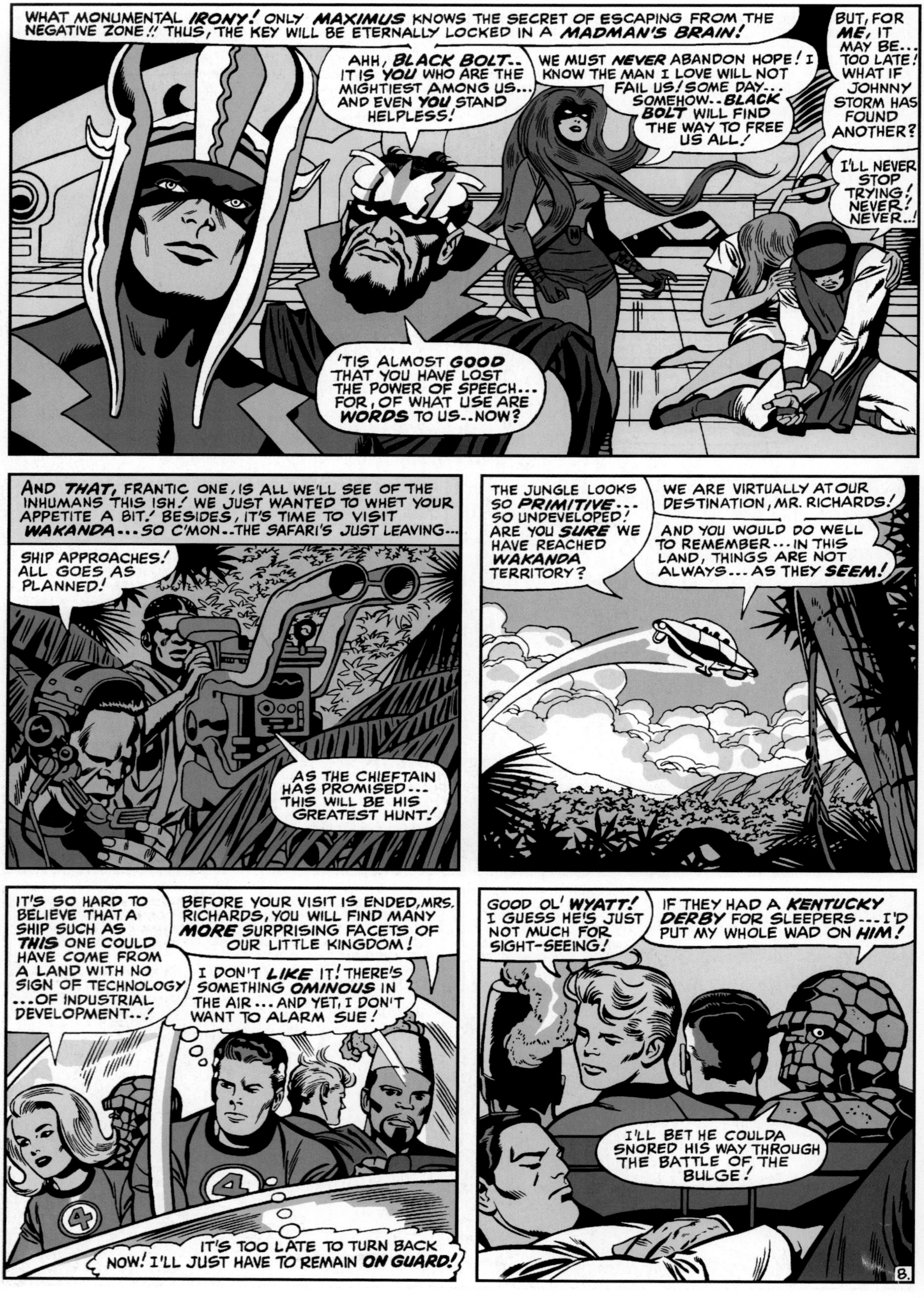
WHAT MONUMENTAL IRONY! ONLY MAXIMUS KNOWS THE SECRET OF ESCAPING FROM THE NEGATIVE ZONE!! THUS, THE KEY WILL BE ETERNALLY LOCKED IN A MADMAN'S BRAIN!
AHH, BLACK BOLT.. IT IS YOU WHO ARE THE MIGHTIEST AMONG US... AND EVEN YOU STAND HELPLESS!
'TIS ALMOST GOOD THAT YOU HAVE LOST THE POWER OF SPEECH... FOR, OF WHAT USE ARE WORDS TO US..NOW?
WE MUST NEVER ABANDON HOPE! I KNOW THE MAN I LOVE WILL NOT FAIL US! SOME DAY... SOMEHOW..BLACK BOLT WILL FIND THE WAY TO FREE US ALL!
BUT, FOR ME, IT MAY BE... TOO LATE! WHAT IF JOHNNY STORM HAS FOUND ANOTHER?
I'LL NEVER STOP TRYING! NEVER! NEVER...!
AND THAT, FRANTIC ONE, IS ALL WE'LL SEE OF THE INHUMANS THIS ISH! WE JUST WANTED TO WHET YOUR APPETITE A BIT! BESIDES, IT'S TIME TO VISIT WAKANDA... SO C'MON..THE SAFARI'S JUST LEAVING...
SHIP APPROACHES! ALL GOES AS PLANNED!
AS THE CHIEFTAIN HAS PROMISED--- THIS WILL BE HIS GREATEST HUNT!
THE JUNGLE LOOKS SO PRIMITIVE... SO UNDEVELOPED! ARE YOU SURE WE HAVE REACHED WAKANDA TERRITORY?
WE ARE VIRTUALLY AT OUR DESTINATION, MR. RICHARDS!
AND YOU WOULD DO WELL TO REMEMBER... IN THIS LAND, THINGS ARE NOT ALWAYS... AS THEY SEEM!
IT'S SO HARD TO BELIEVE THAT A SHIP SUCH AS THIS ONE COULD HAVE COME FROM A LAND WITH NO SIGN OF TECHNOLOGY ...OF INDUSTRIAL DEVELOPMENT..!
BEFORE YOUR VISIT IS ENDED, MRS. RICHARDS, YOU WILL FIND MANY MORE SURPRISING FACETS OF OUR LITTLE KINGDOM!
I DON'T LIKE IT! THERE'S SOMETHING OMINOUS IN THE AIR... AND YET, I DON'T WANT TO ALARM SUE!
IT'S TOO LATE TO TURN BACK NOW! I'LL JUST HAVE TO REMAIN ON GUARD!
GOOD OL' WYATT! I GUESS HE'S JUST NOT MUCH FOR SIGHT-SEEING!
IF THEY HAD A KENTUCKY DERBY FOR SLEEPERS---I'D PUT MY WHOLE WAD ON HIM!
I'LL BET HE COULDA SNORED HIS WAY THROUGH THE BATTLE OF THE BULGE!
8.

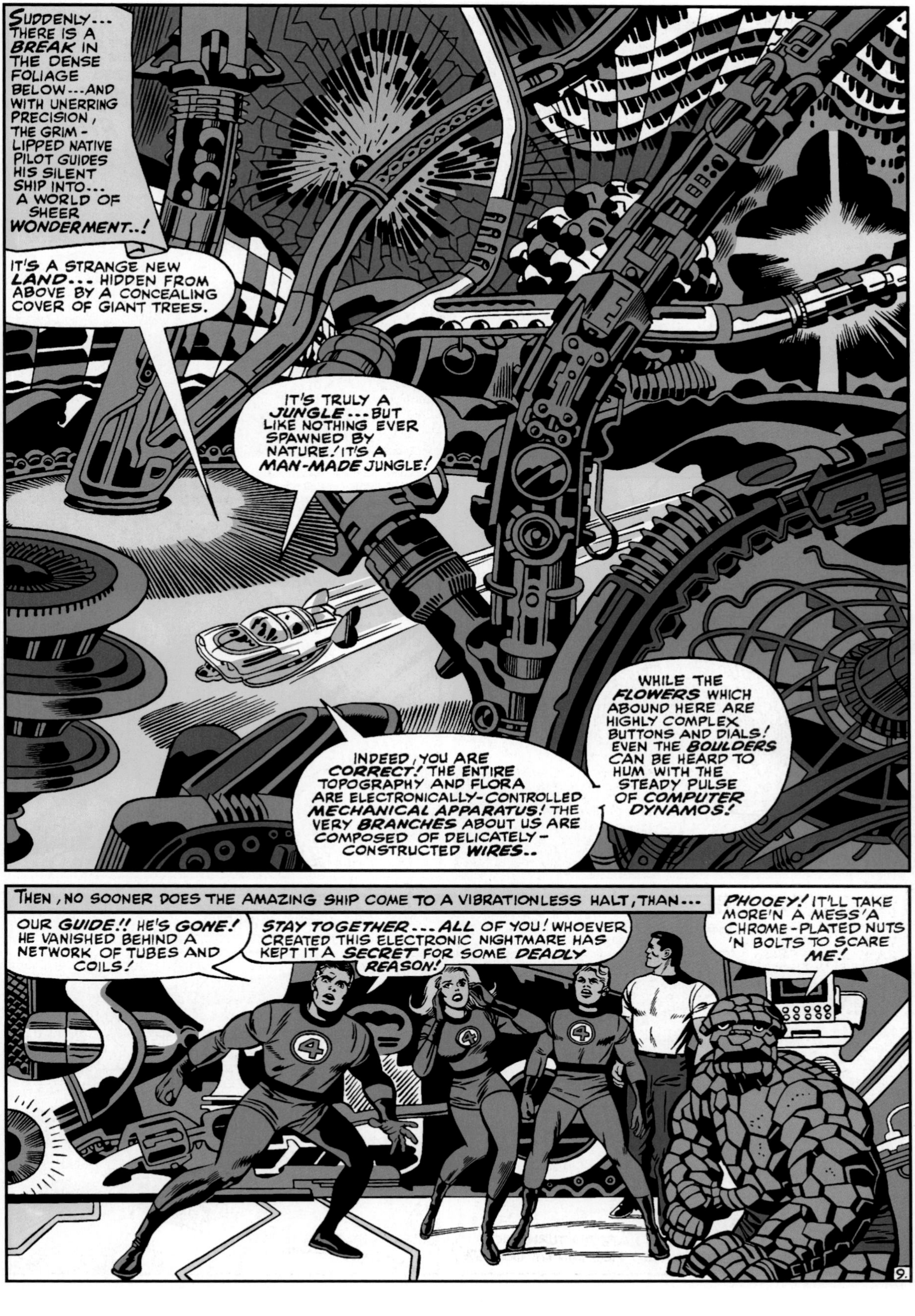
SUDDENLY... THERE IS A BREAK IN THE DENSE FOLIAGE BELOW---AND WITH UNERRING PRECISION, THE GRIM-LIPPED NATIVE PILOT GUIDES HIS SILENT SHIP INTO... A WORLD OF SHEER WONDERMENT..!
IT'S A STRANGE NEW LAND... HIDDEN FROM ABOVE BY A CONCEALING COVER OF GIANT TREES.
IT'S TRULY A JUNGLE...BUT LIKE NOTHING EVER SPAWNED BY NATURE! IT'S A MAN-MADE JUNGLE!
INDEED, YOU ARE CORRECT! THE ENTIRE TOPOGRAPHY AND FLORA ARE ELECTRONICALLY-CONTROLLED MECHANICAL APPARATUS! THE VERY BRANCHES ABOUT US ARE COMPOSED OF DELICATELY-CONSTRUCTED WIRES..
WHILE THE FLOWERS WHICH ABOUND HERE ARE HIGHLY COMPLEX BUTTONS AND DIALS! EVEN THE BOULDERS CAN BE HEARD TO HUM WITH THE STEADY PULSE OF COMPUTER DYNAMOS!
THEN, NO SOONER DOES THE AMAZING SHIP COME TO A VIBRATIONLESS HALT, THAN...
OUR GUIDE!! HE'S GONE! HE VANISHED BEHIND A NETWORK OF TUBES AND COILS!
STAY TOGETHER...ALL OF YOU! WHOEVER CREATED THIS ELECTRONIC NIGHTMARE HAS KEPT IT A SECRET FOR SOME DEADLY REASON!
PHOOEY! IT'LL TAKE MORE'N A MESS'A CHROME-PLATED NUTS 'N BOLTS TO SCARE ME!
9.

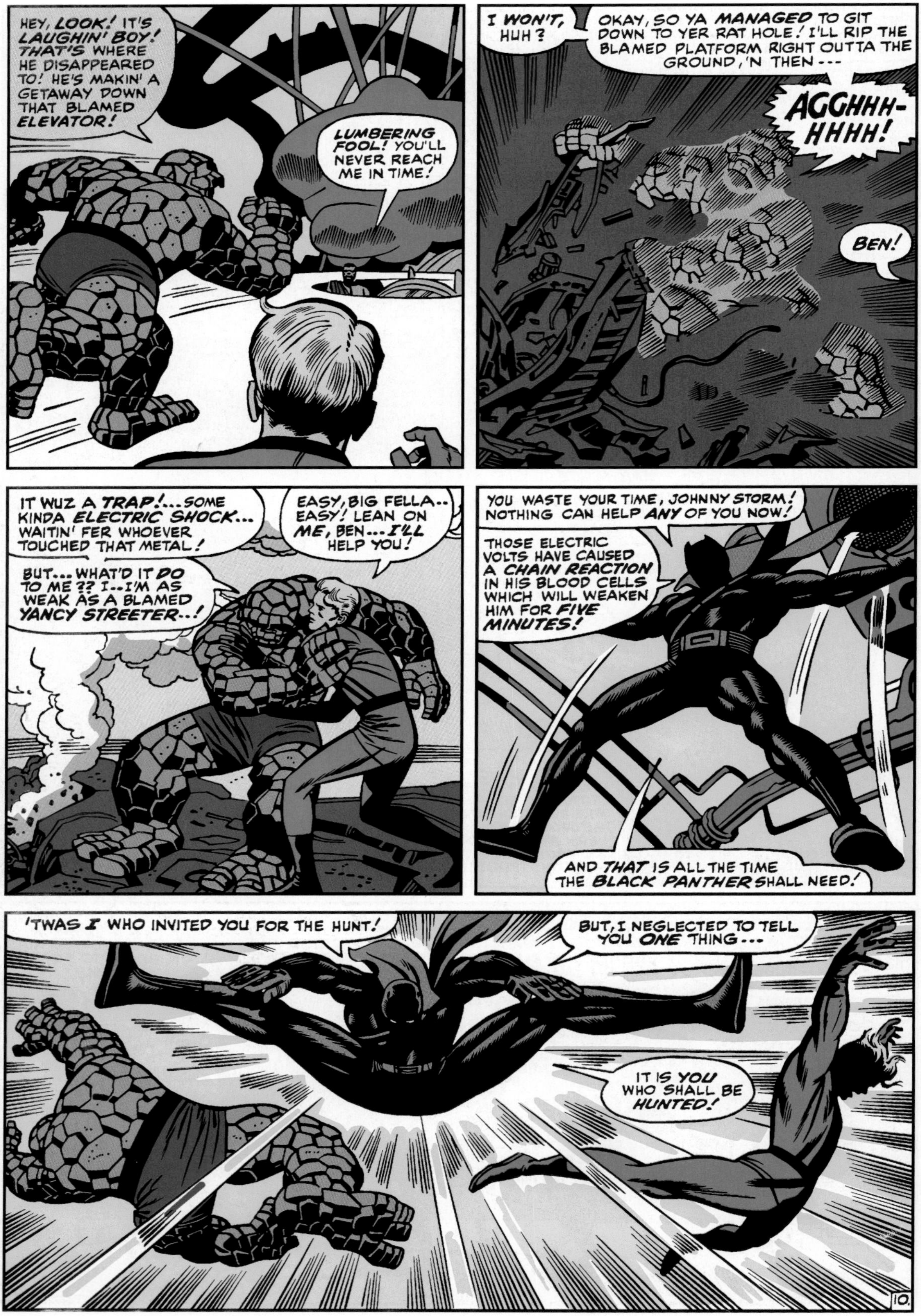
HEY, LOOK! IT'S LAUGHIN' BOY! THAT'S WHERE HE DISAPPEARED TO! HE'S MAKIN' A GETAWAY DOWN THAT BLAMED ELEVATOR!
LUMBERING FOOL! YOU'LL NEVER REACH ME IN TIME!
I WON'T, HUH?
OKAY, SO YA MANAGED TO GIT DOWN TO YER RAT HOLE! I'LL RIP THE BLAMED PLATFORM RIGHT OUTTA THE GROUND, 'N THEN ---
AGGHHH-HHHH!
BEN!
IT WUZ A TRAP!... SOME KINDA ELECTRIC SHOCK... WAITIN' FER WHOEVER TOUCHED THAT METAL!
BUT... WHAT'D IT DO TO ME ?? I--I'M AS WEAK AS A BLAMED YANCY STREETER--!
EASY, BIG FELLA.. EASY! LEAN ON ME, BEN... I'LL HELP YOU!
YOU WASTE YOUR TIME, JOHNNY STORM! NOTHING CAN HELP ANY OF YOU NOW!
THOSE ELECTRIC VOLTS HAVE CAUSED A CHAIN REACTION IN HIS BLOOD CELLS WHICH WILL WEAKEN HIM FOR FIVE MINUTES!
AND THAT IS ALL THE TIME THE BLACK PANTHER SHALL NEED!
'TWAS I WHO INVITED YOU FOR THE HUNT!
BUT, I NEGLECTED TO TELL YOU ONE THING ---
IT IS YOU WHO SHALL BE HUNTED!
10.

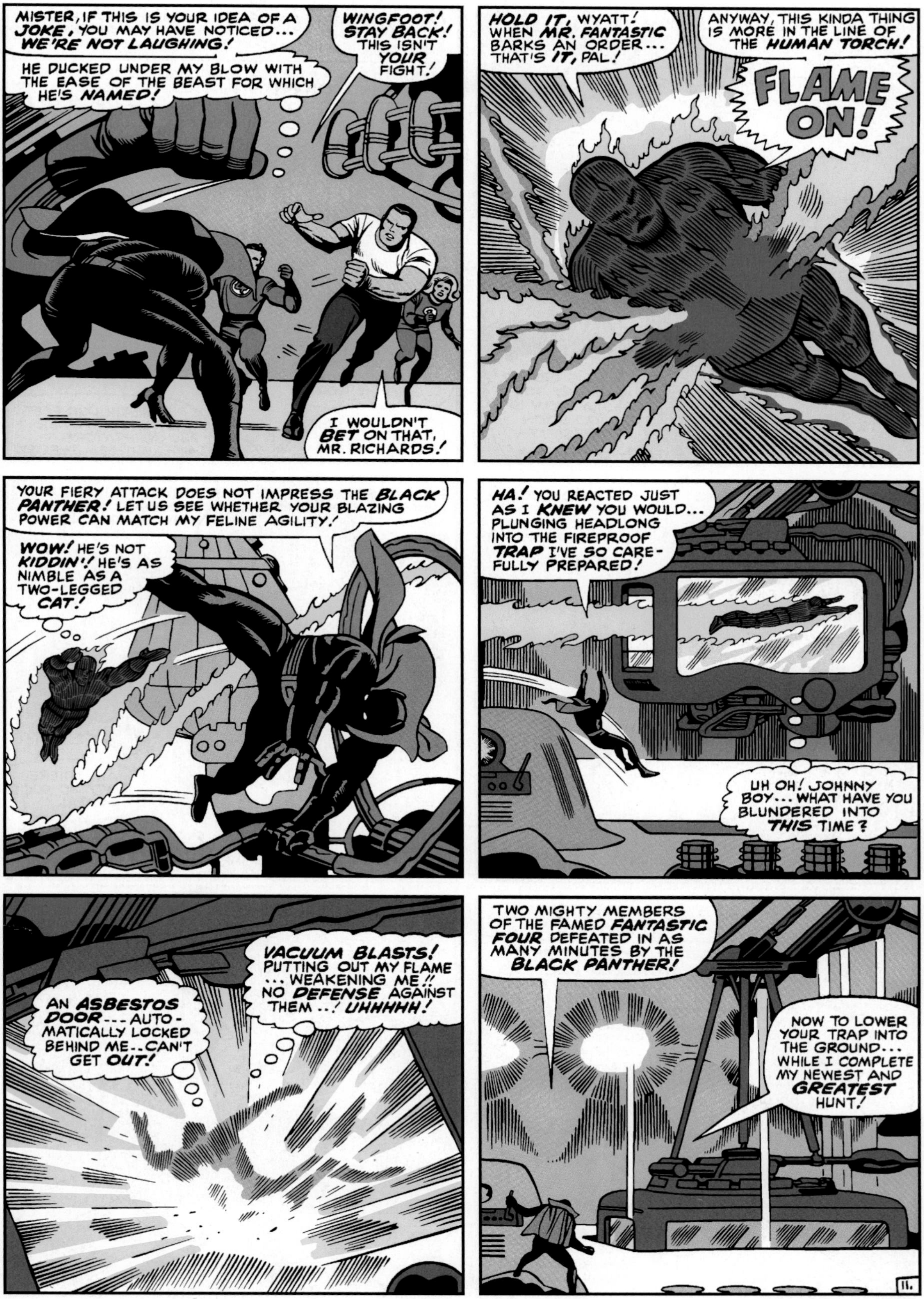

MISTER, IF THIS IS YOUR IDEA OF A JOKE, YOU MAY HAVE NOTICED... WE'RE NOT LAUGHING!
HE DUCKED UNDER MY BLOW WITH THE EASE OF THE BEAST FOR WHICH HE'S NAMED!
WINGFOOT! STAY BACK! THIS ISN'T YOUR FIGHT!
I WOULDN'T BET ON THAT, MR. RICHARDS!
HOLD IT, WYATT! WHEN MR. FANTASTIC BARKS AN ORDER... THAT'S IT, PAL!
ANYWAY, THIS KINDA THING IS MORE IN THE LINE OF THE HUMAN TORCH!
FLAME ON!
YOUR FIERY ATTACK DOES NOT IMPRESS THE BLACK PANTHER! LET US SEE WHETHER YOUR BLAZING POWER CAN MATCH MY FELINE AGILITY!
WOW! HE'S NOT KIDDIN'! HE'S AS NIMBLE AS A TWO-LEGGED CAT!
HA! YOU REACTED JUST AS I KNEW YOU WOULD... PLUNGING HEADLONG INTO THE FIREPROOF TRAP I'VE SO CAREFULLY PREPARED!
UH OH! JOHNNY BOY... WHAT HAVE YOU BLUNDERED INTO THIS TIME?
VACUUM BLASTS! PUTTING OUT MY FLAME... WEAKENING ME!! NO DEFENSE AGAINST THEM...! UHHHHH!
AN ASBESTOS DOOR--- AUTOMATICALLY LOCKED BEHIND ME.. CAN'T GET OUT!
TWO MIGHTY MEMBERS OF THE FAMED FANTASTIC FOUR DEFEATED IN AS MANY MINUTES BY THE BLACK PANTHER!
NOW TO LOWER YOUR TRAP INTO THE GROUND... WHILE I COMPLETE MY NEWEST AND GREATEST HUNT!

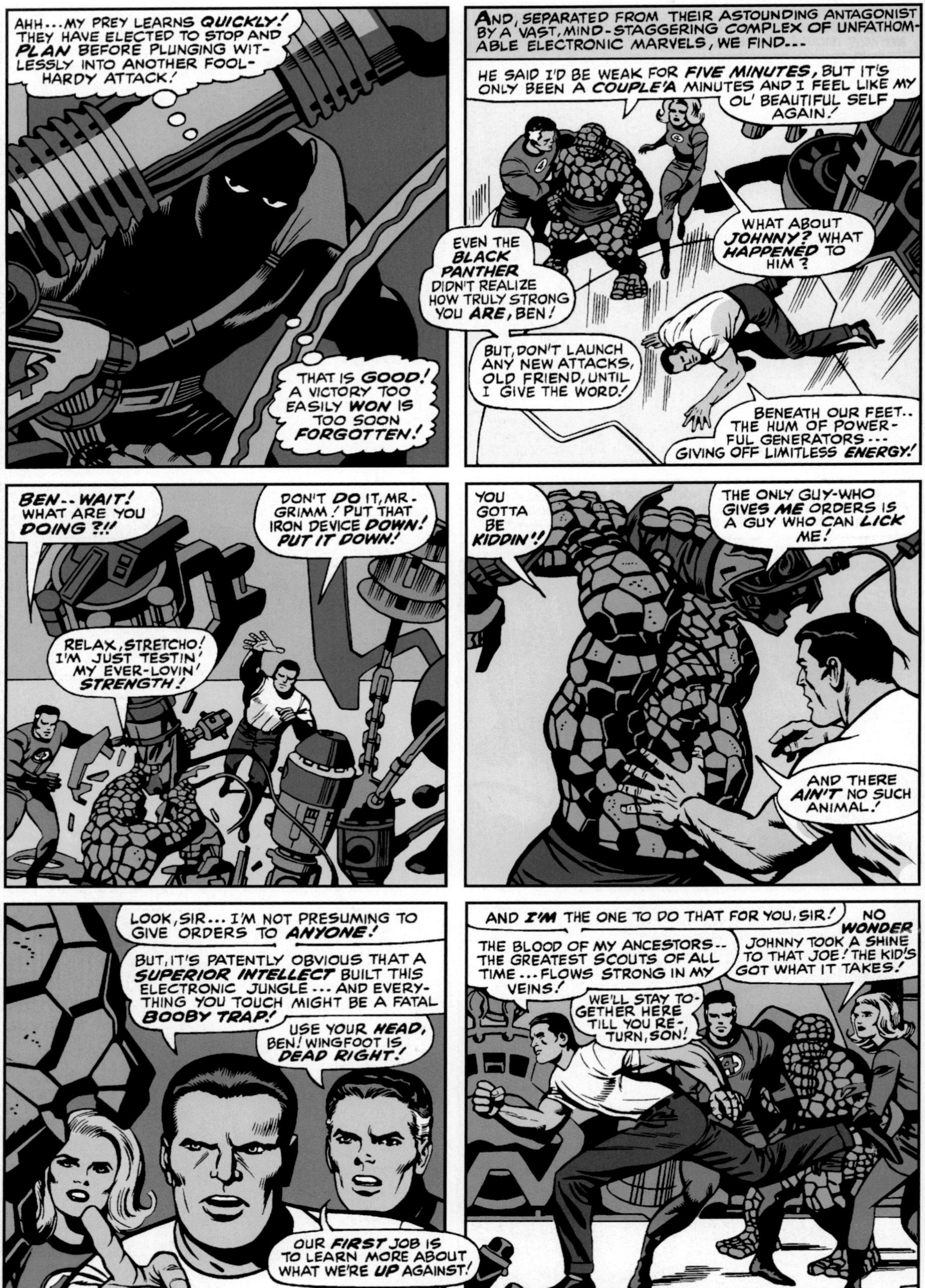
AHH...MY PREY LEARNS QUICKLY! THEY HAVE ELECTED TO STOP AND PLAN BEFORE PLUNGING WITLESSLY INTO ANOTHER FOOLHARDY ATTACK!
THAT IS GOOD! A VICTORY TOO EASILY WON IS TOO SOON FORGOTTEN!
AND, SEPARATED FROM THEIR ASTOUNDING ANTAGONIST BY A VAST, MIND-STAGGERING COMPLEX OF UNFATHOMABLE ELECTRONIC MARVELS, WE FIND...
HE SAID I'D BE WEAK FOR FIVE MINUTES, BUT IT'S ONLY BEEN A COUPLE'A MINUTES AND I FEEL LIKE MY OL' BEAUTIFUL SELF AGAIN!
EVEN THE BLACK PANTHER DIDN'T REALIZE HOW TRULY STRONG YOU ARE, BEN!
WHAT ABOUT JOHNNY? WHAT HAPPENED TO HIM?
BUT, DON'T LAUNCH ANY NEW ATTACKS, OLD FRIEND, UNTIL I GIVE THE WORD!
BENEATH OUR FEET.. THE HUM OF POWERFUL GENERATORS... GIVING OFF LIMITLESS ENERGY!
BEN..WAIT! WHAT ARE YOU DOING?!!
DON'T DO IT, MR. GRIMM! PUT THAT IRON DEVICE DOWN! PUT IT DOWN!
RELAX, STRETCHO! I'M JUST TESTIN' MY EVER-LOVIN' STRENGTH!
YOU GOTTA BE KIDDIN'!
THE ONLY GUY-WHO GIVES ME ORDERS IS A GUY WHO CAN LICK ME!
AND THERE AIN'T NO SUCH ANIMAL!
LOOK, SIR... I'M NOT PRESUMING TO GIVE ORDERS TO ANYONE!
BUT, IT'S PATENTLY OBVIOUS THAT A SUPERIOR INTELLECT BUILT THIS ELECTRONIC JUNGLE... AND EVERYTHING YOU TOUCH MIGHT BE A FATAL BOOBY TRAP!
USE YOUR HEAD, BEN! WINGFOOT IS DEAD RIGHT!
OUR FIRST JOB IS TO LEARN MORE ABOUT WHAT WE'RE UP AGAINST!
AND I'M THE ONE TO DO THAT FOR YOU, SIR!
THE BLOOD OF MY ANCESTORS.. THE GREATEST SCOUTS OF ALL TIME... FLOWS STRONG IN MY VEINS!
NO WONDER JOHNNY TOOK A SHINE TO THAT JOE! THE KID'S GOT WHAT IT TAKES!
WE'LL STAY TOGETHER HERE TILL YOU RETURN, SON!
12

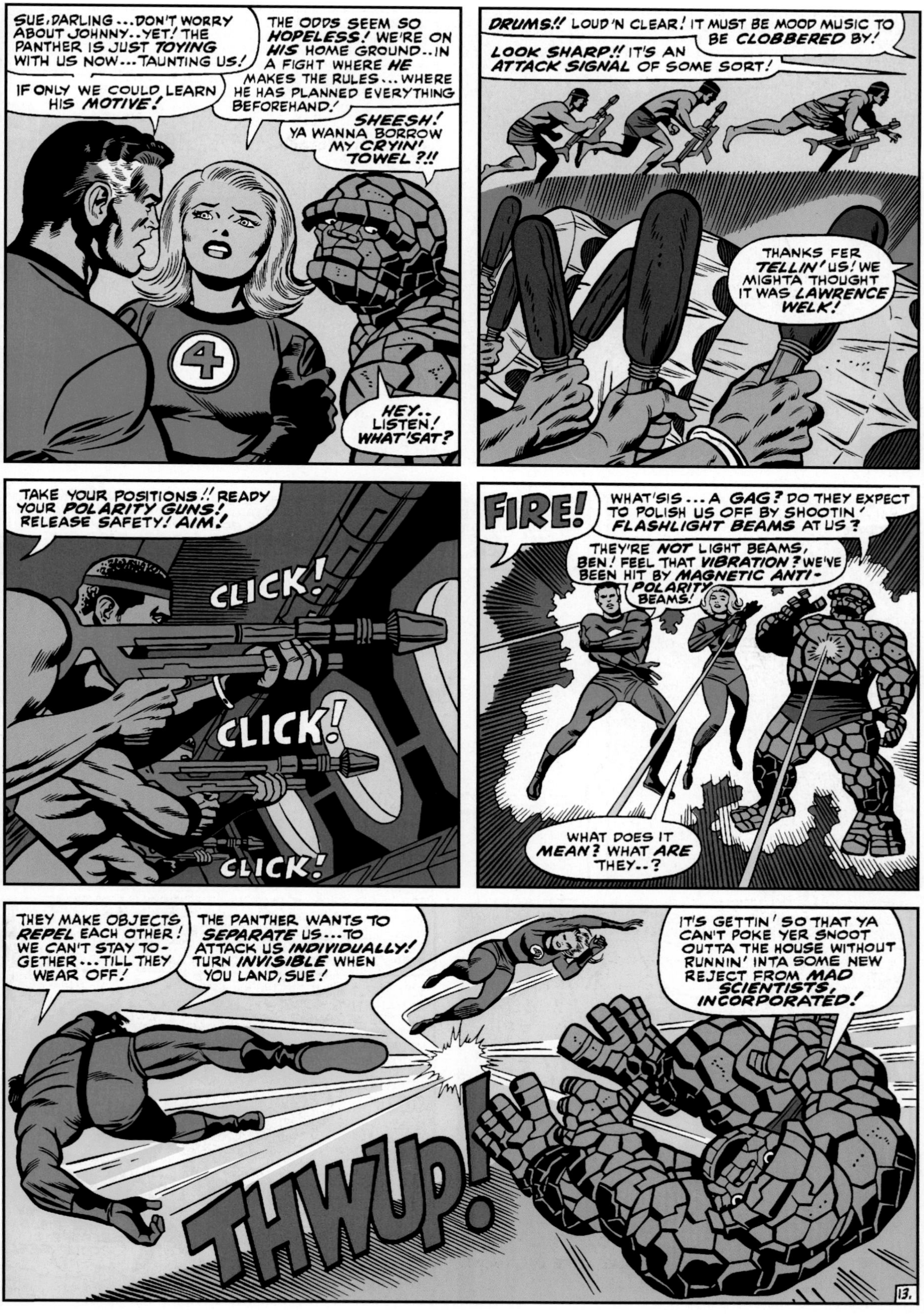
SUE, DARLING ... DON'T WORRY ABOUT JOHNNY.. YET! THE PANTHER IS JUST TOYING WITH US NOW... TAUNTING US!
IF ONLY WE COULD LEARN HIS MOTIVE!
THE ODDS SEEM SO HOPELESS! WE'RE ON HIS HOME GROUND.. IN A FIGHT WHERE HE MAKES THE RULES... WHERE HE HAS PLANNED EVERYTHING BEFOREHAND!
SHEESH! YA WANNA BORROW MY CRYIN' TOWEL ?!!
HEY.. LISTEN! WHAT'SAT?
DRUMS!! LOUD 'N CLEAR! IT MUST BE MOOD MUSIC TO BE CLOBBERED BY!
LOOK SHARP!! IT'S AN ATTACK SIGNAL OF SOME SORT!
THANKS FER TELLIN' US! WE MIGHTA THOUGHT IT WAS LAWRENCE WELK!
TAKE YOUR POSITIONS!! READY YOUR POLARITY GUNS! RELEASE SAFETY! AIM!
CLICK!
CLICK!
CLICK!
FIRE!
WHAT'SIS ... A GAG? DO THEY EXPECT TO POLISH US OFF BY SHOOTIN' FLASHLIGHT BEAMS AT US?
THEY'RE NOT LIGHT BEAMS, BEN! FEEL THAT VIBRATION? WE'VE BEEN HIT BY MAGNETIC ANTI-POLARITY BEAMS!
WHAT DOES IT MEAN? WHAT ARE THEY..?
THEY MAKE OBJECTS REPEL EACH OTHER! WE CAN'T STAY TO-GETHER... TILL THEY WEAR OFF!
THE PANTHER WANTS TO SEPARATE US... TO ATTACK US INDIVIDUALLY! TURN INVISIBLE WHEN YOU LAND, SUE!
IT'S GETTIN' SO THAT YA CAN'T POKE YER SNOOT OUTTA THE HOUSE WITHOUT RUNNIN' INTA SOME NEW REJECT FROM MAD SCIENTISTS, INCORPORATED!
THWUP!
13.

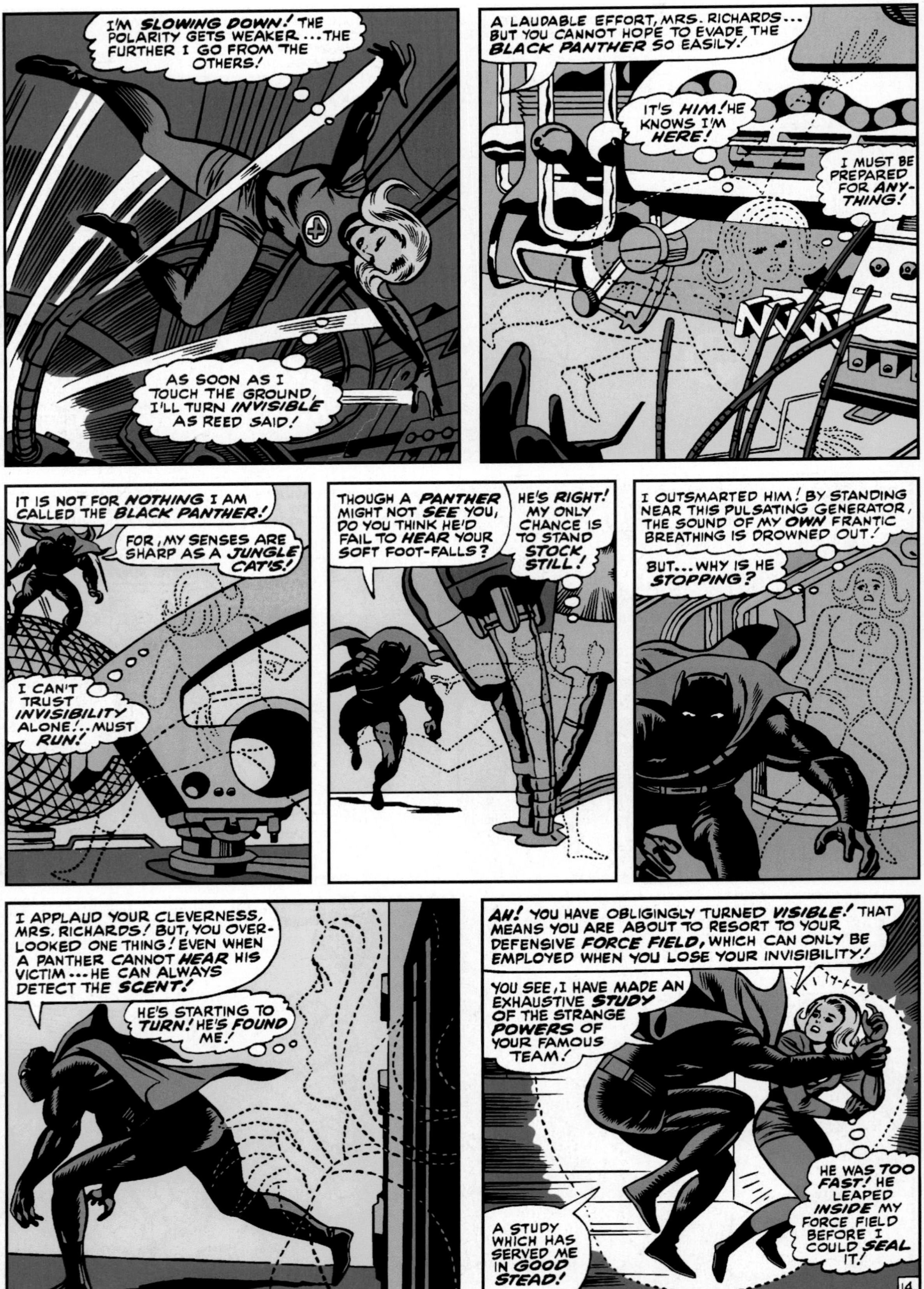
I'M SLOWING DOWN! THE POLARITY GETS WEAKER... THE FURTHER I GO FROM THE OTHERS!
AS SOON AS I TOUCH THE GROUND, I'LL TURN INVISIBLE AS REED SAID!
A LAUDABLE EFFORT, MRS. RICHARDS... BUT YOU CANNOT HOPE TO EVADE THE BLACK PANTHER SO EASILY!
IT'S HIM! HE KNOWS I'M HERE!
I MUST BE PREPARED FOR ANYTHING!
IT IS NOT FOR NOTHING I AM CALLED THE BLACK PANTHER!
FOR, MY SENSES ARE SHARP AS A JUNGLE CAT'S!
I CAN'T TRUST INVISIBILITY ALONE!.. MUST RUN!
THOUGH A PANTHER MIGHT NOT SEE YOU, DO YOU THINK HE'D FAIL TO HEAR YOUR SOFT FOOT-FALLS?
HE'S RIGHT! MY ONLY CHANCE IS TO STAND STOCK STILL!
I OUTSMARTED HIM! BY STANDING NEAR THIS PULSATING GENERATOR, THE SOUND OF MY OWN FRANTIC BREATHING IS DROWNED OUT!
BUT... WHY IS HE STOPPING?
I APPLAUD YOUR CLEVERNESS, MRS. RICHARDS! BUT, YOU OVERLOOKED ONE THING! EVEN WHEN A PANTHER CANNOT HEAR HIS VICTIM... HE CAN ALWAYS DETECT THE SCENT!
HE'S STARTING TO TURN! HE'S FOUND ME!
AH! YOU HAVE OBLIGINGLY TURNED VISIBLE! THAT MEANS YOU ARE ABOUT TO RESORT TO YOUR DEFENSIVE FORCE FIELD, WHICH CAN ONLY BE EMPLOYED WHEN YOU LOSE YOUR INVISIBILITY!
YOU SEE, I HAVE MADE AN EXHAUSTIVE STUDY OF THE STRANGE POWERS OF YOUR FAMOUS TEAM!
A STUDY WHICH HAS SERVED ME IN GOOD STEAD!
HE WAS TOO FAST! HE LEAPED INSIDE MY FORCE FIELD BEFORE I COULD SEAL IT!
14.

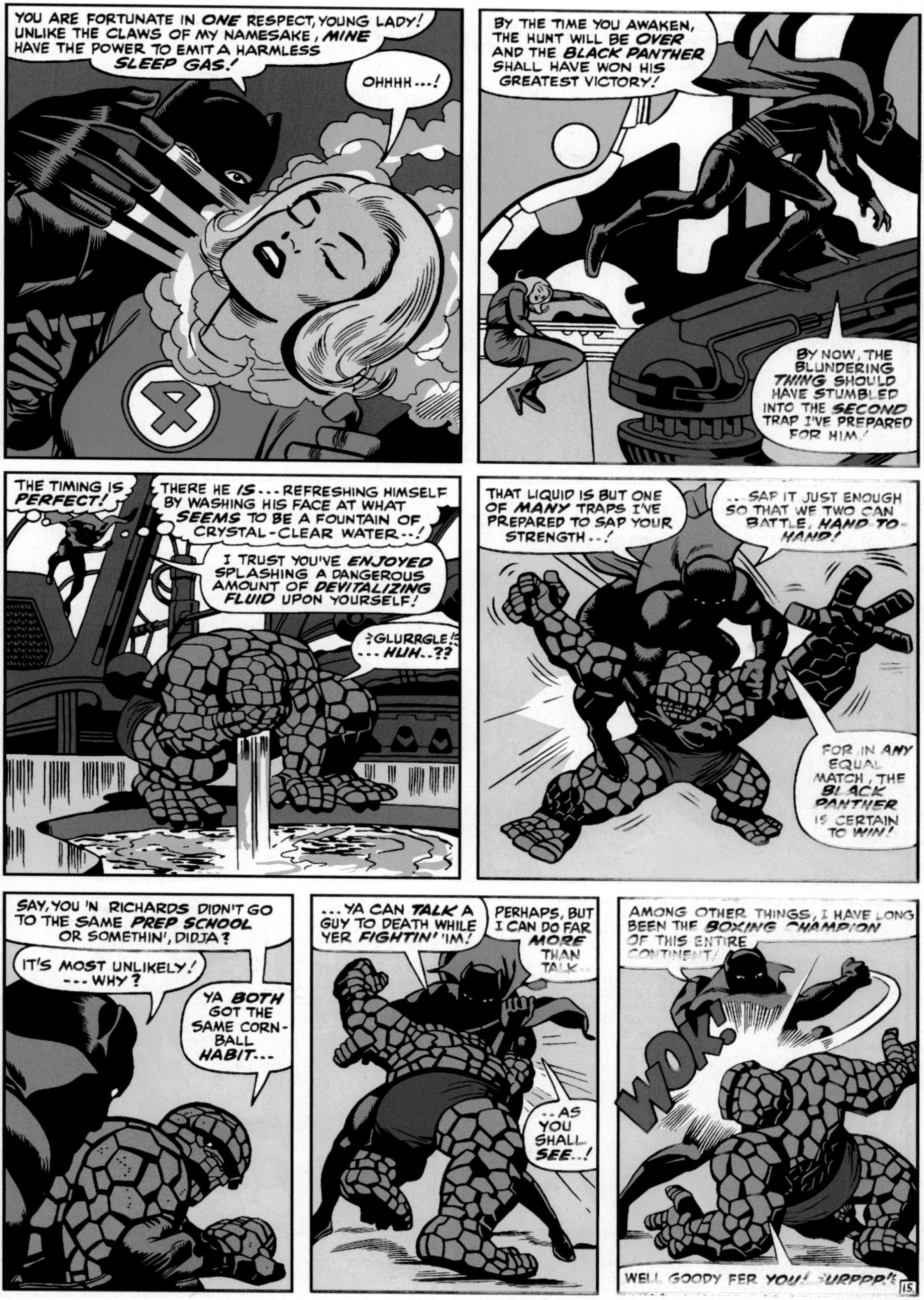
YOU ARE FORTUNATE IN ONE RESPECT, YOUNG LADY! UNLIKE THE CLAWS OF MY NAMESAKE, MINE HAVE THE POWER TO EMIT A HARMLESS SLEEP GAS!
OHHHH...!
BY THE TIME YOU AWAKEN, THE HUNT WILL BE OVER AND THE BLACK PANTHER SHALL HAVE WON HIS GREATEST VICTORY!
BY NOW, THE BLUNDERING THING SHOULD HAVE STUMBLED INTO THE SECOND TRAP I'VE PREPARED FOR HIM!
THE TIMING IS PERFECT!
THERE HE IS... REFRESHING HIMSELF BY WASHING HIS FACE AT WHAT SEEMS TO BE A FOUNTAIN OF CRYSTAL-CLEAR WATER--!
I TRUST YOU'VE ENJOYED SPLASHING A DANGEROUS AMOUNT OF DEVITALIZING FLUID UPON YOURSELF!
GLURRGLE! ...HUH..??
THAT LIQUID IS BUT ONE OF MANY TRAPS I'VE PREPARED TO SAP YOUR STRENGTH..!
..SAP IT JUST ENOUGH SO THAT WE TWO CAN BATTLE, HAND-TO-HAND!
FOR IN ANY EQUAL MATCH, THE BLACK PANTHER IS CERTAIN TO WIN!
SAY, YOU 'N RICHARDS DIDN'T GO TO THE SAME PREP SCHOOL OR SOMETHIN', DIDJA?
IT'S MOST UNLIKELY! --- WHY?
YA BOTH GOT THE SAME CORN-BALL HABIT...
...YA CAN TALK A GUY TO DEATH WHILE YER FIGHTIN' 'IM!
PERHAPS, BUT I CAN DO FAR MORE THAN TALK..
..AS YOU SHALL SEE..!
AMONG OTHER THINGS, I HAVE LONG BEEN THE BOXING CHAMPION OF THIS ENTIRE CONTINENT!
WOK!
WELL GOODY FER YOU! ..URPPP!
15

JUST STAY THERE, WISE GUY... TILL I GIT TO MY FEET! THAT'S ALL I ASK!
I SHALL BE HAPPY TO OBLIGE YOU!
FOR, AFTER ALL... UNTIL YOU STAND, I'LL BE DENIED THE EXQUISITE PLEASURE OF FLOORING YOU AGAIN!
GOTTA STEADY MY-SELF! CAN'T FALL APART JUST 'CAUSE HE WEAKENED ME WITH THAT PHONY WATER!
THEN SUDDENLY... WITH FEROCIOUS SPEED TOTALLY BELYING HIS MAMMOTH BULK, THE THING STRIKES BACK...!
POW
MEBBE THIS'LL SHUT YER YAP FER A WHILE!
NUTS! IF NOT FER DRINKIN' THAT BLASTED WATER, I'DA DEMOLISHED 'IM WITH THAT WHAP! BUT, I'LL BEAT 'IM ANYHOW!
YOUR COURAGE IS TRULY A MATCH FOR YOUR FAME!
BUT YOUR SKILL, ALAS, CANNOT NEARLY COMPARE WITH MINE!
YEAH? WE'LL SEE ABOUT THAT!
HE'S CHARGING INTO ME LIKE A MADDENED RHINO! I'VE GOT TO SIDESTEP, AND THEN...
LOOK OUT!! IF YOU UPSET THAT HIGH-VOLTAGE REFRIGERATION UNIT, IT'LL FREEZE YOU ALIVE WITHIN SECONDS!
BAM!
UNHHH! NOW YA TELL ME!!
TOO LATE!!
YOU ARE INDEED FORTUNATE, THING!
YOUR OWN MASSIVE STRENGTH WAS BEGINNING TO RETURN AGAIN AT THE EXACT MOMENT OF IMPACT!
THUS, YOU WILL SURVIVE THE DEEP FREEZE... THOUGH IT WILL TAKE YOU A WHILE TO THAW OUT!
AND NOW FOR YOUR LEADER... THE ONE WHOM I CONSIDER THE MOST DANGEROUS FOE OF ALL!
BUT, EVEN THE FABULOUS MR. FANTASTIC WILL BE NO MATCH FOR ME!
16

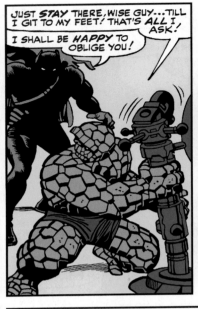

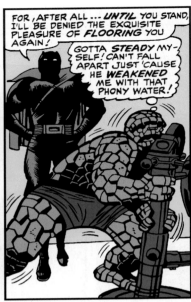

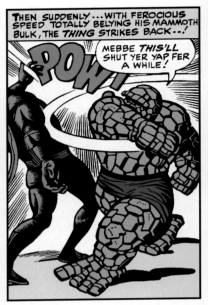

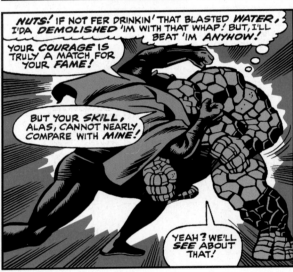

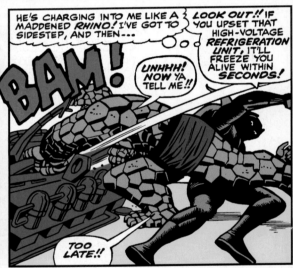

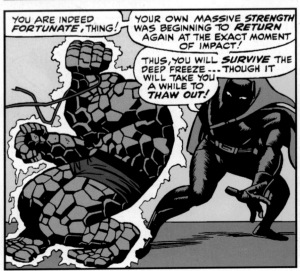

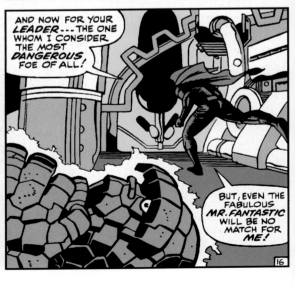

MEANWHILE, WHAT OF *WYATT WINGFOOT?* (...WE THOUGHT YOU'D NEVER ASK!)

REAL JUNGLE, AT LAST! BUT, WHAT'S *THIS?*

A HIDDEN *OBSERVATION POST*--- THE WAKANDAS HAVE BEEN SECRETLY *MONITORING* THE F.F.!

OUR CHIEFTAIN MUST DEFEAT ONLY *ONE MORE* TO ACHIEVE HIS GOAL OF *TOTAL VICTORY!*

THE *BLACK PANTHER* SHALL NOT *FAIL!*

BUT THEN, WITH THE STEALTHY SILENCE OF HIS PROUD, RED-SKINNED FOREBEARS, THE INDIAN YOUTH *STRIKES!*

IF I CAN CRIPPLE THE BLACK PANTHER'S *COMMUNICATIONS,* IT MAY HELP THE *F.F.!*

BAM!

LUCKY FOR ME THEY WEREN'T EXPECTING AN ATTACK! NOW IF THEY'LL JUST STAY *OUT* LONG ENOUGH..!

THERE! THEY WON'T BE ABLE TO SPY ON ANYONE *ELSE* WITH THESE ELECTRONIC SCANNERS!

AND NOW, I'D BETTER GET BACK TO THE *OTHERS*... WHILE I STILL *CAN!*

KRAK!

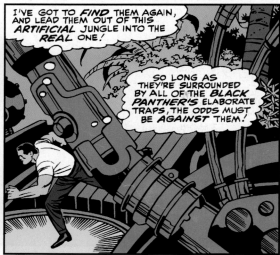

I'VE GOT TO *FIND* THEM AGAIN, AND LEAD THEM OUT OF THIS *ARTIFICIAL* JUNGLE INTO THE *REAL* ONE!

SO LONG AS THEY'RE SURROUNDED BY ALL OF THE *BLACK PANTHER'S* ELABORATE TRAPS, THE ODDS MUST BE *AGAINST* THEM!

BUT, MINUTES LATER, AS THE COURAGEOUS YOUTH REACHES HIS DESTINATION ---

I'M TOO *LATE!!* THEY'RE *GONE!*

WAIT...WHAT'S *THIS?* THE GROUND... IT FEELS *WARM!*

IS THERE SOME SORT OF *DYNAMO* BENEATH ME, OR.. CAN IT *BE..?!!*

THE INTENSITY OF THE HEAT KEEPS *VARYING!* THERE CAN BE ONLY *ONE* EXPLANATION ...

IT'S THE *TORCH!* HE'S TRAPPED *BENEATH* ME... AND HE'S TRYING TO *SIGNAL*.. TO CATCH MY ATTENTION!

NO MATTER WHAT-- I MUSTN'T *FAIL* HIM!

17.

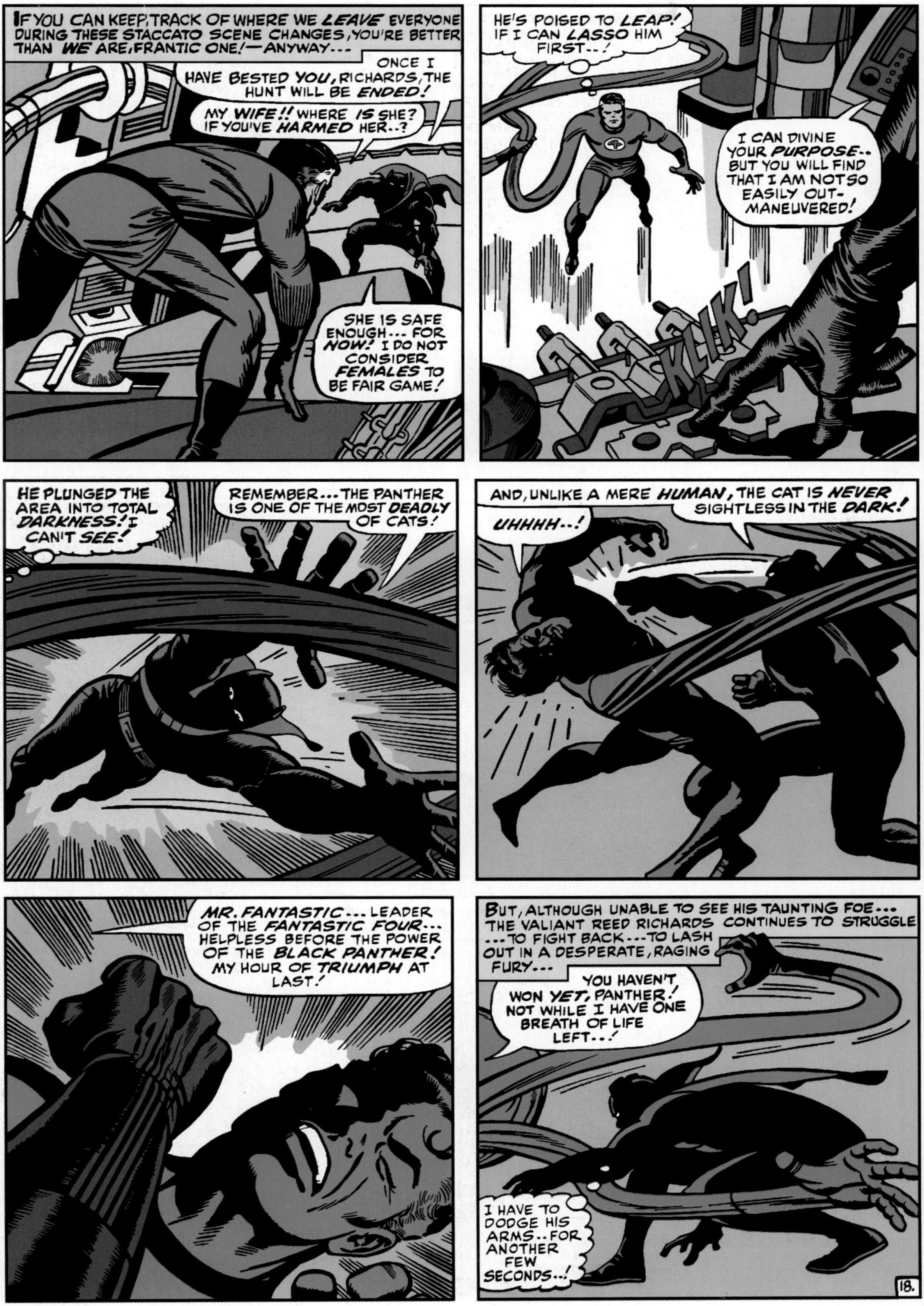

IF YOU CAN KEEP TRACK OF WHERE WE LEAVE EVERYONE DURING THESE STACCATO SCENE CHANGES, YOU'RE BETTER THAN WE ARE, FRANTIC ONE! — ANYWAY...
ONCE I HAVE BESTED YOU, RICHARDS, THE HUNT WILL BE ENDED!
MY WIFE!! WHERE IS SHE? IF YOU'VE HARMED HER..?
SHE IS SAFE ENOUGH... FOR NOW! I DO NOT CONSIDER FEMALES TO BE FAIR GAME!
HE'S POISED TO LEAP! IF I CAN LASSO HIM FIRST..!
I CAN DIVINE YOUR PURPOSE.. BUT YOU WILL FIND THAT I AM NOT SO EASILY OUT-MANEUVERED!
KLIK!
HE PLUNGED THE AREA INTO TOTAL DARKNESS! I CAN'T SEE!
REMEMBER... THE PANTHER IS ONE OF THE MOST DEADLY OF CATS!
AND, UNLIKE A MERE HUMAN, THE CAT IS NEVER SIGHTLESS IN THE DARK!
UHHHH..!
MR. FANTASTIC... LEADER OF THE FANTASTIC FOUR... HELPLESS BEFORE THE POWER OF THE BLACK PANTHER! MY HOUR OF TRIUMPH AT LAST!
BUT, ALTHOUGH UNABLE TO SEE HIS TAUNTING FOE... THE VALIANT REED RICHARDS CONTINUES TO STRUGGLE ...TO FIGHT BACK...TO LASH OUT IN A DESPERATE, RAGING FURY...
YOU HAVEN'T WON YET, PANTHER! NOT WHILE I HAVE ONE BREATH OF LIFE LEFT..!
I HAVE TO DODGE HIS ARMS.. FOR ANOTHER FEW SECONDS..!
18.

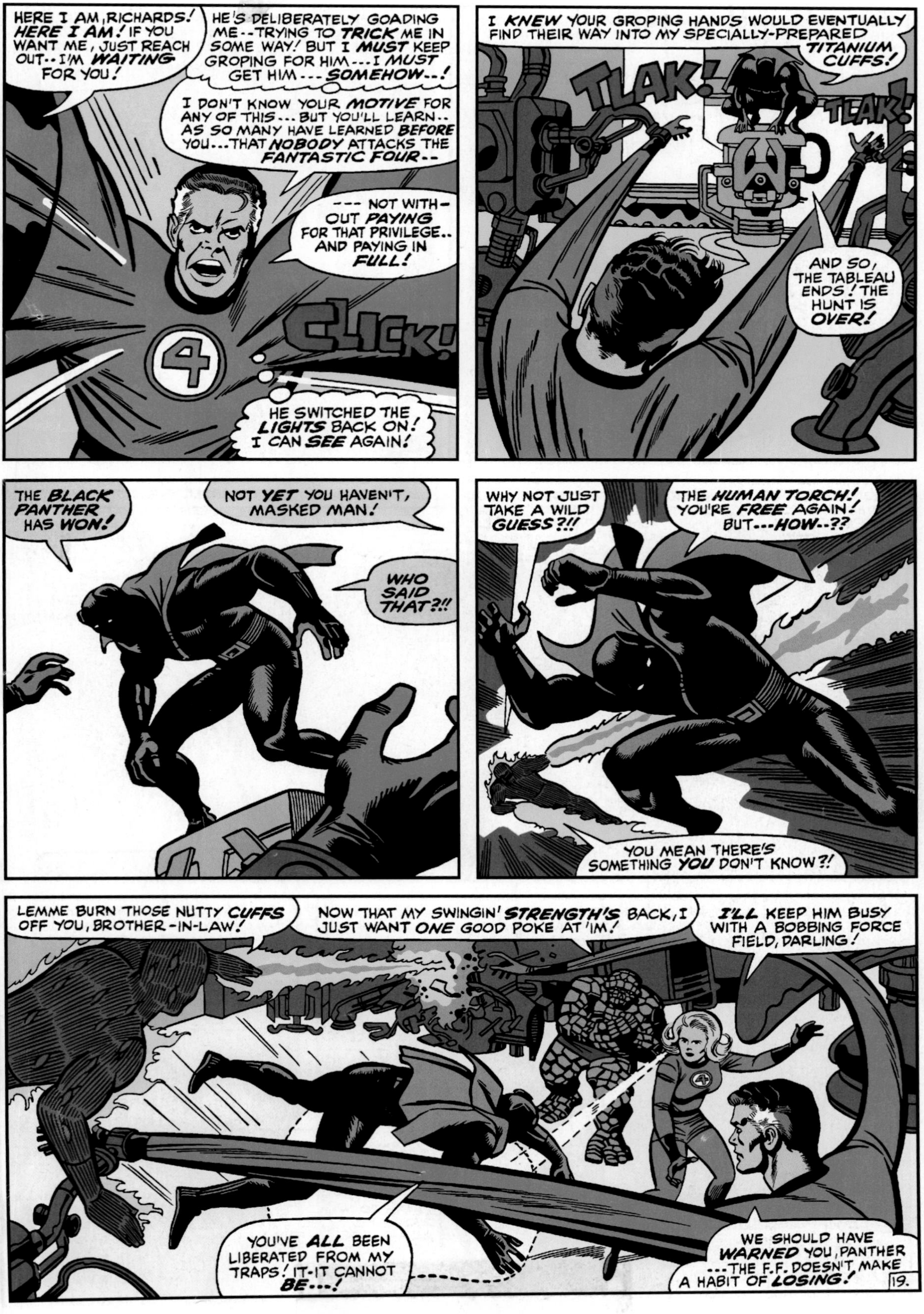
HERE I AM, RICHARDS! HERE I AM! IF YOU WANT ME, JUST REACH OUT-- I'M WAITING FOR YOU!
HE'S DELIBERATELY GOADING ME--TRYING TO TRICK ME IN SOME WAY! BUT I MUST KEEP GROPING FOR HIM---I MUST GET HIM---SOMEHOW--!
I DON'T KNOW YOUR MOTIVE FOR ANY OF THIS---BUT YOU'LL LEARN-- AS SO MANY HAVE LEARNED BEFORE YOU---THAT NOBODY ATTACKS THE FANTASTIC FOUR--
---NOT WITH-OUT PAYING FOR THAT PRIVILEGE-- AND PAYING IN FULL!
CLICK!
HE SWITCHED THE LIGHTS BACK ON! I CAN SEE AGAIN!
I KNEW YOUR GROPING HANDS WOULD EVENTUALLY FIND THEIR WAY INTO MY SPECIALLY-PREPARED TITANIUM CUFFS!
TLAK!
TLAK!
AND SO, THE TABLEAU ENDS! THE HUNT IS OVER!
THE BLACK PANTHER HAS WON!
NOT YET YOU HAVEN'T, MASKED MAN!
WHO SAID THAT?!!
WHY NOT JUST TAKE A WILD GUESS?!!
THE HUMAN TORCH! YOU'RE FREE AGAIN! BUT---HOW--??
YOU MEAN THERE'S SOMETHING YOU DON'T KNOW?!
LEMME BURN THOSE NUTTY CUFFS OFF YOU, BROTHER-IN-LAW!
NOW THAT MY SWINGIN' STRENGTH'S BACK, I JUST WANT ONE GOOD POKE AT 'IM!
I'LL KEEP HIM BUSY WITH A BOBBING FORCE FIELD, DARLING!
YOU'VE ALL BEEN LIBERATED FROM MY TRAPS! IT-IT CANNOT BE---!
WE SHOULD HAVE WARNED YOU, PANTHER ---THE F.F. DOESN'T MAKE A HABIT OF LOSING!
19.

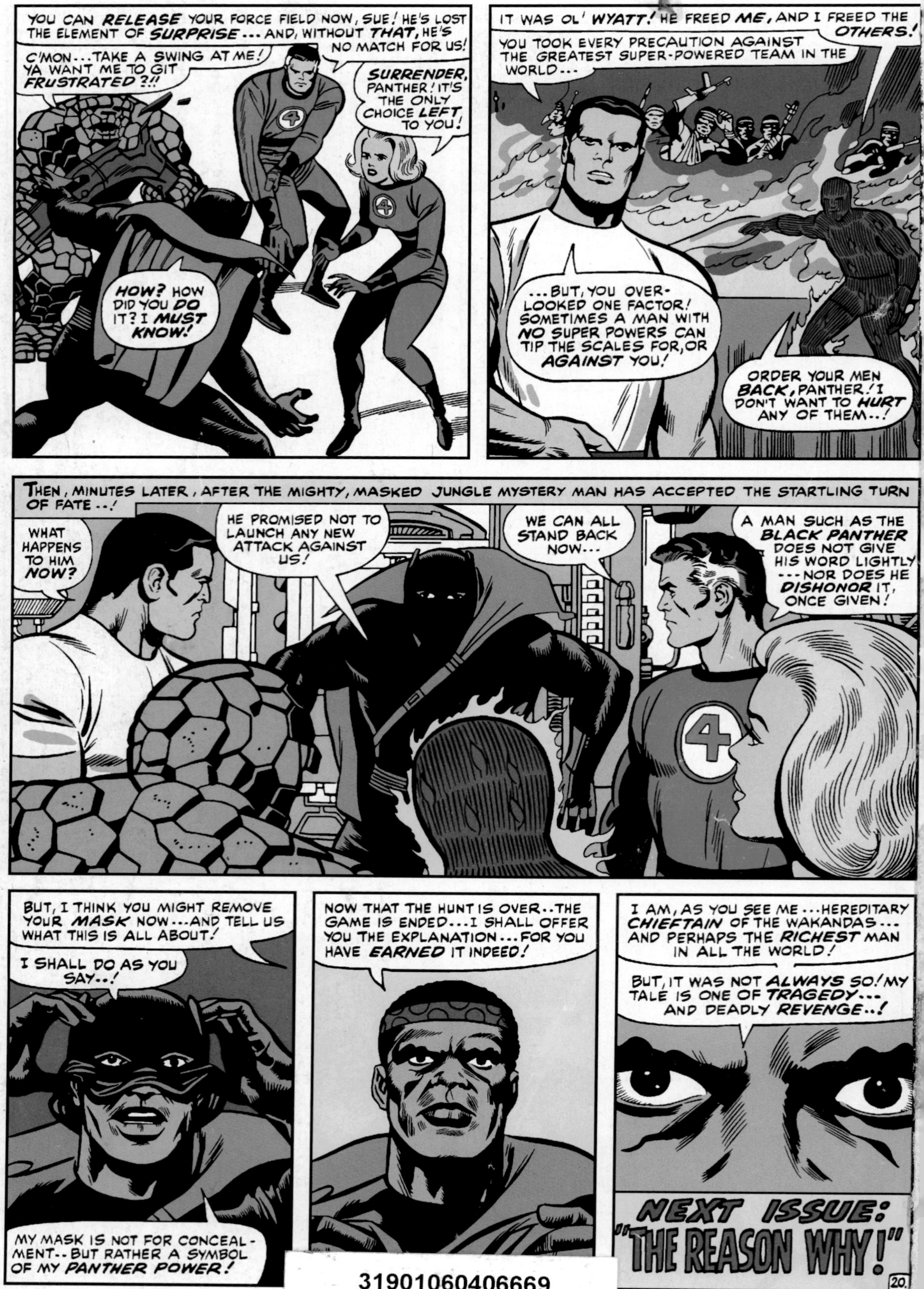
YOU CAN RELEASE YOUR FORCE FIELD NOW, SUE! HE'S LOST THE ELEMENT OF SURPRISE... AND, WITHOUT THAT, HE'S NO MATCH FOR US!
C'MON... TAKE A SWING AT ME! YA WANT ME TO GIT FRUSTRATED?!!
SURRENDER, PANTHER! IT'S THE ONLY CHOICE LEFT TO YOU!
HOW? HOW DID YOU DO IT? I MUST KNOW!
IT WAS OL' WYATT! HE FREED ME, AND I FREED THE OTHERS!
YOU TOOK EVERY PRECAUTION AGAINST THE GREATEST SUPER-POWERED TEAM IN THE WORLD...
...BUT, YOU OVER-LOOKED ONE FACTOR! SOMETIMES A MAN WITH NO SUPER POWERS CAN TIP THE SCALES FOR, OR AGAINST YOU!
ORDER YOUR MEN BACK, PANTHER! I DON'T WANT TO HURT ANY OF THEM..!
THEN, MINUTES LATER, AFTER THE MIGHTY, MASKED JUNGLE MYSTERY MAN HAS ACCEPTED THE STARTLING TURN OF FATE..!
WHAT HAPPENS TO HIM NOW?
HE PROMISED NOT TO LAUNCH ANY NEW ATTACK AGAINST US!
WE CAN ALL STAND BACK NOW...
A MAN SUCH AS THE BLACK PANTHER DOES NOT GIVE HIS WORD LIGHTLY ---NOR DOES HE DISHONOR IT, ONCE GIVEN!
BUT, I THINK YOU MIGHT REMOVE YOUR MASK NOW... AND TELL US WHAT THIS IS ALL ABOUT!
I SHALL DO AS YOU SAY..!
MY MASK IS NOT FOR CONCEAL-MENT.. BUT RATHER A SYMBOL OF MY PANTHER POWER!
NOW THAT THE HUNT IS OVER..THE GAME IS ENDED...I SHALL OFFER YOU THE EXPLANATION...FOR YOU HAVE EARNED IT INDEED!
I AM, AS YOU SEE ME...HEREDITARY CHIEFTAIN OF THE WAKANDAS... AND PERHAPS THE RICHEST MAN IN ALL THE WORLD!
BUT, IT WAS NOT ALWAYS SO! MY TALE IS ONE OF TRAGEDY... AND DEADLY REVENGE..!
NEXT ISSUE: "THE REASON WHY!"
20